Margaret Gallo
January

Ice

Women on Ice

Feminist Essays on the
Tonya Harding/Nancy Kerrigan Spectacle

edited by
Cynthia Baughman

Routledge New York and London

Published in 1995 by

Routledge
29 West 35th Street
New York, NY 10001

Published in Great Britain by
Routledge
11 New Fetter Lane
London EC4P 4EE

The Stacey D'Erasmo article, "An American Tragedy," is reprinted by permission of the author and *The Village Voice*. Abigail M. Feder's article, "'A Radiant Smile from the Lovely Lady': Overdetermined Femininity in 'Ladies' Figure Skating," originally appeared in somewhat different form in *TDR* 38, 1 (T141), Spring 1994.

Printed in the United States of America on acid-free paper.

Library of Congress Cataloging-in-Publication Data

Women on ice: feminist essays on the Tonya Harding/Nancy Kerrigan spectacle / edited by Cynthia Baughman.
    p. cm.
Includes bibliographical references.
ISBN 0-415-91150-8 (cl.) — ISBN 0-415-91151-6 (pbk.)
1. Women skaters—Social conditions. 2. Women skaters—Conduct of life. 3. Women in mass media. 4. Stereotype (Psychology) in mass media. 5. Feminist criticism. I. Baughman, Cynthia.

GV850.A2W66   1995   95-24887
796.91'2 — dc20 — dc20   CIP

Dedicated to Hannah Knipple in appreciation of the exuberance with which, at age ten, she is inextricably both artist and athlete, and to the memory of Trish Squires.

CONTENTS

ACKNOWLEDGMENTS

My gratitude goes first to the contributors to this volume, a number of whom provided much more than their essays; special thanks to Sam Stoloff. Many other friends and colleagues fostered the development of this book with encouragement and expertise: Jeanne Allen, Sally Banes, Lauren Berlant, Thomas Bohn, Susan Bordo, Margaret Dieter, Mary Fessenden, Mary Beth Haralovich, John Hess, Janice Levy, Dennis Lynch, Liz Lyons, Dick Moran, Marcelle Pecot, Bill Rowley, Michael Serino, Steve Skopik, and Stephen Tropiano. Susan Kuc deserves special recognition for her timely inspiration and guidance. Peter Agree was a steadfast friend and source of wisdom. Nichole Gantshar generously shared her archive of skating videotapes, and her vast knowledge of figure skating. Cecilia Cancellaro was a patient and perceptive editor, and Claudia Gorellick, also of Routledge, provided valuable help and advice. Many thanks to Kimberly Herald for her scrupulous editing and assitance with the manuscript.

Karen Wheeler, of the Ithaca College Department of Cinema and Photography managed numerous details with her characteristic skill and good humor, as did Barbara Yonkin and Carmen Ferrara of the Park School of Communications staff. Trish Squires, Kent Loeffler, and Garrett Frawley provided valuable research assistance.

Finally, I am grateful to Ithaca College and the Park School of Communications, for material support, course release time, and a Faculty Summer Research Grant.

Cynthia Baughman
1995

INTRODUCTION

The Iran-Contra hearings, the William Kennedy Smith trial, The Gulf War, Anita Hill, Rodney King, the Bobbitts, the Menendez Brothers, O.J.... The Tonya Harding-Nancy Kerrigan affair both belongs in this chain of recent media spectacles and seems somewhat anomalous there. For despite the husband, henchmen, lawyers, and Olympic officials on the fringes of events, the principals were both women, and the territory at stake—a particular place in a women's sport and all that place demanded (skills and outfits) and conferred (medals and deals)—was women's territory. Is that why it is a little bit embarrassing to admit to being interested in Tonya and Nancy? To having consumed it with rapt fascination? Or is it the unseemly proliferation of the spectacle, across not only all the print media, but an unprecedented number of television genres—nightly news, talk shows, tabloid shows, late-night comedy, the Olympic broadcasts, made-for-TV movies, skating specials, and even commercials—which make this familiar show contemptible? Or is it because the immediate issues at stake here are not major political challenges: violation of the constitution, sexual harassment, date rape. Yes, a woman was assaulted, but not in a way which is part of a pattern that is the subject of national debate. The assault on Nancy Kerrigan certainly had something to do with her being female, but not in a way which is immediately identifiable, or around which one might obviously organize or litigate.

As the affair unfolded, many feminist critics and scholars found themselves watching, reading, and discussing it avidly, though occasionally with that abashed note of apology or bemusement which can attend an investment in the "lowest" forms of women's popular culture—soap operas, talk shows, romance novels. "This is the Superbowl for feminists," said a colleague of mine one evening at a party, when the women had charged to turn on the television when the Olympic skating events—men's singles—(not even the "ladies" events) came on. The men stayed in the kitchen. And as the public debate crystallized around taking sides—an alignment with Nancy's working class virtue or Tonya's working class *resentment*; Nancy's elegance or Tonya's thighs; Nancy's moment of victimization in Detroit, or Tonya's history of victimization in her childhood and marriage—feminists found themselves both drawn to take sides and dismayed to see that once again women were being divided from each other with only two sides to take. Either/or poles have long circumscribed women's real and imagined possibilities—virgin or whore, career girl or mother, feminine ideal or lesbian—but it was surprising and disturbing to see them so heartily established and roundly relished as they were here, officially sanctioned by the categories by which women figure skaters are judged: artistry and technique, or the "artistry" and "athleticism" which the commentators and sportswriters so often tell us are opposing categories in these athletes.

In this volume, feminist scholars from a variety of disciplines take a closer look at the Harding/Kerrigan affair, and its multiple manifestations and meanings, than was possible as the events unfolded. Scholars from the fields of dance, theater, journalism, English literature, film studies, television studies, American studies, philosophy, and politics, as well as literary and journalistic writers, examine the events, how they were transmitted, and how they were received. These analyses enlarge the context for understanding the drama of Tonya and Nancy and the many questions it raised. They also contribute to analysis of a national culture in which media spectacles are experienced both privately and collectively.

Ironically, the scandal of Harding/Kerrigan may have given figure skating the kind of boost which determined women's organizing has given, and continues to provide, to women's sports such as tennis, golf, and basketball. In the first section of this volume, "Skating," the writers bestow upon women's figure skating the first serious critical attention which it has received, studying its history as a spectacle of femininity, its gender conventions, and its rhetorical vocabulary. Jane Feuer, theorizing the figure skating film as a subgenre of the musical, places Kerrigan and Harding in the tradition of feminine spectacles which included Hollywood star and Olympic medalist Sonja Henie. Abigail Feder examines the gender conventions of the contemporary world of figure skating, Laura Jacobs looks at its history as dance, and Ellyn Kestnbaum closes her essay with some answers to the question, "What would constitute feminist figure skating?" In "Fear of Falling," Judith Mayne turns from the choreographed movements of skating to its accidents, and employs psychoanalytic theories of the female spectator to ask how falls function, not only for the skater, but for her audience.

In "Pairs," five writers examine the acceptable and the unacceptable pairings and oppositions that the Harding/Kerrigan affair conjured up. Marjorie Garber juxtaposes the "scandalous" doctored *Newsday* photo of Tonya and Nancy sharing the same ice, with pair scandals of a different sort, the same sex pairs at the Gay Games, to challenge our notions of what constitutes an acceptable coupling. Lynda Zwinger and Robyn Wiegman examine the threat which women's sports pose to "heterovisuality"—the desire for images of women consistent with the desires of heteronormative culture. Diane Raymond considers the Tonya/Nancy dualism in light of another pair of dualistic positions currently being offered to women by the popular press, "victim feminism" and "power feminism." Melanie Thernstrom responds to repeated popular comparisons of the two women to fairy-tale rivals, particularly Cinderella and her wicked stepsister. What ideology—and what truths, if any—about competition between women are encoded in Cinderella's story of good and bad sisters?

As cable channels proliferate, and technology and legislation evolve so that cameras go more places, and are in more hands, we not only have umpteen channels, we also are privy to new vantage points: courtroom cameras, helicopter cameras, video monitors, backstage cameras, and home video recording.

In the section, "Television Spectacles," Sandy Flitterman-Lewis, Mimi White, and Lynn Spigel employ psychoanalytic feminist film criticism to analyze the way in which Tonya and Nancy were represented across television genres, and through several video forms. Flitterman-Lewis examines Nancy Kerrigan as fetishistic icon, and, reading Tonya Harding as the masochistic subject of melodrama, develops an aesthetics of the backstage camera. In "A Skater is Being Beaten," Mimi White invokes Freud's famous essay on childhood eroticism to explain some of the power of what is surely one of Tonya Harding's most powerful performances: her breakdown on the ice during her Olympic free skate. Lynn Spigel examines the ways in which television cast Tonya and Nancy as characters in maternal melodramas. Jill Dianne Swenson turns to television news, examining the questions posed and the sources employed in network and tabloid coverage of the "Skategate" story. Her content analysis reveals that the disdained tabloid shows ask a wider range of questions of a wider range of sources, to tell a more comprehensive story than does network news which fingers its "golden rolodex" of upper-class male sources and is stuck on canonical questions such as, "What did Tonya know and when did she know it?"

Tonya and Nancy were pressed into the service of many national and personal fantasies. Stacey D'Erasmo and Sam Stoloff examine their place in a fantasy of an America with a fluid, unrestrictive class structure. Marsha Kinder shows how the Tonya/Nancy "Dream Scheme" cast the Olympics as a national, rather than international event—our event.

Patricia R. Zimmermann and Zillah R. Eisenstein examine how public attention to the bodies of Tonya and Nancy contributes to racialized, gender-inflected fantasies of nation building. In "Dreaming of Tonya," Cynthia Baughman reports on a personal fantasy deployment of the skater.

The essays in this volume aim to contribute to our understanding of contemporary national fantasies about women's strength and women's beauty; they also aim to contribute to our understanding of how any media spectacle is packaged, sold, and consumed; and they introduce eloquent and incisive critique of the movements and conventions of one of the most popular women's sports. This book was written out of both a fascination with the Harding/Kerrigan story as it unfolded, and out of a fascination with how the story became an elaborate media event; it is written from the dual perspective of the consumer/audience member, and the critic. By unpacking the layers of meaning in this media spectacle, the book hopes to provide a model for the analysis of others which await us.

I >   < Skating

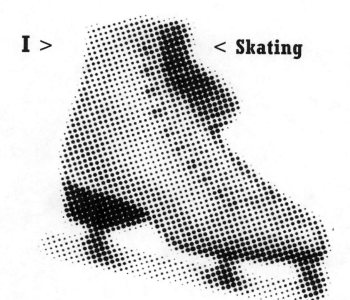

< Jane Feuer

Nancy and Tonya and Sonja
The Figure of the Figure Skater in American Entertainment

Introduction

An unanticipated by-product of the 1994 Lillehammer Olympics was the video re-release of eight films from the star of the previous Norwegian Olympic games, Sonja Henie (1912–1969). Although her films had been shown regularly on AMC and I specialize in Hollywood musicals and have always had a special interest in figure skating, I never thought to include them in a study of the Hollywood musical. Even though I took a keen interest in the Nancy and Tonya brouhaha, having followed both their careers for many years previously, it never occurred to me to think about Sonja Henie at all until I was asked to contribute to this book at the same time as the Henie films became available from Fox video. By coincidence (or, in the case of Fox, planning), I viewed Sonja Henie's black and white Fox films of the late thirties and early forties at the same time as the Lillehammer Olympics and the attendant tabloid coverage of the Nancy and Tonya debacle. The coincidence provided me with the occasion for bringing to bear on figure skating many of my concerns as a film and television scholar: the ice-skating film as musical; the difference between the studio system's and contemporary media's constructions of celebrity; and even the meaning of skating itself as a longstanding form of popular entertainment that spans the studio and the contemporary eras and that combines elements of sport with elements of dance, in the process attempting to merge two very contradictory ideological fields (not least because sport is coded as masculine in our society; dance as feminine).

Sonja Henie was, arguably, the most fabulously successful figure skater ever. She maintained a public skating career from the age of eleven to her death at the age of fifty seven. She was thought at one time to be the richest woman in Hollywood; she had a carefully constructed Hollywood star image, spawned all kind of commodity tie-ins, became the subject of a tell-all "Mommie Dearest" exposé some fifteen years after her demise, and remains virtually unknown to most Americans under the age of fifty. Thus she's the perfect example of a figure skater who rose and fell in the public's estimation, and the prototype for the kind of media frenzy surrounding Nancy Kerrigan and Tonya Harding today.[1]

I want to use Sonja to place in historical perspective the image of the star figure skater. Eventually, I want to make the argument that tabloid TV exposure is better for Tonya's image than for Nancy's. But I want to do this *through* an analysis of Sonja Henie in particular and figure skating stardom in general. For I believe it is not the case that skating is a throwback, old-fashioned, wholesome form of entertainment like Big Band music or state fairs. Just as the construction of stardom has evolved through changes in media, so has the image of the skater as it moves from film portrayals and live spectacles in the studio era to television coverage and a different kind of live spectacle in the 1990s. Although it is not my subject, one can note the rise in status of the sexy male figure skating star to teenybop idol as just one indication that we have moved into what might be called a "postmodern" era in skating, one that contrasts with the traditional imagery of a holiday on ice. I will argue that the Nancy and Tonya affair is also symptomatic of the emergence of figure skating as a postmodern form of entertainment in the age of tabloid TV.

The Figure Skater as Star

I would like to begin with a simple yet elegant proposition culled from many years of studying show business: *a star's image has to be constructed before it can be deconstructed*. Sonja Henie, for example, received some bad publicity during the War because of her friendship with Hitler, but her 1940 memoir *Wings on my Feet* totally mystifies her own life story. Similarly, a star such as Judy Garland spent years building up her MGM image before her later career made "Over the Rainbow" into a tragic ballad about her own life. Star image construction in the studio era was like that. A vast publicity machine existed not to drag stars through the dirt but rather to glorify them and cover up their alcoholism, their promiscuous sexual escapades, their homosexuality, or even their working-class origins. For both Joan Crawford and Sonja Henie, exposés referred to as "mommie dearest" and "sister dearest" were published many years *after* their deaths.

This kind of mystification of stars is no longer possible in today's world of images nor is it considered desirable. Tabloid TV tends not to have time for the construction process, or, as in the case of Nancy Kerrigan, the build-up is compacted. According to a cartoon in the *Pittsburgh Post-Gazette* entitled "The Nancyometer," all three stages of Nancy's notoriety—the attack, the Olympics, and the fallout—occurred between January 4 and Feb. 27, 1994. Nancy had about a month to establish her star image in the public eye before the process of deconstruction began with the bitchy remarks about Oksana's crying, the surly visit to Disneyworld, and the satirical demystification of Nancy's image on *Saturday Night Live* on March 12, 1994. In the world of postmodern star image construction and deconstruction, Nancy didn't stand a chance.

Of what, typically, does a figure skater's image consist? The conventional image is of a child-like fairy-tale princess. Sonja Henie, for instance, although about twenty-five when she began her U.S. film career, looked far more like Twentieth Century Fox's other major female star of the 1930s, Shirley Temple, than she did like an adult movie star.

Shirley and Sonja

In fact, for the 1938 box office year, Shirley and Sonja were the number one and two female stars, respectively. Both had blond curls, round faces and dimples. The resemblance was terrifying. Sonja herself had been a child sports star in Norway, winning her first championship at the age of eleven and her first Olympics at sixteen. In her films, Sonja often starts out as a naive Scandinavian or Swiss in folk costumes with see-through puff sleeves or in traditional village costumes. In *Sun Valley Serenade*, her best-remembered film (not because of her but because of the Glen Miller songs), she plays a refugee adopted by the hero. Thinking she will be a small child, he decorates her room with dolls and toys. When the child-woman arrives, aside from her sexual aggressiveness, one could well imagine her playing with those dolls. Later, especially in those films where she becomes a skating star, she becomes more sophisticated. Indeed her last film at Fox, *Wintertime*, gives us a darker-haired, slimmer-faced Sonja who dresses like Joan Crawford, skates like a dream, speaks English, and even acts like a grown-up. *Wintertime* would be her last and least successful Fox film. But the child-star image is never truly demystified in her films. This child-star tradition continues today with Oksana Baiul and Michelle Kwan, giving us the best of both sporting and celebrity traditions: the child star and the superathelete—Shirley Temple on ice. In this sense figure skating today is a direct descendent of traditional entertainment practices embodied in the Ice Capades and in classic Hollywood musicals. This is true both in terms of narrative form and processes of star image construction.

"Alice in Wonderland" from *My Lucky Star* (1938)

When traditional figure skaters do films or TV specials, they tend to be cast in fairy-tale narratives. Sonja would often do the first skating "number" in a film at a village festival; her later skating spectaculars would take the form of children's stories such as *Alice in Wonderland* as often as they would employ sophisticated sequined show business styles.

Similarly, Olympian Carol Heiss would be cast as an innocent, virginal Snow White, as if to cushion the power of her skating. As late as 1994, Dorothy Hamill, by now a mature woman, was cast as Cinderella in a skating TV special designed to coincide with Lillehammer. Entitled, *Cinderella: Frozen in Time*, the April 16, 1994 broadcast took the form of a narrated fairy tale on ice performed at a rink for a live audience with the usual balletic choreography and virginal costuming. Oksana's 1994 Olympic gold performance as the Swan had its precedent in a number Sonja frequently performed in ice shows, the Dying Swan, a balletic rendition Sonja claimed to have stolen from the famed ballerina Anna Pavlova. Sonja's feathered costume (to judge from photos in her 1940 book) bore a striking resemblance to the one Oksana wore at the Olympics. This is the stereotyped image of the Russian ballerina as bird-like creature, an image easily parodied in the opening segment of the Nancy-hosted *Saturday Night Live* when a similarly clad Russian ballerina appeared in the audience in drag.

Showing her maturity, Dorothy Hamill still enacts the myth of the fairy princess as she impersonates Cinderella.

Carol Heiss as Snow White

The traditional figure skater, then, is portrayed as a wounded bird, a child or a fairy tale princess. If we look at the conceptual opposition which structures figure skating and its media coverage—artistry vs. athleticism—(brought out in several other essays in this book), we can see that the traditional figure skating star image comes down heavily on the "artistry" side. If figure skating is a combination of dance and sport, the traditional image as conveyed by Sonja Henie emphasizes dance and minimizes athleticism in order to present a child-like version of femininity to the public. As in ballet, such femininity can only be an illusion requiring tremendous strength to perpetuate.

Dorothy Hamill as Cinderella

In this sense neither Nancy nor Tonya fit the traditional image, but Oksana did. Nancy is considered an 'artistic' skater, but still more 'athletic' than Oksana. According to an intricate explanation given on TV (explained in full in Appendix 2 of this book), they actually *tied* in the judges' numerical votes. Nancy lost on a technicality because the artistic scores (in which Oksana was marginally better) were given final preference over the technical scores. In terms of "artistry" which is not quite but almost synonymous with "femininity," Oksana is to Nancy as Nancy is to Tonya. One might say that the entire Lillehammer contest ended by glorifying and reestablishing the most traditionally feminine mode of the figure skater as ballerina. Oksana has the body of Russian ballerina Natalia Makarova which was considered the perfect classical ballet body.

Yet there is a world of difference between the body of Oksana and the body of, say, Sonja Henie, although both in their ways present an infantalized version of a woman's body. In the one case there is the "waif look" currently popularized in the sphere of fashion by model Kate Moss; in the other case, the flat chest and huge powerful thighs of an athlete contrasting with that round-faced blond doll of a head. In a sense, Sonja did more to foreground the contradiction between athleticism and artistry than Oksana does today, at least in terms of body language. This is where the idea that, as one TV commentator put it, "Tonya skates like a man," becomes interesting, because, compared to Oksana, Nancy now 'skates like a man' too. Even when she skates out to her position on the ice, she is very "tomboyish." I believe 'Hepburnesque' was the term used by TV commentators to describe this quality. This appellation doesn't jive with her being a "perfect lady" and "the girl next door." In one tabloid tape, we see her striding into the rink after her "attack." She is doing a little jig—a real jock. From my sixth row center position at the skating exhibition, I could see Nancy sneaking out to the edge of the rink to begin her performance; she moved more like Bonnie Blair than like a Russian ballerina. Nancy's skating is praised for its "elegant line," a balletic quality to be sure but one less pliantly feminine than Oksana's extreme flexibility. No American skating star has approached the balletic apex of femininity that Oksana occupies today and that Michelle Kwan promises to occupy in the future. In terms of feminine body images, competitive skating has regressed rather than progressed.

Before she spoke on TV, it was easier to perpetuate Nancy's image as an ice princess. I remember seeing her in competition prior to the 1992 Olympics and seeing her live in the 1992 traveling exhibition of World and Olympic champions. At that time I found her skating elegant and mysterious, enhanced as it was by her beauty. I saw her fall many times but I never heard her talk until after the attack. Ice princesses don't talk to the press or they talk with a charming and child-like foreign accent or with the aid of a male interpreter (Sonja, Oksana). Ballerinas don't talk. And the old studios knew that fairy tale princesses *shouldn't* talk without a script or without the presence of a publicist. Nancy's mystique could only be ruined by tabloid coverage.

Figure Skating Films as Fairy-tale Musicals

In addition to their narrative prototypes and the child-like femininity they foster, figure skating films are fairy tales in yet another sense: they meet all of the criteria for the fairy-tale subgenre of musicals detailed at length by Rick Altman in *The American Film Musical*. Of Sonja's Fox films, only one falls entirely outside of the fairy-tale model and that one was re-released as Irving Berlin's *Second Fiddle*, not as a Sonja Henie film per se. This 1939 film was already a parody of the backstage musical or what Altman calls the show musical. Featuring a behind-the-screen setting, it satirized the contemporary search for Scarlett O'Hara by casting Sonja as a skating school teacher who becomes a star and gets involved with her studio's publicist (played by Sonja's real life lover Tyrone Power). Even in this sophisticated story, most of the skating takes place on a little pond in Minnesota accompanied by a phonograph. There is even a children's skating number early in the film when Sonja is still a schoolteacher (presumably she teaches gym).

Before I go on to discuss them as fairy-tale musicals, perhaps I should say a few words as to why I consider these figure skating spectaculars to be musicals at all. With Altman, I believe that the Hollywood musical is defined by a dual-focus between narrative and numbers. This opposition is one of structure, not content. Therefore a film with a comic romance plot that alternates story portions with nightclub numbers and skating numbers and that resolves in successful coupling is a musical, just as MGM films which used Esther Williams water ballets as numbers were musicals. Figure skating is the content of the show that is put on, but structurally it occupies the same space as dancing does in other musical films.

Sonja Henie's other Fox films constitute the most important group of fairy-tale musicals outside of the MacDonald-Chevalier-Lubitsch-Mamoulian films at Paramount in the late 1920s to early 1930s, the Astaire-Rogers series at RKO throughout the 1930s, and Vincente Minnelli's important fairy-tale musicals at MGM in the late 1940s and 1950s (*The Pirate, Yolanda and the Thief, An American in Paris, Gigi*). According to Altman, the fairy-tale musical is characterized by its setting in an imaginary kingdom which is thrown into chaos through royal love problems. The governmental plot parallels the love story. This is where the link to actual fairy tales is clearest, and even *Snow White and the Three Stooges* fits the pattern perfectly. The Sonja Henie film which most closely approximates the early Paramount fairy-tale musicals is *Thin Ice* (1937), in which Sonja plays a skating instructress in a large Swiss hotel who romances a prince unbeknownst to her. The scandal of the prince falling for a lowly hotel employee throws both the government of his imaginary kingdom and the kingdom of the hotel into chaos. Many of the other Fox films are closer to the Fred and Ginger films in which a hotel or an ocean liner substitutes for a literal kingdom. Of Sonja's Fox films, *One in a*

Million, Thin Ice, Sun Valley Serenade and *Wintertime* are set at resorts or hotels.

For Altman, the fairy-tale musical bears a close link to its contemporary Hollywood genre, the screwball comedy. Indeed many of Sonja's films feature elements of screwball romance. These are the films in which Sonja talks too much (but never while skating) in her charmingly accented English, as in *Sun Valley Serenade* (1941) or *Iceland* (1942) in both of which she attempts to trick co-star John Payne into marriage. *Happy Landings* (1938), filmed at the height of the screwball craze, sustains a madcap plot which culminates in a double wedding involving Sonja, Don Ameche, Caesar Romero and Ethel Merman followed by a coda in which all four lovers skate together as Sonja pulls them in a conga line.

Sonja skates on a big white rink in *Everything Happens at Night* (1939)

Finally, the Sonja Henie Fox films alternate a dream world with a "real" world, the thematic center of the fairy-tale type. There is usually a contrast between the more realistic (although not very realistic) realm of the narrative and the spectacular world of the skating interludes. Although in some ways the skating numbers mimic the spectacle of Busby Berkeley production numbers, in other ways they represent a dream world expressed in the castles and palaces of the Paramount films and in the big white sets of the Fred Astaire and Ginger Rogers films.

Even more representative of the real world/dream world duality are the dream sequences and dream ballets that permeate fairy-tale musicals and that lend a fairy-tale aura to all other musicals that contain them. The Henie films frequently present the skating numbers as the fantasy of someone in the narrative. *One in a Million* has an early dream sequence from the viewpoint of impresario Adolph Menjou in which he imagines 'Greta Mueller' in a spectacular Berkeleyesque ice-show number. After the dream skating sequence, putting Greta in an ice show becomes his fantasy in the narrative as well. In *Second Fiddle* an enormous Beverly Hills swimming pool magically transforms into an ice rink so that Sonja may skate to an Irving Berlin number about missing snow in the summer. In *Everything Happens at Night*, the dream world illustrated by the big white set is introduced from the hero's point of view as he wipes off the ice with his foot and sees Sonja's smiling face emerging from it.

The transition to the dream sequence

There is an imbalance between the narrative portions of Sonja's films in which she often talks too much and the skating spectacles in which of course she doesn't talk at all. Such an imbalance is also part of the entertainment heritage that contributes to figure skating today. As in all Hollywood musicals of this period, the narrative is resolved by a couple coming together. But whereas in a typical musical, the couple will signify their union by singing and dancing together, in the Sonja Henie films, this was usually not possible. None of her leading men—Tyrone Power,

Richard Greene, John Payne, Cornel Wilde—were skaters, and anyway a skating finale with these virile heroes might have compromised their masculinity. Instead, Sonja will either skate alone at the end of a film after the love plot has been resolved or she will skate with a phantom male partner who stands in for the hero. The movie ends with Sonja being lifted into the air by her male courtier. The effect is to enhance Sonja's own star power, and in a curious way to foreground her athletic power. It is this effect which makes Sonja Henie films so susceptible to camp readings. On the other hand, the effect might be said to be traditional: in classical ballet the prima ballerina is attended by the prince but in many respects he is *supporting* her, quite literally in the finales of classical ballets and many Balanchine ballets. The final shot of Sonja in many of her films echoes this tradition. The ballerina is the only star but her power is purely feminine.

Postmodern Figure Skating/Postmodern Stardom

Until now I have been discussing the traditional image of the figure skater as exemplified by Sonja Henie. Carol Heiss, Peggy Fleming, Dorothy Hamill, Kristi Yamaguchi and Oksana Baiul also occupy this position. With her ultra-athleticism and bad-girl persona, Tonya Harding clearly falls outside of this image. But I believe that Nancy in part falls outside of it too, not so much in her skating as in her overall star persona. Nancy's first appearance as the star of a regular (i.e. non-skating) TV show was already deconstructive of her nice-girl image. The *Saturday Night Live* appearance, however wooden, fell squarely within *postmodern* rather than traditional entertainment practices. The opening monologue in which Nancy took questions from the audience completely satirized her all-American-girl image. Her attire in the hosting segments might almost be described as Lesbian Chic: the mini-skirted black suit followed by jeans, t-shirt and vest. In the skits, her outfits parodied the traditionally feminine figure skating costumes as well as her role as spokesmodel for Disneyworld: the Mexican waitress with puffed sleeves, Tinkerbell and even Snow White. In a manner of speaking all those dainty and sequined outfits on all those powerful athletic bodies are parodies of the feminine. Only Oksana with her child's body appeared truly feminine. Nancy's skating costumes tended to follow the 'elegant' and 'Hepburnesque' component of her image: costume designer Vera Wang stated that Nancy wanted her costumes to be modeled on a traditional evening clothes tuxedoed look. Even in some of her skating exhibitions, Nancy fell outside of the traditional ice princess, prima ballerina mold. Neither her costuming for the Worlds and the Olympics nor her choreography were especially balletic.

One might generalize by saying that figure skating today is mired in traditionalism at the level of competition but is moving toward postmodern entertainment practices in exhibition skating. The competition/exhibition opposition of course correlates with the amateur/professional one that almost defines skating today. The correspondence is not exact (there are amateur exhibitions) but in general we can say that competitive skating lines up with athleticism (relative to exhibition skating, that is), ballet, traditional star images and amateur entertainment; whereas exhibition skating lines up with artistry, modern and postmodern dance styles, hip star images and professional entertainment.

As I discussed at length in *The Hollywood Musical*, musicals, while themselves representing professional entertainment for profit, always sought to ally themselves ideologically with amateur entertainment, with folk art, and with singing and dancing for love rather than money. Sonja Henie remained an amateur for many years despite rumors that her father was taking payoffs. Until 1994, turning professional meant the end of Olympic competition. Ironically, Sonja turned professional with her first film, *One in a Million* and yet the film itself completely celebrated amateurism, bringing it into the center of the classic Hollywood musical tradition. In the film, impresario Adolph Menjou tricks Sonja into participating in an open-air skating exhibition on a glorious plaza at St. Moritz. This almost disqualifies her from Olympic competition, until it is revealed that she was not paid for her performance. At the end of the film she wins the Olympics and decides to turn professional and star in ice shows in America, echoing Sonja's real life trajectory.

Although Olympic (amateur) competition tends to favor the traditional image of the female figure skater, professional skating has moved toward hipper and more MTV-like forms of dance and music. Two TV specials that followed in the wake of Lillehammer emphasized this difference. CBS's *Artistry on Ice* framed the tour of Olympic and World Champions in a more traditional vein while *Fox on Ice* (broadcast May 16, 1994) gave us cutting-edge MTV skating. The CBS show provided an especially clear illustration, since it was a recorded version of the live show I'd viewed just a few days previously. It was less traditional than Olympics' coverage because it presented exhibition skating as an art form rather than a competition and because it included some of the more avant-garde men's performances such as Elvis Stojko's Van Halen and Elvis Presley medley and Phillipe Candeloro's shirtless number, both of which elicited much teenybop behavior from the audience. But CBS chose not to include the most postmodern number in the show—Brasseur and Eisler's gender-bending strip tease in drag, in which gender and subsequently supporting and supported positions were reversed. The selections tended towards the more conservative numbers in the live show, especially when Nancy Kerrigan was involved. In the taped TV version, she skated in a rather sedate red dress to a patriotic song. But in the live show that I viewed in Pittsburgh, she did two different—and far sexier—numbers: the showbizzy "One Look" to Barbra Streisand in the red dress and her Madonna Vogue number in bare midriff and hot pants. Not surprisingly, the Madonna number *was* featured on the Fox show. In addition, CBS went all out with the "artistry" framing device in which skaters were introduced in gold portrait frames while the announcer intoned "glimmering across a frozen canvas, the skaters create memorable works of art for us to appreciate."

The art gallery "frame" as metaphor

In case we didn't get the point, the show's credits were set off against a museum portrait gallery. Nancy wasn't exactly framed but she was shown at her most "elegant" in a rose arbor as the announcer informed us "beauty and grace are Nancy Kerrigan's legacy." The entire CBS show brought out her innocent ultra-femme amateur image. In fact, some of the poses were right out of a Snow White fairytale, and the skating echoed that of Carol Heiss in 1960.

Fox on Ice, by contrast, brought figure skating to the MTV generation, even showcasing the postmodern hand-skating of Gia Guddat and Gary Beacom, nowhere seen during the Olympics coverage and certainly not part of CBS's conception of *Artistry on Ice*.

The ice numbers were framed not as works of art but as little music videos with more rapid editing and with numbers motivated by song lyrics, a practice that is forbidden in Olympic competition. Nancy Kerrigan's image, curiously enough, was more like that of the sexy Katarina Witt

Three views of Nancy in *Artistry on Ice*

Postmodernism on ice

or the bad girl Tonya Harding than like the Miss America contestant constructed during the Olympics and on CBS.

Conclusion

Tonya Harding could never have made a career in the traditional figure skating image. Tonya was never "artistic." Her skating reputation was made on the basis of her triple jumps and power. Her image prior to the

Nancy as hot Madonna on Fox

attack was one of an "athlete," so that when she became newsworthy, it
was easy to add on "working class" and "slut." Then Tonya could be
opposed to Nancy, who was artistry/middle class/princess.

Nancy Kerrigan has more in common with contemporary performers such as Michael Jackson and contemporary politicians such as Gary Hart than she does with stars spun out by the studio publicity machine. This is because in recent years, television coverage of celebrities has become adversarial as well as promotional. Tabloid TV coverage of Nancy and Tonya managed to build them up and tear them down at the same time and via the same stories. Ultimately, both the careful construction of a star mystique and the brutal deconstruction of the same serve to perpetuate the star as a celebrity in the public eye. But Michael Jackson was supposed to endorse Pepsi and Nancy was supposed to endorse Cheerios. It is only for those seeking a wholesome image that deconstruction is harmful. If Sonja Henie had appeared on a float with Mickey Mouse, she would not have been miked since legend has it that her favorite English word was "fuck."

Tonya was never a star skater because she was not even marginally feminine/artistic enough. But she proved to be a better actress than Nancy *off* the ice. Also, curiously, her image off the ice became more feminine than Nancy's. Tonya found her greatest talent on tabloid TV. Since she was unable to construct a figure skating image in the first place, deconstruction could only help her. She was better (i.e. more feminine) on tabloid TV than on the ice. And since all TV is now tabloid TV, Tonya starting benefiting from deconstruction at the same time as Nancy began her post-Olympics downslide. Tonya got better and better, more melodramatic, more convincing on TV. Nancy couldn't keep it together. She was too awkward, jock-like in front of the cameras. Her finest moment came when she sobbed to Jane Pauley about her victimization after the Mickey incident. Unlike Tonya, however, she couldn't repeat the performance on cue. According to an item in the *Pittsburgh Post-Gazette* (Aug. 8, 1994):

> Disgraced figure skater Tonya Harding may have a future in acting if her performance to date in the movie *Breakaway* is an indication. Harding, playing a waitress who finds $1 million of mob money in a refrigerator and runs off to Tahiti with it, is doing great in her first flick, says co-star Emilio Estevez.
>
> "Instinct, that's what Tonya has. Instinct," he says. "She's a nice little actor…. Tonya has the raw talent. I think she could do rather well in films. She's got a really great look, she's got a fantastic body, she's very photogenic."

Allow me to offer a suggestion for Tonya's future acting possibilities. One thing we've learned from the Nancy and Tonya telefilms thus far is that "skate-ins" (i.e. skating doubles) don't work—we know it's not the same person acting and skating and we know what Nancy and Tonya look like skating. Therefore I believe the ideal role for Tonya Harding would be to star in a biopic/exposé of Sonja Henie. Not only does the perfect "Sister Dearest" account of Sonja's life already exist, but Tonya could do her own skating. Since, according to *People* magazine, the public has become weary of Nancy Kerrigan, she might want to appear as herself as well. I can see Tonya now, alternating a Shirley Temple sweetness on camera with backstage bitchiness as she says "you tell that sonofabitch Zanuck to get his ass off the polo ponies and meet me on the set. I show that sonofabitch he don't fool with Sonja."

< NOTES >

1 In the process of re-viewing and re-searching Sonja, I also sought out other Hollywood figure skating films (there weren't many) of which I studied two: the amazing *Ice Follies of 1939*, considered the greatest failure of Joan Crawford's career; and *Snow White and the Three Stooges*, a 1961 Fox technicolor fairy tale in which 1960 Olympic gold medalist Carol Heiss's two skating sequences formed a welcome respite from a film in which she played Snow White and the Three Stooges played the seven dwarfs. I wasn't able to locate *Lake Placid Serenade* (1944) which *Cinemania* described as "a flimsy musical romance about an ice-skater played by real-life skating queen Vera Hruba Ralston." I did locate two books which I also read: Sonja's 1940 memoirs *Wings on My Feet* and the 1985 exposé by Sonja's brother, *Queen of Ice, Queen of Shadows: The Unsuspected Life of Sonja Henie*. In addition to this, I attended (live and in person) the Campbell's Soups 1994 Tour of World Figure Skating Champions on May 4, 1994 in Pittsburgh, a traveling show which was broadcast on CBS under the title "Artistry on Ice."

References

Altman, Rick. *The American Film Musical*. Bloomington: Indiana University Press, 1987.

Feuer, Jane. *The Hollywood Musical*, Second Edition. London: Macmillan/ British Film Institute, 1993.

Henie, Sonja. *Wings on My Feet*. New York: Prentice-Hall, 1940.

Strait, Raymond and Henie, Leif. *Queen of Ice, Queen of Shadows: The Unsuspected Life of Sonja Henie*. New York: Stein and Day, 1985.

Sonja Henie: Annotated Filmography

One in a Million (1937)—Henie's screen debut—being trained for a future

Olympics by her Swiss innkeeper father. Sets formula for films to follow. Early number has a "dream sequence" in which Greta Mueller is transported into a Berkeleyesque spectacular ice-show number. She skates in a glorious open-air plaza in St. Moritz. The Olympics competition recreates Sonja's own triumph in 1936 at the Munich Olympics. She skates at the finale but as a solo, not as a pair with her American boyfriend from the narrative. Adolph Menjou as sleazy entrepreneur who envisions the future of the ice show based on what Sonja was actually doing in live performance at the time. Has all-girl band, girl nightclub singer, and the Ritz Brothers who do a comic skating number.

Thin Ice (1937)—Skating instructress in a large Swiss hotel romances prince. With Tyrone Power. Classic fairy-tale musical. Chaos in kingdoms of middle Europe parallels chaos of couple. Features both government in chaos and hotel in chaos over scandal between prince and skating teacher at hotel. Prince and Cinderella—typical class differences overcome by love. They fall in love by skiing together (with body doubles) since she skates solo. Also uses typical mistaken identity plot: she thinks he's a journalist. Skating numbers take place in huge hotel/nightclub rink. Uses skating 'chorus' and mirrors to double rows of skaters.

Happy Landings (1938)—This is the one with Don Ameche, Caesar Romero, and Ethel Merman. The formula is typical: a screwball comedy romance interpersed with night club numbers and skating spectacles. This one actually has a skating spectacle in a night club in which she wears that sequined tuxedo and does showbizzykicks and chorus girl steps. Its most interesting feature is the ending, featuring a double wedding followed by all four of the lovers skating together, ending with Sonja pulling them in a skating conga line. It's a screwball ending but also a musical one in that it ends "on stage." It differs from the ones in which she skates alone or accompanied by a phantom prince/lover skate-in.

My Lucky Star (1938)—Salesgirl in a department store sent to college and stages annual winter ice show in her boss's department store. She is hired to exhibit sporting outfits for the store, and we see her changing skiing and skating and ice hockey outfits four times a day, which alienates her from the other students. Although politically incorrect, she wears some really fabulous furs, including an all-leopardskin item that has to be seen to be believed. Includes ice ballet to *Alice in Wonderland*.

Second Fiddle (1939)—Began as satire on the choosing of Scarlett O'Hara with Sonja as a skating school-teacher; romance with studio's publicity man (Tyrone Power). Typical behind-the-screen show musical. Very interesting dream sequence to an Irving Berlin song about missing the snow in summer. The enormous L.A. swimming pool magically transforms into an ice rink on which Sonja skates romantically with an anonymous male partner.

Everything Happens at Night (1939)—Sonja vies for affections of two reporters with only a few skating scenes.

Sun Valley Serenade (1941)—Glen Miller's manager agrees to keep an eye on a pretty Norwegian refugee.

Iceland (1942)—Sonja's penultimate Fox film, romance and rink. WWII troop musical. Sonja falls for American soldier (John Payne) stationed in Iceland. Fairy-tale plot and setting but not as pure as the early films. Bizarre international skating number (Hula, Tango, Asian dancing, all on skates with anonymous male partner). Most of the film is taken up with the cumbersome plot whereby she tries to trick Payne into marriage. After the successful couplings, we see a solo finale. Sonja, attired in a military ensemble with a huge Yankee Doodle feather in her cap, skates to various American military service patriotic anthems, e.g. "Halls of Montezuma"; "Navy"; and "Air Force." An "army" of soldier/skaters backs her up—so that even though the movie is supposed to be in Iceland, it's really about American patriotism in the war. Iceland is viewed as a backward country with quaint and archaic courtship practices. The whole thing is rather imperialistic.

Wintertime (1943)—Last film for Fox. Sonja as a Norwegian skating star saving a run-down winter resort in Canada which she visits with her rich uncle. Lots of skating, good acting, great clothes.

It's a Pleasure (1945)—RKO; Sonja's only color feature film.

The Countess of Monte Cristo (1948)—Universal-International.

Abigail M. Feder

"A Radiant Smile from the Lovely Lady"

Overdetermined Femininity in "Ladies" Figure Skating

A casual observer of the figure skating coverage at the 1994 Olympics might have supposed that in the figure skating world Nancy Kerrigan had always been the princess and Tonya Harding the white trash whore. In a limited sense they would not have been wrong: Kerrigan and Harding were contrasted in figure skating coverage, especially television coverage, long before the attack on Kerrigan at the 1994 U.S. National Championships. But what might surprise some is that the contrast did not always favor Kerrigan. In the short-hand of figure skating identification, Kerrigan was the elegant lady, Harding the "tough cookie." The ubiquity of this short-hand identification was remarked on by Frank Deford: "everybody who makes reference to Harding, like her or not, is bound to say: 'a tough cookie.' It's like an official part of her name, a position, like: Tonya Harding, shortstop, or Tonya Harding, soprano; Tonya Harding, tough cookie" (52). While Kerrigan had more "tel-appeal" as a skating personality, a stereotypical "ice princess," Harding had more legitimacy as an athlete, especially among sports writers who usually cover men's sports.

Femininity and athleticism are mutually exclusive concepts in American culture. Even in recent years, when the fitness craze extended to both sexes, women were constantly reminded that all signs of their athleticism must be kept invisible. In an Arid deodorant commercial that ran extensively in recent years, the young man says to the camera, "To me, it just isn't sexy when a woman sweats;" the young woman says, "Sure, a guy is going to sweat sometimes; but who wants to be close to a guy who smells?" In our culture "it is assumed that sports success *is* success at being masculine. Physical achievement, and masculine activity, are taken to be the same" (Willis, 123).

I became interested in exploring singles figure skating when I observed that, although the athletic requirements do not appear specifically gendered, the narrative surrounding the women's competition is sickly sweet in its presentation of the competitors' femininity. I discovered, as I will detail below, that in the original (short) program, for which the requirements are set by the International Skating Union (ISU), gender differences are built in. However in the free (long) program, for which the athletes choose their own material, there is little difference between the skills performed by men and women. Both are required to perform complex footwork and a variety of spins and jumps; no competitor would be taken seriously who does not have several triple jumps, and for both men and women the triple Axel is the most difficult jump performed (although two male and one female competitor have performed a quadruple jump). Judging ranges from the fairly objective to the extremely subjective: jumps are judged on height and clean take-offs and landings; skaters are judged on how well they "relate" to their music. They are awarded two sets of marks, for technical merit and artistic impression.

Perhaps it is because of the equality of the skills performed that the narrative surrounding competition is so overdetermined in its construction of the women skaters' femininity: "Even if ideology cannot totally submerge itself as common sense, it can at least forward plausible suggestions for the reinterpretation of events. Ideology can never afford to let contradictory interpretations of reality go free from at least a crippling ambiguity" (Willis, 127). The almost hysterical assertion of gender difference presented in coverage of figure skating succeeds in tangling the ideological issues until they are almost beyond debate. The idea that men may not have a "natural" physical superiority is no longer out of the question: Evy Scotvold, the coach who trained U.S. skaters Nancy Kerrigan and Paul Wylie, once said of Japan's Midori Ito, "The only man I've ever seen outjump her is [1988 Olympic gold medalist] Brian Boitano" (Swift, 1992a:20), an opinion echoed by former Olympic champion Scott Hamilton during CBS coverage of the 1992 games (see also Deford and

Starr, 1992:52). Boitano himself said of Tonya Harding, "'She jumps like a male skater.... There's an incredible strength and control in her jumping'" (Swift, 1992:63). When physical capabilities no longer distinguish men and women, femininity is overdetermined to keep female athletes from being labeled as masculine or lesbian. This phenomenon can be observed elsewhere in women's sports from the obsession with tennis player Monica Seles' latest "do," to Florence Griffith-Joyner's long nails and lace stockings, to professional golfer Jan Stephenson posing for a Marilyn Monroe style pin-up poster: "The more successful a female athlete, the more she tries to embody the culturally appropriate gender role...a role essentially at odds with her athleticism" (Faller, 154). This is, of course, assuming that the athlete wishes to avoid such a label; an out lesbian, such as Martina Navrotilova, does not need to bother.

"Femininity," wrote Susan Brownmiller, "must constantly reassure" (15)—reassure that, no matter their accomplishments, women athletes are still "just girls" underneath. Successful women athletes risk being labeled "mannish," with generally unspoken implications of lesbianism close to the surface. The connection between femininity and reassurance was made explicit in a 1982 *Sports Illustrated* article on the above-mentioned Stephenson: "Stephenson did a lot for the image of women's golf in 1981. That was the year in which Billie Jean King admitted she'd had a lesbian affair and almost knocked a wheel off the apple cart of women's sports. And all during that perilous time, there was Stephenson out front on the sports pages, looking good and playing better" (McDermott, 31). Women must precariously negotiate their societally contradictory roles of woman and athlete. Nancy Therberge summarizes one strategy, Jan Felshin's theory of the female apologetic in sports:

> Felshin characterized the social dynamic of women in sport as an anomaly.... As an extension of this, women in sport advance an apologetic for their involvement. The apologetic affirms a woman's femininity despite her athletic endeavors and thus "legitimates the woman's role in sport by minimizing the anomaly." This legitimation is not complete, however, and social conflict over the contradictions inherent in women's sport activities persists. (344)

Figure skating's "apology" is actually incorporated into the competition, where costume, makeup, and gesture feminize and soften the athletic prowess required for executing triple jumps and flying sit-spins. The fact that female competitors are still officially called "Ladies" under U.S. and International Skating Union rules (a fact which even the typically unselfconscious U.S. television reporters felt the need to explain to its audience) is only the beginning (ABC, 11 January, 1992). Television coverage is framed in vignettes featuring soft-focus lights, stars in little girls' eyes, glittery costumes, and flowers from adoring crowds. "A dream is a wish your heart makes when you're fast asleep" is the music accompanying the shots of a little girl falling asleep surrounded by stuffed animals wearing skating medals which introduced ABC coverage of the 1992 U.S. National Championship; "You look wonderful tonight" sang Eric Clapton over close-ups of the 1992 female Olympic medal hopefuls before the finals. In contrast, the framing device that introduced the men's finals played the percussive background to a Genesis song which has accompanying lyrics: "I can feel it coming in the air tonight," while computer animated lightning signaled each explosive editing cut. While the women were shown in flowing movement, in worried close-ups or applying makeup, the men were pictured doing their most difficult jumps, raising their hands in gestures of triumph. Spots publicizing the '94 men's Olympic competition featured more explosive shots of men jumping or pumping their arms in triumph to rock music, while the voice-over punched out their names: "Boitano. Petrenko. Browning. Elvis.... The battle will be epic!" The teaser for the ladies' final featured Frank Sinatra singing, "Yes, you're lovely, with your smile so warm, and your cheeks so soft, that there's nothing for me but to love you, and *the way you look tonight*" over shots of the women spinning, smiling, bowing, waving and hand-kissing to the crowd.

There is always an emphasis on the women skaters' physical beauty (and a corresponding denigration of the sport), which is related to their exchange value and the commodification which is the ultimate reward of Olympic victory. An insidious duality is established by labeling some women as athletic and others as artistic, with the artistry associated with physical beauty and a slender body type. Finally, the women competitors are never allowed to own their success, but are always identified in relationship to family, either biological or their extended skating family; they are especially identified with their mothers.

The anxiety about the success of women athletes is most obviously symbolized by the Olympic practice of sex-ID testing, which proves how closely sports success and masculine identity are connected in our culture.

The idea of certifying female athletes as females originated more than 25 years ago. Athletic directors said they were trying to guard against male impostors, but a more subtle message was also being sent, said Alison Carlson, a member of the athletic federation's committee and a tennis coach. A successful female athlete "challenges society's notion of femininity," Ms. Carlson said, so both the athletic directors and the women themselves felt it important to prove they were real women. (Kolata, E6)

In order to compete, women athletes must strive for strength, speed, and competitiveness—all those qualities which our society codes as masculine: "As an athlete becomes even more outstanding, she marks herself out as even more deviant.... To succeed as an athlete can be to fail as a woman, because she has, in certain profound symbolic ways, become a man" (Willis, 123). So in order to avoid being coded as overly masculine or a lesbian, the athlete will participate in her own construction as a hyperfeminine creature. This is more true in figure skating than in any other sport. Because of its element of theatre, figure skating provides more opportunities for adornment and display, those familiar tropes of femininity with which the American public is comfortable. But even as they have become embraced as stars, female skaters have often been negated as athletes.

Women in figure skating are caught in a trap that Naomi Wolf could have labeled "the bind of the Beauty Myth": a woman must live up to popular notions of beauty in order to compete successfully, both on the ice and in the commercial endorsement sweepstakes. The spectacle of their beauty is one factor in the fabulous popularity of women's figure skating, and why the women's competition is one of the few that is more popular than the men's equivalent (the valorization of male athletes is reversed in those sports "whose 'aesthetic' properties encode them as suitably 'feminine'" [Whannel, 104]): "When Katarina Witt won her second gold in '88, the prime time ratings...topped out past 35, the sort of number that baseball and basketball never fetch and that football obtains only for the Super Bowl itself" (Deford, 46). But the sport is taken less seriously precisely because its competitors are beautifully dressed and made-up women: "The preservation of youthful beauty is one of the few intense preoccupations and competitive drives that society fully expects of its women, even as it holds them in disdain for being such a narcissistic lot." (Brownmiller, 167). One particularly overwrought male columnist wrote, "Figure skating—Should be dropped altogether. What used to be a genuine competition is now what *Cats* is to musical comedy, a costumed, overwrought, pretentious joke. And what kind of game is it where the winner gets to wear cosmetics and skate on tour?" (Lincicome, 1).[1]

The concern with spectacle can be seen in the obsessive attention to women's costumes. In 1992 skating fashion found its way from the sports pages to the "Living Arts" section of the *New York Times,* because top fashion designers, including French haute couture designer Christian LaCroix, were making skaters' costumes. Vera Wang described the outfits she designed for Nancy Kerrigan: "Nancy wanted me to translate the look of couture evening wear to the ice" (Louie, 1). What was not pointed out is that all these costumes, in addition to sequins and tiny skirts, have some simulated nudity, whether it is a plunging neckline, a cutout back or "sheer illusion sleeves" (Louie, 1); "Appearance, not accomplishment, is the feminine demonstration of desirability and worth.... Feminine armor is never metal or muscle, but paradoxically, an exaggeration of physical vulnerability that is reassuring (unthreatening) to men" (Brownmiller, 51).

"So why do they play into it?" a male friend asked me. "What if they competed in full body coverings like the men?" As it turns out, both men and women are limited in their choice of costumes by the rules. Debi Thomas, who won the bronze medal at the 1988 Olympic games, skated her short program in a sequined body stocking rather than a short skirt. Although she skated her program "flawlessly," according to a Canadian magazine ([O'Hara, 49] which might be expected to be free from U.S. partisanship), she received low artistic impression marks. If, as speculated, artistic impression for women skaters is connected to a particular kind of unthreatening femininity, perhaps the scores were connected to her costume and to gold medalist Katarina Witt's, which made her look "like a member of the Rockette's chorus line" (O'Hara, 49). After this competition, the ISU adopted new rules on costuming which specified that "Costumes for Ladies cannot be theatrical in nature [?!]. They must have skirts...covering the hips and posterior. A 'unitard' is not acceptable" (USFSA Rulebook, 112). This rule eliminates the most sensible (and unisex) costume available to all skaters, the unitard.

Dick Button, a former Olympic gold medalist who has covered skating for ABC for decades, commented in a 1992 interview about the women's Olympic competition: "The dress helps. The easiest thing is to get here. The hardest is to get that last 1 percent. You can't have anything out of place. Tonya Harding's dresses don't help" (*New York Times,* 1992:B13). Harding's 1992 Olympic costumes, although they had the ubiquitous short skirt and a cutout back, were also high necked with shoulder pads and a faintly military air about them, the kind of power lines usually reserved for the men (in fact, in 1988 both gold medalist Brian Boitano and silver medalist Brian Orser wore outfits with military shoulders and trim). At the 1992 World Championships which followed the Olympics, Harding had softened both her music and the lines of her costume for her short program; her artistic impression scores went up.

Women find their greatest popular acceptance in sports that are considered "feminine," yet then are denigrated as lesser athletes. Nancy Kerrigan, according to numerous print and television profiles of her family, wanted to play ice hockey like her older brothers. But there were no teams for girls and her parents "felt figure skating would be more appropriate": "You're a girl. Do girl things," her mother recalled telling her (CBS, 29 February, 1992). Women are ghettoized into certain sports, then the sports are seen as less serious because mostly women participate in them. The coverage of the sports identifies the competitors as women first and then athletes. When Nancy Kerrigan took to the ice to skate her free program at the 1992 U.S. Nationals, Dick Button said, "Doesn't she look elegant," and Peggy Fleming agreed, "She looks like a little angel," thereby framing her program not as the competition of a serious athlete, but as the display of a beautiful woman. Verne Lundquist, commentator for CBS coverage of the Olympics, said of Kerrigan, "She has such an elegant presence…and then to skate that well," as if the beauty were natural and the skating skill an unexpected surprise in an Olympic athlete. An interview in *Gentlemen's Quarterly* with two-time Olympic gold medalist Katarina Witt pointed out this practice (even as it presented Witt in a centerfoldlike pose): "Coverage of the 1988 Winter Olympics at times degenerated into an overheated symposium on Katarina's sex appeal—from the shape of her legs to the lush arrangement of other body parts, most notably those that Katarina refers to matter-of-factly as her boobs and her butt" (Cook, 130).

Witt may be able to laugh at her objectification. In fact, she is laughing all the way to the bank, with several highly lucrative commercial endorsements, ice shows, and TV sports commentary jobs. But the message that women, no matter how accomplished, will always also have to live up to highly unrealistic standards of physical beauty harms women and girls far from the spotlight of the Olympic winner's circle. An article in *People* magazine dropped the comment that 1992 Russian pairs champion Natalia Mishkutenok looked a little "chunky"; the following week *People* ran a cover story bemoaning the tragedy of a young TV star who, after years of being the butt of fat jokes in the context of the show, now suffers from anorexia. Somehow, they seemed to have missed the connection. Objectification is about power.

> The female athlete is rendered a sex *object*—a body which may excel in sport, but which is primarily an object of pleasure for men. A useful technique, for

if a woman seems to be encroaching too far, and too threateningly, into male sanctuaries, she can be symbolically vapourised and reconstituted as an object, a butt for smutty jokes and complacent elbow nudging. (Willis, 122)

Although the coverage of the 1992 Olympics seemed to tend closer to the worshipful than the smutty, the latter is hardly unknown in skating: "In Europe, anyway, by far the most popular photograph of any skater in recent years is not of anybody jumping, but of Witt coming completely out of the top of her outfit after a simple spin" (Deford, 50). In 1994, the frequent reiterations of the story of Harding's costume coming undone, combined with tabloid broadcasts of Harding stripping out of her wedding dress at a party on home video, served as signs of her "sluttishness" and sloppiness.

In a lecture on sports photography, University of Washington professor Diane Hagaman emphasized the need for sports photos to be a "good quick read…eyecatching [and able to] entice readers to read the text." They must also reinforce the image conveyed by the text, be it winning or losing, endurance or conflict. Therefore, sports photography depends on "highly conventionalized images" (Hagaman, 1992). For example, the narrative surrounding Nancy Kerrigan in 1992 always emphasized her beauty and elegance; she could not step onto the ice without the commentators, male or female, remarking how "lovely–elegant–angelic–sophisticated" she was. Not surprisingly, therefore, many different newspapers and magazines caught her in the same arabesque pose (called a "spiral" in skating) from the end of her program, one long leg extended out behind her, arm extended out front, a very balletic pose (see Silverman).

Television editing can also manipulate our perception and lend credence to narrative. An impression of speed and choppiness can be emphasized by use of cuts, which instantaneously switch from one shot to another; while flow and grace can be emphasized by use of dissolves, which gradually replace one shot with another. Kerrigan's 1992 Olympic long program was broadcast with nine dissolves and eight cuts; in contrast the program of French skater Surya Bonaly, a former gymnast who is commonly described as a choppy skater and dynamic jumper, had only four dissolves to thirteen cuts. Hagaman, who was looking at particular gestures representing victory, defeat, injury, and endurance in sports photography did not observe gender differences in these particular gestures. But in figure skating, despite the similarity in skills performed, certain poses and gestures are gendered female. The most obvious is the forward layback spin, a move meant to show the flexibility of female skaters. Back arched, eyes closed, mouth slightly open, arms extended as for an embrace—in still photographs it looks like nothing so much as popular conceptions of female sexual arousal. The same pose is often used in fashion photography or "beauty pornography," as described by Naomi Wolf: "Beauty pornography looks like this: The perfected woman lies...pressing down her pelvis. Her back arches, her mouth is open, her eyes shut,... the position is female superior, the state of arousal, the plateau phase just preceding orgasm" (132). In figure skating a layback spin is a requirement in the women's original program; men rarely perform this skill. There were more pictures of Yamaguchi in this position than in any other in 1992. The repetition of this image presents a disturbing convergence of racist and sexist images, playing into stereotypes of the sexually submissive Asian beauty. The virginal, elegant Kerrigan, in contrast, is rarely represented this way. In my review of two years worth of skating articles in newpapers and magazines leading up to the 1992 Olympic games, I never saw one photograph of Kerrigan in this pose, although all the other top skaters (Harding, Ito, and Bonaly) were pictured this way at least twice. The notable exception was the picture of Kerrigan which was a prominent part of the cover montage for "*Life* Remembers '92" (1993). An irate reader wrote in response to that cover, "Did you guys forget Kristi Yamaguchi was the gold medal winner for the U.S.A.? 'Racist' is a very harsh word, but I can't think of any other word to explain this inexcusable slight." The editors replied, "All the cover images were chosen for their complementary shape, composition and perspective" (1993a:30). My research indicates that *Life* would have had to pass many representations of Yamaguchi in a layback spin in order to put an atypical Kerrigan photo on its cover.

It is not only the narrative surrounding skating which favors "feminine ladies." The rules and judging are also skewed to reward such skaters. Skating is judged in two categories, technical merit and artistic impression. A maximum technical merit score is predetermined by the difficulty of the program, and then deductions are made for each error. There is a range of possible deductions, making the technical merit score far from objective. By far the most straightforward part of the program to judge is the jumps, because the order of difficulty is agreed upon and the success or failure of a jump is usually obvious. In the original program, for which the requirements are set, the men are expected to do at least two and perhaps three triple jumps, while until a 1995 rule change the women were only *allowed* to do one triple jump. This requirement reduced the most objective end of the scoring—how difficult the jump was and how cleanly it was landed—and gave far more emphasis to the more subjective areas of judgment that fall under "technical merit," along with the already nebulous category of "artistic impression."

The 1992 Olympic competition was filled with soul-searching debate over the direction the sport was going: Would it lose all its artistic beauty and become just a "jump-fest"? The Yamaguchi gold and Kerrigan bronze were hailed by many commentators and sportswriters as a clear victory for artistry over athleticism (see Deford and Starr); this debate undercut the athletic abilities of "artistic" skaters. "Although figure skaters train hard, they are schooled to make the difficult look easy. [They are] 'athlete[s] in disguise' who [skate], with unimpaired femininity, into hearts closed" to less feminine athletes (Guttman, 200-01). Few athletes were more skillful at disguising their athleticism than Yamaguchi, whose jumps at the 1992 Nationals were described as "beautiful, effortless, soft.... She does indeed float like a leaf" (ABC 12 January 1992). Katarina Witt said Yamaguchi "represents the sport in the right way. Because it's figure skating and it's not only sport, there's a big part of artistry involved. And her jumps look just so effortless, so easy and they're still so difficult" (CBS, 19 February, 1992).

Kerrigan is another athlete who has managed to make the signs of her athleticism all but invisible. None of the stereotypical signs of the athlete—grunting, sweating, bulging muscles—ever seemed to disrupt the lady-like Kerrigan package. She was known not for her strong jumps (although, in fact, she is quite a strong jumper), but for her elegance and her line. In contrast, Harding, with her huge jumps, speed, and muscular body was aggressively athletic. Her incompetence as a woman, whether it was her choice of costumes, her hobbies (shooting pool, hunting, fixing cars and drag racing), or her controversial behavior (firing coaches, her rocky marriage, fighting with a fellow motorist on a Portland street) marked her as deviant. Because she was such a strong jumper, she threatened the very notions of sexual difference which to a large extent define masculinity. This "deviance" reduced her value as a television entertainer and commercial spokeswoman long before she was connected to the Kerrigan attack.

What is always close to the surface, but rarely acknowledged, in the narrative of the artistry vs. athleticism debate, is that for the women, artistry is indistinguishable from physical beauty. Japan's Midori Ito came the closest to expressing this when she explained why she relied on her athleticism over artistry: "All I can really do is jump. Figure skating is a matter of beauty, and Westerners are so stylish, so slender. I wish I could be beautiful like them" (Deford, 51). According to a report in USA Today, compiled from interviews with coaches and various books on skating techniques, Ito had the ideal body for figure skating: "a compact body with a low center of gravity" (*USA Today*, 10). Ito did not question this apparent contradiction, but assumed that because she was not "beautiful" she could not be artistic. As Willis said about interviews with female weight-lifters, "the (at least reported) responses of the women…either collude in the sexualisation of the topic or reinforce the standards of male comparison" (131).

Why are artistry and athleticism considered mutually exclusive in Ladies Figure Skating? A baseball player can be called poetry in motion; the balletic grace of Michael Jordan's jumps was admired without implying that he was less of an athlete. Comments on male skaters make it clear that the younger skaters are expected to grow into their artistry—which is related to elegance, showmanship, playing the audience, and choreographic maturity—and become "complete" skaters.[2] Yamaguchi, on the other hand, grew into her artistry and, according to many, out of her athleticism: "Poor Yamaguchi. Paradoxically, in the past, she had always been labeled 'the athlete' in comparison to the artistic Jill Trenary…. then suddenly Yamaguchi found herself written off as some kind of a bush leaguer just because she couldn't hit the triple axel; never mind she can land all the other triples extant" (Deford, 47, 50). Only Ito and Harding among the women have completed the triple axel in competition. Although most of the top men now perform the triple axel, those who do not, such as Christopher Bowman (who won the 1992 U.S. Nationals without a triple axel), and '92 Olympic bronze medalist Peter Barna, are not considered nonathletes, simply less advanced. There were no reporters worrying over the future of the men's competition because some athletes were acquiring new skills. In fact the idea of a man being called "too athletic" is simply ludicrous.

A woman's athleticism is belittled, often undercut in commentary which calls attention away from her athletic ability and right back to her physical appearance. After Kerrigan completed a complicated triple-double combination in 1992, Scott Hamilton commented, "Perfectly done!" and Verne Lundquist chimed in, "That brings a radiant smile from the lovely lady." After Yamaguchi's double axel, Hamilton said, "Look at the height and flow," and Lundquist added, "And then look at the smile." Says Brownmiller: "A major purpose of femininity is to mystify or minimize the functional aspects of a woman's mind and body that are indistinguishable from a man's" (84). Yamaguchi's coach Christy Ness complained about her athlete not being taken seriously: "Kristi doesn't lift weights to be called fluff" (Swift, 1992b:19); yet her weight-lifting was treated with fluffy, patronizing humor. *Sports Illustrated* reported that she had begun to lift "(very, very small) weights" to increase her strength (Swift, 18), while a TNT reporter joked that after getting off practice Kristi thought about "things girls think about—weights!", as if a world class athlete lifting weights was the most unexpectedly comical thing he had ever encountered (TNT, 20 February, 1992). "Frequently, reporting of women's sport takes its fundamental bearings, not on sport, but on humour, or the unusual. The tone is easy to recognise, it's a version of the irony, the humour, the superiority, of the sophisticated towards the cranks" (Willis, 121).

Newsweek presented its version of the athlete vs. artist debate as a fairy-tale, with an insidious, antifeminist moral:

> Surely, there must be a fairy tale that fits here.... It'd be the one about the two stylish gorgeous creatures—swans or butterflies, take your pick—competing against the stronger, more daring beings for the favor of the gods. And, of course, the stronger, more daring beings are certain to win, because spectacular is always better ever after. Only, the stronger, more daring beings reach for too high a sky...and so the stylish gorgeous creatures glide to victory—and, probably, here comes a handsome prince or two, as well.... Oh, truth be told, it wasn't all that neat. The athletes weren't quite that klutzy, and the artists weren't quite that wimpy, but let's not louse up a good fairy tale. (Deford and Starr, 50)

In fact, one of those "daring beings," Midori Ito, took the almost unheard of risk of adding a triple axel late in her long program after she had missed it twice in the competition; her daring was rewarded when she vaulted over Kerrigan to win the silver medal. But "let's not louse up a good fairy tale" with the facts. The moral that America seems most comfortable with is that "ladies" will be rewarded for being "stylish and gorgeous" and punished for being too daring. *Sports Illustrated* had a different take on the same event: "This was a competition incorrectly billed as the athletes vs. the artists.... Yamaguchi and Kerrigan were plenty athletic. They were just minus one jump: the triple Axel" (Swift, 1992b:19). The athlete vs. artist dichotomy was even clearer in the 1988 competition, where preview articles such as one in *Time* magazine set up the competition between Debi Thomas and Katarina Witt as "steely resolve" vs. "stylish allure," with accompanying pictures showing the former lifting weights and consulting with her coach, while the latter flirted with the judges and pouted at the camera (*Time*, 44–46).

"I always tell my girls: think like a man, but act and look like a woman," says former skater turned coach Carol Heiss (Deford, 6). What does it mean to "think like a man?" Men are supposed to be competitive, focussed, and ambitious. They can even be cocky, if they have the skill to back it up—witness the popularity of Charles Barkley and Andre Agassi. Proper masculinity is by definition ambitious and competitive: Canadian skater Kurt Browning had a "job to do," which was winning the gold medal, while of Kristi Yamaguchi it was said, "she would skate even if they didn't give out medals." He was lionized for being a "big game" skater (although, in fact, he did not skate his best at either the 1992 or 1994 Olympics); she was patted on the head for being very steady, consistent. She was allowed ambitions as long as they were couched in terms of little girl dreams, creating a continuity with past champions such as 1976 gold medalist Dorothy Hamill. This connection was made by television interviewers who asked Yamaguchi, "Have you been dreaming of this moment?" and by television visuals which caught Yamaguchi talking to Hamill backstage before her free skate. It all seemed to lend credence to the "A dream is a wish your heart makes" framing device of the 1992 U.S. National Championships. To win the men's final, a competitor would need "all the ammunition you can fire" (CBS, 15 February, 1992), while Ito, the "Queen of the triple jumps" was going to have to be "on her toes" to win (CBS, 19 February, 1992).

The emotions that make for a good competitor do not necessarily make for a feminine woman. Kerrigan's monumental success in the endorsement game, which dates back to before the attack, was always based more on her lady-like demeanor than on her prowess as an athlete. She was admired as a genuine girl who, her father said, has "got all the emotions of anybody. If she's watching TV and something is sad she'll cry, if it's laughter she'll laugh" (CBS, 19 February, 1992). This image of Kerrigan was contrasted to that of the poised (read: inscrutable?) Yamaguchi. Women aren't supposed to have the nerves and ambition to compete. TV is always searching for signs of women's instability, sure that they are always about to crack under the pressure. The framing device for the 1992 Olympic pairs final focussed exclusively on the women, with the implication that the men were a given, stable and solid as rocks:

It's a tale of two women [close-up of Natalia Mishkutenok]. One who has always exemplified grace under pressure [tape showing Mishkutenok lifted, spread-eagled, above her partner's head]. And one who wants so much to win it's sometimes gotten the best of her [close-up of Yelena Bechke looking up into her partner's eyes]—until it was the Olympic games [Bechke receiving a kiss from her partner after a successful original program].... It's also the story of another woman who flew so high [Isabelle Bresseur being thrown by her partner], but couldn't land [Bresseur falling on her double axel, then a cut to Bresseur backstage in tears]. Three different women, who with their partners tonight share one common purpose. (CBS, 11 February, 1992)

Coverage of women skaters always seems to emphasize women's vulnerability, both emotional and physical, rather than their strength and accomplishments. This vulnerability was one of the most common descriptions of Nancy Kerrigan even before the attack that cast her as the nation's number one victim of greed-motivated violence. Along with a reputation for elegance and niceness, Kerrigan built a reputation for crumbling under pressure. At the 1992 Olympics, "Kerrigan...botched her long program...gasping for air and nearly crying afterward" (Deford and Starr, 52). She dropped from second to third and held on to the bronze only because the other top competitors also fell. The same was true of her silver at the 1992 Worlds and even her performance when she won the 1993 U.S. Nationals. Although this did not win her much respect as an athlete—after the 1993 Worlds, Filip Bondy, writing in the *New York Times,* said flatly, "Kerrigan has not come up big in the long program at a major competition since the Nationals in 1991, and she fell apart again today" (1993:6)—it did not seem to affect her marketability. In fact, her vulnerability may have made her more appealingly feminine and less threatening. After the January 1994 attack, Kerrigan and her public relations people seemed to have borrowed a page from Tonya Harding's press book, describing her as "tougher" than people gave her credit for. About two weeks after the attack, Kerrigan's coach Evy Scotvold was quoted as saying, "since the incident, she has become a different cat. She has a different look in her eyes—a peaceful determination with the confidence of a gunslinger" (Hersh, 1994, sec. 4:3).

I find Frigga Haug's notion of "slavegirl competence" a useful framework for thinking of the way in which women both use and are victimized by the figure skating system. It "allows us both to grasp the relation of structural domination within which femininity is subordinated to masculinity, and at the same time to portray women as active, albeit in the context of given constraints" (Haug, 131).

Women are made both supplementary and subordinate to men, they are abused as objects of sex and pleasure.... Yet women also know from their experience that skill is involved in conforming to prevailing rules and orderings. Among other things, we take pleasure in acquiring and endorsing the requisite skills. Our active appropriation of the rules makes us more self-confident in our activities; in availing ourselves of the existing order by actively "exhibiting" our own bodies, we participate in our own construction as slavegirls. (Haug, 144)

During the 1992 Olympic coverage there was one interview with Yamaguchi while she was being fitted by her costume designer. She stood in a red body suit while another woman measured and pinned her, saying: "I think it's important to create the entire mood of the program.... People come to watch you because, you know, it's supposed to be a beautiful sport and the costumes are just part of it" (CBS, 21 February, 1992). She was actively participating in her own construction as a passive object of beauty. Yamaguchi's original program, much praised for the beauty of its choreography, was described by her choreographer Sandra Bezic as the moment when a girl looks in the mirror and realizes she's a beautiful woman. The beauty of Yamaguchi's program played into popular concepts of what Brownmiller describes as "preoccupied gestures that are considered sublimely feminine because they are sensuously self-involved" (73). This sensuous self-involvement was admired by Martha Duffy in an article in *Time:*

They are at their most beautiful, these rarefied athletes, in the six-minute practice session where competitors warm up, a few at a time. Done by a Kerrigan, the waltz jump, a mere half revolution, is a perfection of grace. A double Axel is clear and open, not the whipped-up whir a triple must be. Yamaguchi and Harding may land perfect leaps in tandem.... All the women are intently absorbed, and their jumps look less like stunts than whitecaps bubbling out of waves. (1992a:56)

The model of the "slavegirl" is especially useful when thinking about Kerrigan. During the 1993 Worlds, before Kerrigan skated her long program, NBC broadcast a piece on how her life had been changed by the pressures of fame. The theme was "everyone wants a piece of her." Her mother commented, "It's almost too much. Every once in a while she becomes emotional. And then she'll cry, like, 'I just can't do this, I just can't do any more. All I want to do is skate.'" It was as if she had no choice when it came to signing contracts, filming commercials, and posing for magazine spreads. The NBC report on the pressures of fame included tape of Kerrigan being prepared for filming. She wore a white flowing dress and long loose hair, but she was harnessed, so that she could be flown in front of a backdrop of a gorgeous sky. The illusion constructed was that she was flying when, in fact, she was restrained. This was Nancy Kerrigan as the perfect slavegirl: soaring success, completely confined.

Another way in which the figure skating coverage emphasized the femininity of its ladies was by constantly defining them in the context of their families, either their biological families or their skating family. Biographical sketches of each of the three 1992 U.S. Olympians contrasted the three as being from different worlds, but the story worked like the classic family picture: Kristi Yamaguchi as first-born, businesslike, an overachiever, out on her own—the bio featured shots of Yamaguchi in her work environment and with her coaches. By foregrounding Yamaguchi's move to Canada to train, television was able to portray her as an outsider without ever referring to her race. Tonya Harding was the troubled middle child, firing and rehiring her coach, referring to her coach as her "employee," breaking up and reuniting with her husband, all evidence of a lack of values in the skating world; rebellious and unconventional, she was shown behind the wheel of a truck. Kerrigan (although actually the oldest of the three at 22) was the much-beloved baby of both this skating family and of her biological family in Massachusetts, with whom she is shown in happy domestic settings, ending at the dinner table toasting with milk (you could almost hear the dairy industry chortling with glee). In subsequent newspaper and television coverage, these themes were picked up again and again: stories about Yamaguchi emphasizing her wonderful working relationship with her coach and choreographer, her poise, her consistency ("Kristi's greatest strength is her lack of weaknesses," said Scott Hamilton before her original program); stories about Harding emphasizing her personal troubles, her foolish stubbornness; and stories about Kerrigan always emphasizing her family, especially her "mother and best friend Brenda [who] is legally blind" (ABC, 12 January, 1992), an appealing human interest story that TV milked for all it was worth.

Kerrigan's family was the most overplayed at the 1992 Olympics, but hers certainly wasn't the only family put on display. Families are big in Olympic coverage. Families sell. The U.S. Postal Service brought over a number of athletes' families to see the games in exchange for product endorsements. "Pride and profit, that's why we're in it," said Postmaster General Anthony Frank (CBS, 19 February, 1992). The commercial appeal of family is linked to the commercial appeal of femininity. Before the pairs were to free skate, Charles Kuralt and Scott Hamilton did a special on the mothers in the stands—but only the mothers of the women. Said Hamilton, "Especially for the women in the pairs team the mother must really go through a lot because of the danger involved.... If I was a mother of a child and my little girl was out there and somebody dropped her...." (CBS, 11 February, 1992). Kuralt finished up, "Skaters' mothers pull for their children." By only showing the mothers of women skaters, they reinforced the assumption that the women are children.

Of course, this same touching portrayal can take on the ugly stereotype of the stage mother, who Hamilton calls the "nightmare mother...[who] thinks they know everything about skating, they know more than any coach.... Everybody in the building is against them, everyone hopes their child falls." This seemed to be the case with French skater Surya Bonaly and her mother Suzanne: "the Olympic gold medal...is clearly the tangible object of her adoptive mother's desire.... With apparent manipulative encouragement from her mother, Bonaly has turned into...a chippie...the sort of school kid who would pinch the other students or pull their hair" (Hersh, 1992a, sec.4:2). A woman's success is not her own but a collaborative effort between skater and her biological family or her surrogate family of coach and choreographer. On the "CBS Morning" program preview of the 1992 Ladies Original Program, Harry Smith asked Kerrigan's parents, "Tell me a little about what it takes to get a daughter on the ice in the Olympics. How much work is it? Dad?" When Daniel Kerrigan would have given all the credit to Nancy—"[It's] all her work. She does it all.... She came here on her own"—Smith turned to her mother and persisted: "Doesn't it really take a family commitment, Brenda?"[3] What this coverage never mentioned were those skaters whose families were less than supportive, such as Harding's. Women must be portrayed in relationship; only men can thrive as lone individuals.

And women will be punished for not being good girls. Coverage of Yamaguchi emphasized her steady, professional, but also close and loving working relationship with her choreographer and coach: "Says U.S. coach Don Laws: 'Kristi has the ideal temperament for a skater. She trusts her coach, her parents, and her program'" (Duffy, 1992a:49). Coverage of Kerrigan made her the perfect loving, obedient daughter and best friend of her blind mother. Harding was portrayed as recalcitrant and headstrong and she was "rightfully" punished for not "honoring her mother":

Harding's fourth-place finish in France was not surprising, given how erratically she had trained and her strong-willed decision to defy jet lag and travel fatigue by leaving Portland only three days before the competition began…. Teachman [her fired coach] said "I'm looking forward to working with other skaters who are hard workers, respectful of their coaches and are a joy to work with. I wish Tonya and her new 'employee' all the best." (Hersh, 1992a, sec.3:2)

Many sports writers who normally cover men's sports are dismissive of figure skating. But Harding was different and therefore, for a while at least, admired. She was called "dynamo," a "blond hotspur," "the gallant asthmatic" who had been through so much—who would never give up, and (my personal favorite) "the tough little American buzz-bomb" (Vescey, 19). These writers could barely contain their excitement in 1991, when Harding won the National Championship:

In one energized four-minute free skating program, Harding leapt from nowhere into history as she became the first American woman to land a triple Axel in competition…. Forty-five seconds into her routine, Harding stroked the length of the ice, coiled and sprang to an improbable height. Her ponytail became a blur as she spun. Upon landing, she cried out, "Yes!" The crowd, recognizing history in this 5'1", 105-pound package of fist-clenching grit, roared. (Swift, 1919)

In her only major national commercial, which ran extensively in 1992, Harding skated in an ad for Texaco as a demonstration of the company's "boundless energy." *New York Times* columnist George Vecsey used his admiration of Harding as a backdoor way of insulting skater Todd Eldredge. Eldredge did not choose to compete in the 1992 U.S. Nationals because of a back injury, but was named to the Olympic team anyway because he was the world bronze medalist; Harding, who was also injured, chose to compete, although as the world silver medalist she also would have been given a spot: "She did not get this far by being afraid of falling. Harding did not want to qualify for the Winter Games by the whim of a committee. Drag racers don't do it that way." The obvious implication was that Harding was more macho than Eldredge.

Harding's reputation for athletic prowess survived the attack on Kerrigan somewhat intact. What may surprise readers far more in retrospect is how many writers in 1991–92 described Harding as a refreshingly unaffected presence in the figure skating world, even an innocent. Janofsky admiringly described Harding playing pool in a bar after she won the 1991 National Championship "[w]hile hundreds of everybodys-who-are-anybodys in skating were in the hotel's ballroom attending a huge party…."

In a world of lavish costumes, haunting music and obsessive discipline, where million of dollars await the very best the sport can produce, Harding seems to be an anomaly, a baby-faced, 20-year-old skater either unfamiliar with or unready for what lies beyond the moment. 'She doesn't even have an agent,' said a woman associated with a production company based in New York, her tone one of astonishment.

In 1992, Swift catalogued Harding's hard-knock life (37)—which up until then had been virtually unknown and even after this article was rarely mentioned before the Kerrigan attack—and looked for the fairy-tale ending:

> Lord knows she's trying. Problem is, when life has been dealing you cards from the bottom of the deck for most of your 21 years, the aces and jacks all start to look marked, and it's kind of hard to trust the dealer. Even after winning a couple of hands.
>
> But Tonya Harding, the reigning U.S. women's figure skating champion, is trying.... Trying to fulfill a preposterous childhood dream in which a hardscrabble, dispossessed kid from Portland, Ore., hoists herself above a troubled past and wins the most refined gold medal of the Olympic Games— the women's figure skating title—propelling her toward a happily-ever-after she has never known.
>
> It could happen, and wouldn't it be rich if it did? An ice princess who has her own pool cue...an interloper in the realm of pixies and queens who's as at home doing a brake job as she is performing an arabesque. Aspirant to the throne of some of the most elegant women in the sport...who can curse like a sailor, bench-presses more than her weight and drag races in the summer for kicks.
>
> Harding shatters all stereotypes of the pampered and sheltered figure skater who has spent his or her youth bottled in an ice rink, training. At 21, she has seen a lot of life, and she is unapologetic if the experience has left her just a little rough around the edges. (54–55)

Harding's rough edges were admired when she was at the height of her success; later these same qualities would be identified as the cause of her downfall. For a woman, strong-willed behavior is obviously wrong, and punishment is the "not surprising" outcome. Long before she became connected with any criminal behavior, Harding's rebellion was contained in the moral of her "punishment," her fourth-place finish at the 1992 Olympics; in contrast, quite similar erratic relationships with various coaches by U.S. skater Christopher Bowman (and more serious allegations of illegal drug use) were treated, at least among TV commentators, as just a part of his unconventional personality. Bowman laughed at his own bad boy reputation, nicknaming himself "Hans Brinker from Hell" and skating in exhibition to Buster Poindexter's "I'm Just a Bad Boy," mugging for the cameras with a showmanship that commentators treated with slightly exasperated but affectionate amusement.

Similar showmanship nearly led to an international incident when French skater Surya Bonaly performed a back-flip during warm-ups the morning of the 1992 Olympic original program. She was castigated on television and in the press for intimidating poor Midori Ito—"an illegal trick," all gasped with horror. "Intimidation," they murmured. "What are the ethics involved?" asked Tim McCarver. "I was a little shocked.... I heard that Surya Bonaly did this already the third time this week," reported Witt (who was herself legendary for her ability to intimidate her competition during warm-ups). It was only added as an afterthought that Bonaly always does a back-flip during her warm-up, that although it is illegal in competition, it is a popular part of her exhibition, that as the local favorite in France she was naturally playing to the crowd, and that when she heard that she might have distracted Ito, she apologized. Her "active flamboyance" did not win over the press. Ito won widespread sympathy on American television when she apologized to her whole country for falling during her ladies original program. American audiences could both admire her humble shyness and implicitly bash the Japanese for putting so much pressure on such a sweet girl. It was almost as if Ito was a poor child being held hostage by the power- and glory-hungry Japanese. Coverage of Ito's slip under pressure was handled much more sympathetically in the U.S. press than Harding's.

In large measure, the Olympics are an audition for future commercial endorsements. One of the many ironies of being a successful woman athlete is that the most marketable and potentially lucrative images are those that are farthest removed in the public's mind from associations with filthy money. In 1994 Tonya Harding was repeatedly chastised for saying she had dollar signs in her eyes; meanwhile Kerrigan flew to California in the middle of her rehabilitation to film a Reebok commercial. Harding was condemned as a hotdog seeking the limelight, while Kerrigan was given sympathy because no one would leave her alone, despite the fact that Kerrigan was being paid by Seiko and Reebok to wear their products to each excessively photographed press briefing and Olympic practice. Kerrigan signed a multi-million dollar deal with Disney before the competition began and was featured in not one but three commercials which aired during the finals, adding yet another nail to the coffin of the concept of the Olympics as an "amateur" competition.

If Kerrigan and her agents took great advantage of her image as gallant lady athlete up until the Olympics, the post-Olympic backlash demonstrated how frail that image was. Beginning with her impatience before the medal ceremony, when she misinterpreted the delay in locating the Ukrainian national anthem as gold medalist Oksana Baiul redoing her makeup and snapped, "Oh, give me a break, she's just going to cry out there again. What's the difference?" and her endless comments of "I was perfect" in interviews about the competition to her "this is so corny" remark during the Disney parade, Kerrigan displayed an awkward streak that sent her image plummeting in the week following the games. Her critics felt that she should have taken her money and shut her mouth; the "brutal attack" of January was now a "whack on the knee."

Arguing referree calls is a respected skill in Major League Baseball, and post-game criticism of the officiating is accepted practice in the NBA. But being scrappy and pugnacious is one acceptable model of masculinity to which "ladies" do not have access. Allen Guttman, writing on the history of women in sports, noted that "advertisements are here to stay and that most advertisements will use physically attractive rather than unattractive models" (263), ignoring the fact that advertisements not only reward but also determine what is attractive in our society. Frank Deford, in his preview of the 1992 games, predicted the possibility that a Yamaguchi win would touch off feelings of racism: "And now: what's a good ol' boy to do if there's not only a Toyota in the driveway and a Sony in the bedroom and a Mitsubishi in the family room—but on the screen there, as the band plays the 'Star-Spangled Banner,' is the All-American girl of 1992, and her name is Yamaguchi?" (53). An article in *Business Week* after the Olympics stated that Yamaguchi was not getting the offers a white champion would have gotten ("The environment to 'max out' on her earning potential is not enhanced by the present mood of the country toward Japan," said one agent [1992:40]). Subsequently, Yamaguchi's agent denied the story, telling reporters that they simply had no time to sort through offers.

Yamaguchi has appeared on boxes of Kellogg's Special K, a cereal marketed to dieters. Several months after the Olympics, E.M. Swift wrote in *Sports Illustrated* "Post-Olympic endorsements were down for all athletes in 1992, probably due to the sluggish economy. Still, Yamaguchi did pretty well. She signed lucrative deals with Hoechst Celanese

Corporation, which makes acetate fabric for fashion designers, and DuraSoft contact lenses" (Swift, 1992b:75). Yamaguchi's television commercial for DuraSoft was especially interesting. She tells us that ever since the Olympics, people have been encouraging her to change. A series of comic vignettes follows, with Kristi taking up tennis and hosting a talk show. But when she really wants to change, she goes "blue, green, violet": in other words she changes the color of her eyes, changes them to colors an Asian woman would not normally have.

Post-Olympic endorsements may have been down, but not for bronze medalist Nancy Kerrigan. Long before the attack which made her a household name, Kerrigan had been tagged by Campbell's Soup, Seiko, Reebok, Northwest Airlines, and Xerox to tout their products. Campbell's cited Kerrigan's "all-American charm and her grace and beauty on the ice," (Reisfeld, 91) (all-American as opposed to Japanese American?). In naming Kerrigan one of the "50 Most Beautiful People in the World" in 1993, *People* magazine wrote, "Kristi Yamaguchi may have won the Olympic gold last year, but bronze-medal winner Nancy Kerrigan got the gasps for her Grace Kelly gleam." The article also confirmed that Kerrigan had six-figure endorsement contracts (1993:138). She was labeled the "Irish Katarina Witt" during the 1992 Olympics. Witt was then Diet Coke's poster girl, and Diet Coke–Nutra Sweet was a major sponsor of Ladies Figure Skating. Kerrigan was the only 1992 Olympic skater to have a prior commercial relationship with Coke, having done a Coke Classic commercial in 1988, playing the character of a Russian skater, not herself. Because of these circumstances, I was not surprised that the coverage of the 1992 Nationals and the Olympics focused on Kerrigan to a degree that might have seemed out of proportion to her chances of winning a gold medal.

What are the images of femininity we are presenting for young girls to emulate and for young boys to expect of women? What will it do to a girl's self-image if she is told that Midori Ito, Tonya Harding, or Debi Thomas is not beautiful enough, that Natalia Mishkutonek is chunky? It is not only in figure skating. Speed skating gold medalist Bonnie Blair was shown a few mornings after she finished competing in 1992 being "made over." Her "wholesome image and nice smile" made her attractive as a possible product pitcher, but only with a "new do" and makeup, only when she could conform as closely as possible to societal norms of beauty. The newscaster reporting the story observed, "I'm not sure if she liked that makeover" (CBS, 19 February, 1992). But like it or not, there she was, reassuring the public that despite her lightning speed, she's still "just a girl." The metaphor that Greg Faller uses to describe romance could also apply to commercial endorsement:

> The promise of romantic union [or commercial success?] works like the three golden apples Melanion rolled in front of Atalanta. They will be seduced from their position of culturally unacceptable power and dominance in a masculine pastime to a culturally demanded position of submissive femininity within the patriarchal family. (157)

< NOTES >

An earlier version of this article appeared in *TDR* 38, 1 (T141), Spring 1994.

1 This is the same writer who wrote a subsequent column disguised as his own brother because he was so embarrassed that most of America's 1992 medals had been won by women.

2 This is not to say that the male skaters completely escape the stigma of being involved in a "feminized sport." In his autobiography, four-time world champion Kurt Browning felt the need to write, "Let me just say, 'I like girls.'" Pairs skater Rocky Marval's mother said in an interview, "It was hard to accept a figure skater which is of course known for tutus and ballet."

3 Men's parents are mentioned sometimes, but rarely is a man's success attributed to his parents. One Russian skater was said to be supporting his mother and grandmother on his small stipend. Hamilton gave a eulogy for his mother, who died of cancer before he won his Olympic medal, describing her as "perfect." But her perfection seemed to lie not in active influence, but in unquestioning support: "She always let me be me" (CBS 11 February 1992).

< BIBLIOGRAPHY >

Bondy, Filip. 1993. "Ukraine's Rising Star Sets Worlds Ablaze." *New York Times*. (14 March).

———. 1993a. "Yamaguchi Figures: Gold, Not Gold Medals." *New York Times*. (24 March).

Brownmiller, Susan, *Femininity*. New York: Linden Press/Simon & Schuster, 1984.

Business Week. 1992. "To Marketers, Kristi Yamaguchi Isn't As Good As Gold." *Business Week*. (9 March).

Cook, Alison. 1991. "Das Kapitalist." *Gentlemen's Quarterly*. 61, 7. (July)

Deford, Frank. 1992. "The Jewel of the Winter Games." *Newsweek*. (10 February).

Deford, Frank, and Mark Starr. 1992. "American Beauty." *Newsweek*. (2 March).

Duffy, Martha. 1992. "Spinning Gold." *Time.* 139, 6 (10 February).

———. 1992a. "When Dreams Come True." *Time.* 139, 9 (2 March).

Faller, Greg S. 1987. "The Function of Star-Image and Performance in the Hollywood Musical: Sonja Henie, Esther Williams, and Eleanor Powell." PhD dissertation, Northwestern University.

Guttman, Allen. 1991. *Women's Sports: A History.* New York: Columbia University Press.

Hagaman, Diane. 1992. "The Joy of Victory, The Agony of Defeat: Stereotypes in Newspaper Sports Feature Photography." CIRA lecture, Northwestern University, 6 March.

Haug, Frigga, ed. 1987. *Female Sexualization: A Collective Work of Memory.* London: Verso.

Hersh, Phil. 1992. "Adulation on hold for Tonya Harding." *Chicago Tribune.* (8 March).

———. 1992a. "French Flip Stirs Tempest in Figure Skating's Teapot." *Chicago Tribune.* (21 February).

———. 1994. "Coach says Kerrigan Way Ahead of Schedule." *Chigago Tribune* (20 January).

Janofsky, Michael. 1991. "Wearing Crown Minus the Glitz." *New York Times.* (18 February).

Kolata, Gina. 1992. "Who Is Female? Science Can't Say." *New York Times.* (16 February).

Life. 1993. Cover montage. 16, 1 (January).

———. 1993a. "Letters to the Editor." 16, 3 (March).

Lincicome, Bernie. 1992. "Here's a Sure Cure for Winter Blahs." *Chicago Tribune.* (20 February).

Louie, Elaine. 1992. "Women's Figure Skating Puts Couture on the Ice." *New York Times.* (17 February).

McDermott, Barry. 1982. "More Than A Pretty Face." *Sports Illustrated* 56, 2 (18 January).

New York Times. 1992. "Just This Once, Button Makes Call From Couch." (21 February).

O'Hara, Jane. 1988. "Stars in the Spotlight." *Maclean's.* (7 March).

Reisfeld, Randi. 1994. *The Kerrigan Courage: Nancy's Story.* New York: Ballantine Books.

Silverman, Barton. 1992. Photo. *New York Times.* (22 February).

Swift, E.M. 1991. "Triple Threat." *Sports Illustrated.* 74, 7 (25 February).

———. 1992. "Not Your Average Ice Queen: A Troubled Past hasn't Stopped Tonya Harding from Becoming a Figure Skating Champion." *Sports Illustrated* 76 (January 13.

————. 1992a. "Stirring." *Sports Illustrated.* 76, 8 (2 March).

————. 1992b. "All That Glitters." *Sports Illustrated.* 77, 25:(14 December).

Therberge, Nancy. 1981. "A Critique of Critiques: Radical and Feminist Writings on Sport." *Social Forces.* 60, 2 (December).

USA Today. 1992. "Winter Olympics: Figure Skating." (28 January).

United States Figure Skating Association. 1993. "The 1994 Official USFSA Rulebook." Colorado Springs, CO: The United States Figure Skating Association.

Vecsey, George. 1992. "Skating's Double Standard." *New York Times.* (12 January).

Whannel, Garry. 1984. "Fields in Vision: Sport and Representation." *Screen* 25.

Willis, Paul. 1982. "Women in Sport in Ideology." In *Sport, Culture and Ideoloqy.* Edited by Jennifer Hargreaves. London: Routledge and Kegan Paul.

Wolf, Naomi, 1991. *The Beauty Myth: How Images of Beauty are Used Against Women.* New York: W. Morrow.

Television Coverage

"The Olympic Games" on CBS, February 1992.

"Olympic Highlights" on Turner Network Television, February 1992.

"The 1992 U.S. National Championships" on ABC, 11 January 1992.

"The 1992 World Championships" on ABC, 29 March 1992.

Pure Desire

Peggy Fleming was pure. It began with the neat assonance of her name, her dark hair parted plainly down the side, her high-necked, long-sleeved outfits in ironically exotic 60s cocktail colors—grenadine and chartreuse. Watching her on tape, the directness of her style is striking, a chaste line so similar to another famous and pure Peggy: ballerina Margot Fonteyn, whose real name was Peggy Hookham. Both women excelled in simple strength, an almost royal minimalism that might have verged on the matronly were it not for the delicate hush, the flushes of girlish fervor that marked their connection with the audience. Neither were pyrotechnics. Neither were pyrotechnical, yet both became icons of their art forms, setting standards to which women after them have aspired—and fallen short.

But then, purity for these two was psychogenetically predestined, built into their silhouettes, their synapses, and finding quick affinity in their faces. Providentially, the eras in which they ascended (Fonteyn in the 40s, Fleming in the 60s) could appreciate pearls of understatement—the high drama they made of restraint. Fonteyn, we've since learned, was really more of a vixen than a virgin; no matter, even had she dallied daily, she would have projected the same authoritative innocence. For it was not sexual innocence (which is one-dimensional and grows tedious over time) that was at the heart of this purity, but an innocence of alternatives: the wonder that dancing, or in Fleming's case, skating, could be anything but what it was for them, a deeply accepting, fundamentally wise belief in classical values of line, balance, decorum, and denouement, inspired by a brown-eyed, fire-breathing focus.

Purity means parity—the artist defining the art as much as the art defines her. Thus Fonteyn, the Sleeping Beauty of the century, could take a knowing role like Juliet, a character of Romantic excess and sensual abandon, and not only seem more abidingly self-contained, but shine new light on a stock ingenue. Casting against type, don't forget, is an act of clarification—one of the ways performers learn who and what they are, and glimpse the mystery of themselves.

For athletes, however, there are no new scripts and only a single soliloquy: to win or not to win. In the sports arena, the competitor's persona unfolds against a static and unblinking backdrop. The location may change, but never the scenery (the rink) or the time allotments (two-and-a-half minutes, four minutes). Indeed, even the choreographies of skaters can seem written in Arctic stone; routines remain in competition for two years or longer. While the sportscasters differentiate competitors through details of plot—charting the melodramatic paths that led each to *this moment*—the athlete knows that her true story is wordless, told through body type, technique, stamina, and score power. For the dancer, it has been said, repertory is destiny; for the skater, repetition is all.

And renunciation. For there's another bit of story that's almost always missing with female athletes, especially in skating, and its summer sister in grace, women's gymnastics, and that is a man. There may be a coach, a consort (friendship with a male teammate), and of course, a caravan (family, fans, etc.), but there is nary a prince. Pre-Lillehammer, I can't remember an Olympics where star figure skaters or gymnasts had a guy by their side. With female athletes, the continuum goes from appetite to annunciation—first the wanting, then the being singled out, the receiving gold from on high. These women embody the oxymoron of "pure desire."

It's an opposition worth looking at, for here the concept of deserving through purity, with its echos of immaculate conception, of virgins waiting for a shaft of light, *is* a sexual commentary. In practical terms, the teenage girl athlete, like the ballet dancer, often reroutes her libido into her sport—there's only so much energy in any one day. And the unrelenting schedule of daily before- and after-school practice insures a late-blooming social life. A second, more complex reading—that desire makes one pure—

explains even more. The need to succeed, to master, to be *the one*, brings with it autonomy, momentum, a shedding of distraction, a new feel for and fixing of the boundaries of the self, without which there is no art. The winning skater, each in her own way, is an armored, aesthetic Joan of Arc—complete with silver blades. In fact, the artist and the athlete in their tunnel vision and physical commitment both do violence to the life we call "normal."

This is nothing new. Only two months before the Lillehammer games, a musical version of the famous ballet movie *The Red Shoes* opened on Broadway. As in the 1948 film, its heroine faced the same stern choice—a jealous art or a jealous lover—and her inability to choose, her lust for both, resulted in a bloody death. *The Red Shoes* bombed after ten days in New York City, just three weeks before Nancy Kerrigan got whacked in Detroit. Its story of unswerving devotion to an art form, of torn loyalty and self-immolation, was out of step with a culture that thinks sacrifice is for suckers. It should have opened on ice. Tonya Harding, after all, picked up one of its themes without missing a beat: she too chose not to choose. Along with all the triple jumps that were changing the landscape of figure skating, Harding brought impurity to the sport—she brought her husband.

She brought him last time too. In 1992 Harding arrived in Albertville days after her teammates, coachless and underprepared. It was as if she'd arrived without a chaperone. Rumors flew that she had been fighting with her spouse, or had separated from him, or wasn't really married after all. No one know for sure and Jeff Gillooly (or is it Svengali?) was not mentioned by name. Instead, his presence was felt as a kind of black cloud hovering over Harding's inconsistent, sloppily-presented performances. At Lillehammer in 1994, of course, the cloud was a monsoon. Yet true to Harding's tone of in-your-face strength, she turned up for the short "technical" program in Jezebel-red sequins, skating to the overture from "Much Ado About Nothing." Suddenly this athlete had a hot new script and a spectacular spotlight. But what was her skating really saying?

Fast forwarding through the Olympic competition, I happened to look up and notice that Harding is the only skater who "reads" at top tape speed. Unmistakable in her scarlet short-program costume, she could be the solitary Firebird of Russian folklore, zipping around in hyperspace. In a way, fast forward is the perfect place for her. Harding always smacked of phenomenon, which is what we crave in young artists and athletes. Her full round thighs and strong spade of a back, so unapologetically bold and Bolshoi-esque, give her blading not just speed but depth, dimensional power. Those anvil strokes of the silver blade were great coursing preludes to the mighty triple axels she tossed off from time to time, her claim to fame.

Harding didn't complete any triple axels in Lillehammer. As the sportscasters noted, she also never once completed a practice program. This sense of the incomplete turned out to be definitive. In both her short and long programs, Harding showed a lack deeper than missed triples. She herself was missing. The pseudo-lyricism of those arms might be fine on a flowery Kristi Yamaguchi, but it did not suit Tonya's tough demeanor, her blue eyes boring down a rifle sight. Was her stiff upper body really home to that driven heart? And what about those angsty, turned-in, experimental-dance poses? Harding's costumes, tight, bright, and Vegas-tacky, clanged in compensation for the muscular flash she couldn't muster, for the piece of her character stuck somewhere in Gillooly's hip pocket.

Harding, a big girl, took a lot of media heat for her extra poundage, and admittedly would never be a refined, Peggy Fleming type of artist. Still, she could have made her size and body type work for her. When it comes to performance, less-than-Greek figures, body fat untouched by the rigors of spot training, are forgiven if the athlete performs brilliantly *and* consistently—at which point plumpness can become a plus. One thinks of ballerina Suzanne Farrell's plummy thighs, which gave poetic ballast to her typhoon sweeps through space (other dancers' catty comments be damned). But Harding's innate strength was never properly harnessed or honed, or her sense of hurry (fast forward again) overcome. Her belief in her own raw oomph, despite her I'm-the-best press bytes, needed tempering by equal parts concentration and self-discipline. Unable or unwilling to build an imaginative space in which to consolidate style, a mind-body correspondence, Harding came into the arena a harried image of a skater grasping at shoestrings.

But just picture, for a moment, Harding in one of Fleming's prim costumes (black, to set off that blonde hair), having found a way to let her skating, rather than her husband or herself, say "I want." Suddenly her Free Skate music from *Jurassic Park*, with its eerie opening and glacial lyric line, might have buoyed rather than tired her. And we might have seen Harding the prototype, the super skater of the radial triples and power glide that was so much her early promise. We might have seen the creature Harding thought she could be when she chose that music: high tech, dominating, and larger than life.

Nancy Kerrigan came into the competition torn between her natural New England scowl and the real-life victim script fate handed her. It's not easy to play Damsel in Distress when your inclination is toward shrugging sarcasm. Under Kerrigan's wincing smile—steel. Skating out to her opening poses, though, she seemed to grow taller and less torn, a cool bone structure with ship's-prow posture, a lifted nose scenting clear sailing ahead. And in truth, there wasn't much rough on the horizon. Kerrigan turned in clean, succinct, utterly predictable performances, buttoned-up to the eyelash (no wonder Revlon wanted a contract).

Kerrigan was never a first-class skater; she didn't make you see new possibilities for the sport in the way that Harding did. But she certainly knows what she has and maximizes her gifts. That body line, long and lean with a lovely V-shape from waist to shoulder, was further emphasized by programs built on endless arcs. Kerrigan pushes the notion of flow to its extreme—floe—holding poses halfway around the arena like ice sculptures to be admired from all sides. To this end, Vera Wang's quiet, exceedingly attractive costumes were a perfect foil. Perhaps too perfect. Wang's creations of illusion stretch net and subtle sequins made Kerrigan look like a statuette, a Diana with no arrows—elegant, yes, but dull elegance, more the airs of what used to be called a "conscious beauty" than the crown of giggles and sobs worn by that lyric Lolita, Oksana Baiul.

Kerrigan's style is classic, not classical, and this is key. By presenting herself in the Peggy Fleming lineage of figure skating, she set herself up for risky comparison. For though no one said it, Kerrigan is an example of a skater who has worked doggedly, who has pared away to her essential self and revealed there a personality that doesn't sustain interest. "I was flawless," Kerrigan repeated in frustration, not quite realizing that there are finer, more definitive achievements to reach for.

Consistently unspontaneous, Kerrigan was trapped in her finishing-school deportment and ice princess aura (the ice princess who doesn't warm up has never been a crowdpleaser—does anyone run to a Catherine Deneuve movie?). Even though her programs were punched up with jazz dance elements—straight-arm swings and disco explosions, percussive hops and front layouts—she never broke through the monotonal meter, the feeling of forced fun. She has a tough heart, surely, but a dutiful one. When the music picked up, Kerrigan seemed off a beat, behind it—she's so much happier in a frozen pose.

And that's the way we remember Kerrigan, and why the newspapers were unconsciously on target when they kept printing the same image over and over again: Nancy angled forward in arabesque *alongé*. The archetypal position of both ballet and figure skating (where it is called a spiral), the arabesque presents the performer balancing on one leg, the other leg lifted behind, parallel to the ground. It is an enchanted configuration, celestial, mathematic, mysterious. Dipped down into *alongé* (elongated), the torso drops and the back leg shoots up even higher. And so the arabesque becomes anxious, a picture of narcissism—as if the skater seeks her reflection in water—and a posture of desire, a lengthening reach. Kerrigan's beseeching expression in *alongé*, arm out as if for a tip, was the American-accented leitmotif of Lillehammer: "give me" (the flip side of "Why me?").

I recall now the signature pose shared by those two past Peggys—the ballet position we know as 'attitude.' It is the tiptoed moment of Mercury, messenger of the gods, an arabesque with leg bent behind at a right angle, suggesting the pirouette as he leaves from or returns to earth. Fleming used to hit her attitude in a spin; lofting the leg lower than hip level, softening the silhouette. Fonteyn, on the other hand, held her attitude like a decree: 90 degree angles or nothing!

At Lillehammer, in every one of her programs—her Tchaikovsky Black Swan, her Saint-Saëns Dying Swan, her 42nd Street free skate—gold medalist Oksana Baiul performed a strange, dizzy, sometimes ridiculous move. It was an attitude spooled sideways and grabbed from behind during a vertiginous spin. The giddy wind in Mercury's wings, the whirlpool the white swan drowns in, a skater breakdancing—Baiul delivered messages from ballet and Broadway, blew kisses from skating's past and its future. Turning an archetypal shape into a vortex of pop culture allure, she was Peggy Fleming as a Russkie Romantic, the Little Match Girl in pink marabou (fire, anyone?) If pushed to categorize her, you might call this skating sheer classical fantasy, role playing on a grand scale and clearly a game Baiul's body was built for. An open, acquisitive imagination is the basis of Baiul's leggy, sexy, still-unformed style. Pure potential, she has yet to give big to the sport. But crossing herself each time she steps into the arena's white light, she's an on-ice articulation of the Joy of Man's, make that, Woman's Desiring.

4

What Tonya Harding Means to Me, or Images of Independent Female Power on Ice

On January 6, 1994, I flew into blizzard-blanketed Detroit to watch the National Figure Skating Championships, hoping to see Tonya Harding beat Nancy Kerrigan for the women's title.

That wasn't the only reason I'd come to Detroit, my first trip to a live skating competition since I'd watched friends compete in the 1975 Mid-Atlantic regionals. Having skated myself for a couple of years as an adolescent and having followed the sport on television sporadically since then, as a theatre graduate student interested in performance and cultural studies, I'd recently started to do some serious thinking and writing about what skating means. So I was here to do research—to see all the not-quite-top U.S. skaters who didn't make the TV coverage, to witness a wider range of approaches to the sport. I was also here to have fun—to spend some time with my mother's cousin who lived in Detroit and have her show me around the city, to hang out with a friend-of-a-friend who'd loaned me some videotapes of skating coverage a few months earlier and who'd become a long-distance skating appreciation buddy, and to meet the friends of hers we'd be sharing a hotel room with, and just to enjoy watching lots of skating. I had a few other personal wishes: I wanted to see some artistically innovative ice dancing, despite the recent rulings urging ice dancers away from the theatrical and back to the ballroom (I didn't). I wanted to see returning hero Brian Boitano skate well but not walk away with first place on the basis of reputation alone (I did, thanks to Scott Davis's super free skate). And I wanted to see a female skater who didn't just display herself out on the ice as an object of beauty for the audience to look at, but who looked right back as a thinking subject (I did, thanks to Nicole Bobek's hilarious exhibition performance). But most of all, perhaps, I wanted to see Tonya Harding live up to the potential she'd showed throughout 1991 and win back her title. In that wish, I got both less and more than I'd hoped for.

As my cousin battled snow and traffic into town on my behalf, the radio gave us the news that Nancy Kerrigan had been attacked that afternoon by an unknown assailant. By the next day, when it became clear that Nancy would be withdrawing from the competition, I was disappointed less because I would miss seeing Nancy skate (although I would have liked to see her; she was certainly one of the most accomplished skaters entered in the competition) than because without her there, if Tonya did win it would be more by default than because she'd managed to prove her point.

What point? And why did I care so much? To explain that, let me explain how I think figure skating carries meaning, and what Tonya and Nancy meant to me as of that weekend in Detroit.

Skating and Gender Ideology

Skating as such need not "mean" anything at all; a skater might move in a particular way simply because it feels good, or because it's an efficient way to get from point A to point B. In the context of competition, however, specific moves are very clearly performed in order to denote a level of competence to the judges and thereby garner the appropriate score for technical merit. More and more, in the Ladies'[1] competitions as well as the men's, technical merit means triple jumps. Whereas twenty years ago all the top men but barely a handful of the top women did triple salchows, toe loops, and/or loops, in the 1990s both men and women need all the three-revolution jumps to compete for international medals. Only the three-and-a-half revolution triple axel has remained no-woman's-land, except for Midori Ito and Tonya Harding.

Freeskating programs are judged simultaneously for their artistic impression and to the average spectator, unfamiliar with the individual moves and their respective difficulty, it is on this level that skating means something, connoting what Roland Barthes calls myths or second-order meanings about nationality, class, and especially about gender.[2] There is also a level, corresponding to Barthes's "third meaning"[3] of direct kinesthetic perception of the movement quality, the stretch of a leg or the suspension of a jump in the air, which communicates to the viewer on an emotional, experiential plane separate from any denotation of the skater's flexibility or strength, or any connotations of, say, Americanness or femininity that it may carry. When Nancy Kerrigan hits a new body position perfectly in time with a musical accent, there's a sense of satisfaction that can't be described other than as a feeling of rightness. Similarly, when Tonya Harding flies through a good triple lutz or triple axel (and we saw her do several beautiful triple axels in practice sessions in Detroit, though not, unfortunately, in the runthroughs of her program or in the competition itself), I find the way she hangs in the air more beautiful than the most explosive men's jumps, perhaps because there's a sense of womanly roundness to her jumps missing from those of the more vertically proportioned men.

This "third" level of meaning may in fact be the first that attracts skating fans, but once the issue of choosing between skaters in competition is brought in, of judging artistic merit and of rooting for favorites, the second level of connotation and myth often takes precedence. It might theoretically be possible to objectively quantify the degree of artistry a skater and her coach and/or choreographer have invested in constructing a program, but in practice the valuation of this aspect of skating often comes down to personal preference. Some onlookers have argued that this subjective component of figure skating judging disqualifies it as a true sport. Perhaps so. But the subjectiveness is precisely what makes it so fascinating to me as an object of study.

What we see on the ice, the whole packaged program of skating moves, gesture, gaze, music, costume, and so on, presents on the body of the skater a performance persona that stands as a symbol of a particular way of being in the world, including very much a particular way of being male or female, and our preferences for one skater over another reveal a lot about our ideologies. The perennial debate over the predominance of artistry or athleticism in the sport, and the resultant rule changes or changes in what the judges tend to reward, can be read as a code for femininity or masculinity. Does demanding artistry from male skaters render them effeminate? Does favoring women who can do all the triple jumps masculinize them?

Skaters (and their coaches) know that, like it or not, skaters are judged on their image, and part of putting together a competitive program means packaging their image with professional choreography, music recording, and costuming in the interest of constructing a performance persona that will generate approval from judges and fans. This persona is of course not completely independent of who the skater is off the ice, or who we think she is off the ice. Judges do watch practices, and encounter skaters in hotels and other locations besides the arena in competition cities; they also, like the rest of us, read newspapers and hear rumors, and what they see and hear does influence their opinions of individual skaters. Over the years, for instance, Tonya Harding managed to generate a fair amount of negative press regarding her on-again off-again marriage and coaching relationships that certainly affected public perceptions of her personality (and the events covered certainly have everything to do with who she "really" is as a person, but only Tonya and her intimates know who that is). But to a large extent these factors serve primarily either to confirm or to mitigate what we think we know about a skater from what we see on the ice.

For singles skaters, the gendering of their performance personae relies in large part on their positioning within the economy of spectatorship. In particular, both figure skating practice and media coverage have adhered to conventions of representation that construct spectatorship along gendered lines. For example, television commentary positions male skaters as athletes while emphasizing the beauty of women's performances.[4] In the technical program, requirements for the women such as the layback spin and spiral sequence emphasize the relatively greater flexibility of the female over the male body, whereas the men's requirements of more triple jumps and flying spins emphasize conventionally masculine attributes of speed and athleticism.[5] These distinctions are not just a question of innate physical differences between males and females. By penalizing women, like Tonya, who happen to jump better than they bend (or men who bend better than they jump), the technical program, which as one-third of the skater's total score serves primarily to rank skaters in or out of potential medal-winning standing prior to the free program, exaggerates and reinscribes gender difference by acting as a gatekeeping mechanism to weed out skaters whose strong points deviate too markedly from their respective gender norms.

The spiral sequence requirement, in fact, somewhat backfires in its intended effect. A spiral can be a very beautiful move when performed by either a male or female skater, one that almost defines the essence of skating as distinguished from other forms of aesthetic movement: the skater's body is perfectly still, preferably in an attractive position, and yet it is moving through space, even seeming to change shape as the perspective of the viewer changes in relation to the location of the skater's body, as the blade of the skating foot glides across the ice. But it is not a particularly difficult move. All it requires is being able to skate on one foot, preferably on a curving edge with the free foot held at or above hip level. How much above hip level the foot can be lifted depends much more on natural body build and on time spent stretching and strengthening the thigh muscles off the ice than on skating ability, although of course balance on the blade is important. The guidelines for the Ladies' technical program require at least two changes of position (i.e., at least three different positions) in the spiral sequence, which means that the majority of skaters use the sequence to demonstrate their flexibility by stretching the free foot above their heads, or to demonstrate skating difficulty by changing position more than twice, using one-footed turns as well as changes of foot. Rarely, however, do they take the time to hold a position once attained long enough for it to register as an aesthetic statement.

The spiral, especially in its classic form with the free leg lifted straight back and up, does offer television cameras good opportunities for a straight-on crotch shot. The traditional female skating costume of short skirt over sheer, flesh colored tights barely meet the requirement of "covering the hips and posterior."[6] The ultra-short skirt attached to pants and bodice in fact almost signifies figure skating in and of itself. When eleven-year-old Sonja Henie showed up at the 1924 Olympics in a mid-thigh-length skirt (with the rise of the hemline to upper thigh and then to the juncture between thighs and buttocks a more or less chronological progression thereafter), by dressing in a style only a child could get away with at the time she took women's skating in a more athletically-inclined direction than it had previously followed; only the foolhardy or suicidal would attempt a flying sit spin in the full-length skirts her competitors sported.[7] Skating regulations specify that costumes must be "modest, dignified, and appropriate for athletic competition."[8] But the short skirt does nothing in the service of sartorial modesty. Even if it does cover the upper thighs when at rest, it inevitably flies upward during spins and backward crossovers. And with tights simulating nudity and the pants of the skating dress drawing attention to the groin and lower curve of the buttocks by terminating there, the short skirt only serves to emphasize these sexualized regions of the anatomy. Flesh-colored insets in the bodice that pretend to reveal the cleavage and upper curve of the breasts (or in the case of Tonya Harding's unfortunate costume at the '94 nationals, even more) are not explicitly forbidden, while opaque unitards such as those worn by American skater Debi Thomas in the 1980s, which cover all parts of the body equally and so draw attention to none, have been disallowed. The skating skirt, then, is not really required on the basis of physical modesty, but rather as an explicit marker of femininity. As popularized by Henie in her traveling ice shows and Hollywood films, the skating skirt has allied the female skater visually with the showgirl and the starlet, roles traditionally valued for the beauty and shapeliness of the woman's body rather than for her artistic accomplishments.[9]

Thus, through both costume and conventional choreographic practice female figure skating has come to connote what feminist film theorist Laura Mulvey has termed "to-be-looked-at-ness."[10] For feminists seeking to disrupt the binary of male subject and female object-of-the-gaze and to find positions for a female subject to occupy, figure skating does not offer an easy challenge. Because it is so clearly a spectator sport, skaters are necessarily positioned as objects of the spectators' gaze. Male skaters, perhaps uncomfortable with being thus structurally feminized, often resist this positioning in their skating practice. They may claim athletic agency with glances or gestures that draw attention to jumping feats or they may mitigate the sense that they are displaying *themselves* as objects of the gaze by casting the display in the context of playing a role (for example Kurt Browning taking on the Humphrey Bogart persona from *Casablanca* or Philippe Candeloro as Conan the Barbarian and then as a figure out of *The Godfather* in their 1993 and '94 free programs). Females, on the other hand, have for the most part been complicit in offering their glamorized, eroticized bodies for spectatorial consumption, often curving the arms out and upward to the audience as if presenting themselves as an offering (see Katarina Witt in her 1988 "Carmen" Olympic-gold-winning free program, or Oksana Baiul in the free program that won her the 1993 world championship and 1994 Olympic gold), or curving the arms and shoulders inward and lowering their eyes, thus directing the audience's gaze at the body (see Kristi Yamaguchi's 1992 *Blue Danube* technical program, and Baiul again).

The majority of figure skating spectators may in fact be girls and women, but the images of femaleness presented on the ice so thoroughly reinforce the gendered functions of looking that as a female spectator looking at a female skater my only options in most cases are to position myself as a consumer (implicitly male) of the skater's beauty, or to identify with the skater as she-who-is-looked-at (and judged on how good she looks). Male skaters do, yes, sometimes invite me to appreciate them as objects of beauty and of desire, but more often they ask me to admire them as heroic athletes/athletic heroes. It's rare to come across a female skater who allows me not only to admire but also to identify with her in her heroic feats. For at least several days beyond her victory in Detroit, Tonya Harding served that function.

Images of Women: Nancy and Tonya

When I watched the 1992 Albertville Olympics on television, I more or less accepted the media's easy characterizations of Tonya as the artless athlete, Nancy as the personification of elegance whose athleticism was not worth mentioning, and Kristi Yamaguchi as the complete skater who blended athletic excellence (no triple axel, but a triple lutz-triple toe loop combination few other women have dared to try) with choreographic nuance. But in 1993, as I looked back at videotapes of these and other skaters' past performances in trying to figure out how they were feminized by the conventions of figure skating, or how they feminized themselves, I was able to make finer distinctions. Kristi, for instance, characterized as "the little waif" by Dick Button in the ABC coverage of the 1990 U.S. nationals, by 1992 at age 20 was still presenting herself as a demure—but available—girl child. A year later, as a professional, she was able to skate with a hipper, more self-assertive attitude, but throughout her amateur career the image she projected was of delicate fragility and willingness to please. With her solid technique and thin build she was able to execute difficult triples easily without a great deal of height. Nancy's jumps are bigger, if less consistent up to the 1993–94 season, but less emphasized as well as less powerful than Tonya's (and Midori's), which even when they end up crashing really soar. Despite Tonya's failures during and since Albertville, I found myself appreciating her more and more—not necessarily who she really was, but what she represented on the ice. By mid-January of 1994, the knowledge that Tonya may well have been guilty of a criminal attack on her competitor made it difficult to watch her performances with quite the innocence I once had, but for the sake of this analysis I want to put this knowledge aside. Certainly any allegations that surfaced subsequently had nothing to do with what I felt as I sat in the Joe Louis Arena on January 8 willing Tonya to victory.

A close reading of Nancy's and Tonya's 1992 Olympic free programs, as televised by CBS Sports, makes explicit many of the meanings associated with these two skaters going into the 1994 competition. These performances do not show either skater at her best, but they are fairly typical of each skater's style. Both women skated just about equally well (or badly) that day, Nancy falling from second place after the technical program to third, and Tonya pulling up from sixth to fourth.

For her free program in Albertville, Nancy wears a white dress, sheer over the arms, shoulders, and upper chest. The heart-shaped top of the opaque part of the bodice follows the upper curve of the breasts and cleavage in the center. Her hair is pulled back into a neat bun, circled by a white scrunchie. The slim, straight, simple lines of the dress suggest elegance and sophistication; the firmly controlled hair bespeaks a certain primness or at least sexual modesty, and the whiteness evokes purity, whereas the revelation of the upper body through the sheer cloth and the accentuation of the breasts (as well, of course, as the short skirt) eroticize a body that is simultaneously marked as inviolate. This conjunction of virginal and nubile images suggest a bridal gown; indeed, this dress was designed by Vera Wang, a noted designer of bridal clothes.

The opening pose is straight and simple, the stillness of Nancy's face conveying serenity, purity, and inner focus. The music begins, a horn-like call into the void, leading into a slow, flowing melody. Nancy pushes into an opening glide, leading into the space with her chest (the seat of the heart and so metonymically of the soul), reaches her hands straight up as if to the heavens and then clasps them across her heart. She curls into a low, compact pose, then unfolds upward, her arms crossing her chest then reaching back as her chest reaches forward. This program, her body seems to say, will channel something pure and ineffable, from the heavens or from the music, through the pure and intensely focused body and soul of Nancy Kerrigan.

Easily, with erect, noble posture, Nancy executes a double axel and a triple flip, landing with open arms, palms up in welcoming display. A circle of one arm while stroking to gain speed serves as a simple herald of the upcoming triple toe loop–triple toe loop combination, the second jump of which unfortunately today becomes a single. She swings into a flying camel spin, one arm crossing her mouth and then opening to the side, as if freeing her voice. She steps into a shallow sit spin, gaze focused down and inward toward her center as her hands reach forward from the waist as if to express what she sees there. She rises with a high swing of the free leg to end the spin, then turns into a still pose, left hand on hip, right upraised triumphantly.

Throughout this opening section, Nancy's expression remained still and serene, innerly directed as her body flowed through securely executed technical elements (except the botched combination) and clear, fully stretched positions that seem to be an expression of an intense private experience we have been privileged to peek in on. As the character of the music changes into something jazzier and more rhythmic in the next section, and the choreography follows with sharp up-and-down movements of the hands beside the body in poses and then a footwork sequence accentuating the hips, Nancy's face remains unchanged, so still as to be practically expressionless. Evidently this section is meant to be sexy (someone in the stands seemed to think so, as a whistle is audible on the tape), but you wouldn't know it from the skater's face.

Stroking forward around the corner with her chest reaching forward and arms straight back and down, Nancy becomes briefly a sharp projectile cutting into the space, what I find to be the most active image in the program. She turns into a triple salchow jump, then a change-foot combination spin, moving on each foot from classic camel position to a low, turned-in variation in perfect synchrony with chirping pulses in the music. As this rhythmic middle section of the program concludes, she poses with a supposedly jazzy side-to-side undulation of the arms and ribcage that is particularly halfhearted in this performance (compared to this same move at other competitions).

To transition into the more flowing final section she pivots, then strokes into another still pose, legs scissored apart, forward and backward, chest forward and arms back as if storing tension to launch herself forward. When she does, it is in smooth movements appropriate to the music, reiterating the cutting edge motifs in the extended chest and the scissored-apart legs. A curved upward reach of the arm announces the next important element, a triple lutz (which becomes a single), followed by a low waltz jump into a bent, turned-in landing reminiscent of the change-foot spin earlier, unfolding into a back spiral. This final section consists largely of smooth gliding moves with angular, uplifted positions of the upper body. Crossovers to gain speed lead into an outside spread eagle, arms dropped straight down, then floated up to an asymmetrical V-shape (the leading arm higher), turning directly into a triple loop jump. Nancy circles in a two-foot curve, outside arm raised as the inside arm circles to a low diagonal opposite, then strokes into a low forward glide. The next jumping pass is two walley jumps, the second ornamented with one hand curved overhead, followed by a triple toe loop marred by touching down the skating hand and free foot. Then, arms and chest open, Nancy prepares for a series of star turns traveling in synch with the music into a death drop. This is followed by a backward glide on both feet, legs spread sideways with the outside knee bent and hip thrust to the side as the outside arm reaches overhead with slow tension, palm out and fingers spread, toward the center of the curve. Next comes an Ina Bauer glide with both arms raised to a V, back crossovers with arms opening as preparation, then forward-leaning front crossovers into Nancy's trademark front spiral. While her free hand grasps the free leg to hold it extended back above her head, her skating arm reaches forward, presenting the position with upcurved gaze and the only genuine smile of this performance, now that it's almost over and the skater can relax. As she continues to hold the spiral, Nancy turns her head downward and bends her free arm in to shade her brow in modesty or even shame, then stretches forward and up again in open offering. Finally, she exits the spiral to slide into a final, backward arching pose on one knee and one skate, hands reaching upward with one elbow straight and the other angled down.

Tonya wears a white, high-collared dress with an open oval in back, embroidered with large gold wedge shapes arranged to form floral patterns. Shoulder pads and gold fringe on the cap sleeves suggest military epaulets. Tonya's blonde bangs are teased and the rest of her hair pulled back into a pony tail by a gold scrunchie. (The military connotations were even stronger in her technical program costume the same year, a similarly styled black dress with vertical lines rather than flowers adorning the bodice.)

Her music starts with low throbbing strings, soon joined by heroic horns. After an initial reach upward, Tonya twists right into a change-foot camel spin, a single straight body position held for six or more revolutions on each foot, with a clear increase of speed at the change of foot, one arm at a time reaching down next to the skating thigh, extending straight forward, and crossing over the chest, while the other arm reaches back above the free leg. From her exiting back crossovers, she executes a back-outer-to-front-inner three turn, a move that gives an image of opening or unfolding the body, announcing herself to the world, enhanced by the upward and outward circle of the arms and the forward stretch of the free leg.

After a brief spiral, Tonya turns into back crossovers, shifting in a wide two-footed stance away from and then back toward the center of the curve she is making by bending the outside knee and thrusting the corresponding hip sideways while straightening the other leg, then reversing sides. I find this simple move, which recurs throughout the program as a kind of motif, extremely sensuous, especially as one arm, palm up, follows the sideways flow of the hips out and in, as if to draw energy (or the viewers' gaze) into the circle. The other arm then circles forward and back to prepare a triple lutz. Stroking forward around the corner after this jump, Tonya swings her arms forward and back in opposition to her feet as if marching. Then the arms open, and one circles forward, up, and to the side, as she turns backward and into the opposite circle to set up a triple axel. She launches herself into the full three-and-a-half revolutions, but she is tilted off center and her landing leg gives way immediately, collapsing her to the ice. After rising, she strokes resignedly into a moderately complex straight-line footwork sequence, arms crossing and reversing up and down, wrists flexed, pulling backward when both are down to thrust her upper body forward like an arrow into the space. One foot bends up in front of the opposite shin with arms bent up in front of the chest, elbows out, as if winding up to gain power. Tonya swings her arms forward and back during the crossovers, again as if marching, before she jumps into a triple toe loop-double toe loop combination (intended to be triple-triple).

The music segues into a bluesy slow section featuring a saxophone melody line, the mood now lazy and indulgent. Tonya circles, turns, and sways from hip to hip, rolling her shoulders and passing her hands, usually gently curved, close to her chest, or hips and waist, and reaching away in loose, relaxed gestures that she follows with her gaze. She seems to be enjoying the sensuality, although she doesn't always stretch an arm or leg to its full extension before moving on to the next element. Her arms reach up from her chest and then clasp back to it during a layback spin. She flows through a triple loop jump to a back spiral, made difficult by opening the leg around the side instead of lifting it back directly, but not in a particularly high or stretched spiral position. After stretching out her arms and body as she leans into a sustained deep forward outer edge, she bends back in an Ina Bauer with arm circling open above her lifted chest, then three-turns into a triple flip followed by a forward spiral.

She hits a pose (somewhat tentatively today compared to other performances) as the music changes to a strong beat, more rock-and-roll and a little raunchy. Tonya circles her head quickly, ponytail swinging wildly, and kicks one foot forward high in front of her face. As she resumes skating, the choreography of her arms is now sharply alternating, forward and back, and up and down with elbows bending and straightening, hands closing to fists and opening to spread fingers. An intended triple salchow-double toe loop combination turns into double salchow, step and three turn, triple toe loop. She does some quick turns, whipping her head sharply, gathers speed for a double axel, then finishes with a fast combination spin that sends her ponytail flying as she switches sharply from camel to sit to layback position, then changes feet to a back sit and back upright spin with her head tilted back to face the ceiling. She exits with a quick turn and head roll into a disco-like ending pose with a knowing look to the audience.

There is much to appreciate in both these performances, despite the missed jumps that left these two skaters behind Kristi's cleaner performance (marred only by a hand down on triple loop and a singled triple salchow) or Midori's success on the second of two triple axel attempts. They are, however, very different in the images they project.

Nancy is often described as "elegant" and "sophisticated," including descriptions by Scott Hamilton in the CBS commentary for this performance. These characterizations are inspired by her erect carriage and the long, slim lines of her body. Although she was not in fact born to wealth and privilege, the way she holds herself as she skates, along with her choice of costumes, suggests finishing school polish and a kind of haughty distance.

The stillness of her visage seems an appropriate evocation of purity and ethereality in the opening and closing sections of the program, but in the middle rhythmic section I find it particularly disturbing. Nancy seems neither to be enjoying these movements for herself nor performing them for us. Instead her body moves through positions that might be considered provocative on the dance floor, while facially she dissociates herself from the impropriety being displayed by her body, refusing it, and us, access to the soul she seemed to be expressing so intensely in the first section. Shading her eyes during the final spiral similarly suggests a dissociation from the sexual display implicit in that move, although the smile before and after otherwise offers it willingly.

The fact that her still expression in the middle section, though no longer appropriate, is the same one she wore in the opening soulful section calls into question all the sincerity and depth it seemed to betoken in that context. Probably this blank look just represents what Nancy looks like when she's concentrating on what she's doing. But the utter lack of connection between the movements of the body and the face, where we look for signs of the intelligence guiding those movements, suggests that that intelligence is elsewhere, that the body skating in front of us is an empty shell, a wind-up doll or robot performing movements programmed by some external source. And especially when she raises her chin, she seems to offer up her face to the viewer as a mask of beauty, like a model or starlet posing for the camera but not wanting to crack a smile for fear of wrinkles.

Nancy's choreography often asks her to change clearly and quickly from one position to the next. She almost always does so right on the music, and her body shapes are almost always extremely clear, each limb precisely positioned. This attests to careful schooling of her body to do what she wishes it to. It also, despite the constant flow of her skating, provides a series of distinct pictures or poses, each self-contained and "correct." In a long move, such as her spiral, she may hit one position and then continue to grow through it, in this case with the upper body only as the lifted leg remains still, but the emphasis is on the position arrived at, not the process of getting there.

Overall, then, the type of woman she appears to be on the ice (and again, let me state that I am speaking of an on-ice persona as I perceive it, not of the real-life Nancy Kerrigan) is one whose appeal is based in physical beauty and discipline to external, culturally sanctioned standards of bodily deportment. She may be deeply spiritual; on the other hand, she may just be innerly focused on skating technique in a way that reads as inner spiritual focus. She is willing to display her body for the sexual enjoyment of the onlooker, but unwilling to assert ownership of her own sexuality. She seems to shut the viewer out of any acknowledged relationship, to be always the perfectly constructed, completed object. As a watching subject I can't project myself into identification with Nancy's subjectivity, because I can't find it; for the same reason I can't imagine a mutual recognition of my own subjectivity with hers. The message to women viewers is: be looked at, be beautiful in face and in bodily movement, don't let a hair or a body part out of place, work at this beauty if necessary but don't show effort and don't show independent thought.

Tonya, on the other hand, elicits most often from commentators the adjectives "strong" and "powerful." In addition to her speed, the choreography of the first section of this program calls attention to rather than hides the muscular effort that goes into setting up the difficult opening jumps, particularly the triple axel; these are clearly presented as athletic feats, not blended into a would-be seamless whole. Combined with her pseudo-military costume and strong, sweeping music, this opening section presents an image of woman as active agent and as conquering hero, an image I find empowering but one seen all too rarely on or off the ice. Of course, Tonya did not conquer the triple axel in Albertville, nor to the best of my knowledge has she done so in competition since then, but the fact that she has continued to attempt this move that is so risky both physically and strategically bespeaks a courage that to me seems worth admiring rather than dismissing as leading to flawed performances.[11]

Tonya on the ice seems to be someone for whom doing is more important than simply being, process more important than product. The middle section of the program in particular demonstrates choreography based on moving through positions rather than arriving at them. The opposing tensions of, for instance, left free leg and right arm stretching slowly forward simultaneously during the middle slow section again highlight muscular effort, while the symbolically self-caressing movements and flowing weight shifts suggest not display but pleasure in one's own body. The spectator, though acknowledged, is irrelevant; this movement just feels good. I find this an empowering image for women in a world that continually constructs us as existing for the pleasure of men. And the final section, with its down-and-dirty bad girl imagery, its controlled lack of control, similarly depicts a woman who makes her own rules rather than fitting into the strictures of the larger society. This is very different from the highly disciplined images of Kerrigan's program.

Parallel Paths Diverge

This first Olympic experience also marks a turning point in the relative fortunes of Nancy and Tonya on and off the ice. Nancy went on to skate well at the '92 World Championships, finishing second to Kristi, and later won the '93 Nationals and the fall '93 Piruetten competition held on the Olympic ice in Norway (although not, as expected, the '93 Worlds), whereas Tonya had problems (equipment failures and missed jumps) at the '92 Worlds, the '93 Nationals (not even qualifying for the world team) and the fall '93 Skate America competition. Those results probably have everything to do with each skater's talents and training habits. Tonya's claim that she was "not controversial, just misunderstood," her stated determination not to give up until winning a gold medal at the Olympics, and her belief that "God is looking out for me"[12] were primarily either mere bravura or perhaps responses to a paranoid delusion that everyone was somehow conspiring to keep her from the skating successes and endorsement contracts she rightfully deserved. Such delusions, if they existed, were not entirely unfounded. I'm not suggesting there was an intentional conspiracy against Tonya (or that even if there was, injuring Nancy would have been an appropriate response). Nor am I suggesting that Tonya would have performed any better in the two years following Albertville had the media been on her side. But Nancy came home from Albertville as crown princess, the amateur heir-apparent to Kristi's gold medals (and more endorsement offers than Kristi herself received, but that's another story, with a racial subtext),[13] while Tonya was written off as an also-ran, a has-been. Was the difference in how Tonya and Nancy were received due just to the difference between third place and fourth, bronze medal versus none? Or was it because the mode of being a woman Nancy projected, on at least as much as off the ice, was more acceptable to collective American ideologies of femininity than Tonya's?

The ABC television coverage of the 1993 national championships, for instance, continually referred to Nancy, in first place after the technical program, as the expected winner and the one to beat, featured her in the opening credit montage that showed former champions and Nancy receiving a hug from Kristi Yamaguchi, and ran a human interest profile on Nancy's life since her bronze medal at Albertville. Tonya, on the other hand, in second place in the tech program, the other former World and Olympic competitor and the only former national champion in the competition, was positioned as just one of the four other skaters challenging the front-runner. The other human interest segment focussed on Lisa Ervin and Nicole Bobek, two up-and-coming 15-year-olds. In fact both Ervin and the other over-20 "veteran" in the final five, Tonia Kwiatkowski, finished ahead of Harding that evening. But in the live telecast, during which ABC's computer readout erroneously showed Harding retaining her lead over the others who skated after her and before Nancy, the relative lack of airtime accorded to Tonya, despite positive comments from Dick Button and Peggy Fleming as she took the ice, seemed like a dismissal. Nancy was the chosen champion, not because she had a stronger record than Tonya (she had for the past year only) or because she skated particularly well at the '93 Nationals (all of the top five women fell and turned triple jumps into doubles), but because she projected an image the judges, and before them the corporations that had hired her to star in their ads, and ABC Sports, wanted to promote. And the figure skating establishment breathed a sigh of relief as the judges rewarded skaters they saw as representing "the conservative, stable past of women's skating, [not the] athletic, unpredictable and erratic side of the sport—and of life—that most of the judges plainly do not like."[14]

Although Nancy and Tonya, of similar ages and with similar competitive histories, invite comparison, they don't represent the two poles of an either/or alternative, but rather are two of many excellent skaters in the United States and in the world. On any given competition day some will be more "on" than others, successfully completing more of the difficult moves in their program.[15] Almost always, the winners are those who skate cleanly with the most difficulty. But finding out who wins, who's the "best" skater, is not the only or in most cases probably the primary reason we watch television coverage of figure skating. And we do watch, especially in Olympic years. In 1994, U.S. television viewership for the Ladies' technical and free programs was inflated because of the controversy surrounding Harding's involvement in the attack on Kerrigan, but during both the 1992 and 1988 Olympics the coverage of the ladies' final was not only the highest rated evening of Olympic coverage, but the second highest rated TV sports event of the year, following only the Superbowl. The proliferation of professional skating competitions on TV since the 1980s, as well as more coverage of amateur events other than the U.S. Nationals and World Championships, not to mention the televising of exhibitions with no competitive structure, attests to a growing interest in watching skating for its own sake. Perhaps some who tune in only for the Olympics are less interested in the skating per se than in witnessing whether our country will add to its medal count (the U.S. has historically been strong in both men's and ladies' singles, less so in pairs and dance), or in seeing young women in skimpy costumes displaying their bodies. Some may particularly enjoy watching the fluid motion of stroking and gliding on the ice, and find it more appropriate to watch on female rather than male bodies. Some prefer the explosive athleticism of triple jumps and flying spins, movement qualities more common among the men. And some enjoy the variety of artistic expressiveness possible through different types of movement on skates to different types of music.

For reasons discussed earlier, this kind of artistic expression is in fact more varied among male skaters (those who watch women's skating only because of discomfort with men using their bodies for aesthetic purposes, and the networks who devote two and three times as much air time to the women's competitions as the men's, are missing something). Men are expected to assert their individuality; women are expected only to be charming and beautiful. Men may be judged as artists, women as works of art. But in the world we live in women need more than charm and beauty to survive. So in figure skating, the one area of sport, and one of the few representational modes in mass culture in general, where what women do attracts more attention than the men, I rejoice when I see a woman out there battling to make her mark through what she does rather than what she looks like. Among recent American skaters, Tonya Harding was the woman who best projected that ideal. I wish that she (or Jeff Gillooly and the other conspirators, if she was telling the truth when she claimed not to have known about the plan to attack Kerrigan until after the fact) could have trusted her own ability to skate well, with or without the triple axel, and that we all could trust the media and the skating establishment to value images of female strength at least as highly as connotations of female to-be-looked-at-ness.

If Tonya had skated as well as she did at the Nationals with Nancy there, she would have finished no worse than second, good enough to make the Olympic team. If she had skated that well at the Olympics she might or might not have earned a medal (the competition was stiff), although a successful triple axel in an otherwise clean program would probably have assured her one, assuming a top six placement in the technical program (which would have been easy to achieve if she'd skated it as well as at the Nationals). But as it is, we'll never know how well she would have done without the distractions of a criminal investigation.

Feminist Figure Skating?

So maybe Harding is no longer the best example of positive female images on the ice. As I continue to enjoy the sport and to deplore the emphasis on the beauty of female *skaters* rather than on the beauty and other positive qualities of the *skating*, I wonder what might constitute a feminist figure skating performance. To answer that question entails also addressing the question of what I mean by "feminist." Is it more feminist for female skaters to emulate men, skating in ways that have been defined as masculine, emphasizing power and triple jumps? Or is it more feminist to emphasize what the female body can do better than the male?

More people watch more of what women do on the ice than what men do (also more females watch skating, and more females engage in it). Figure skating is thus the only sport and one of few realms of public representation where what women do matters more than what men do. Women may be better than men at being aesthetic to look at (although this point is debatable; much depends on who's doing the looking), but in the culture at large looking aesthetic is not considered a very important thing to be good at. As long as skating (and skating coverage) continues to emphasize female skaters as objects of beauty, of interest because of what they look like rather than what they do, and therefore trivialize them in a culture that values "masculine" action over "feminine" appearance, its popularity as a spectator sport will only continue to reinforce cultural perceptions of women as ornamental rather than substantive members of the social body. However, the activity of skating in itself carries the potential for more active representations of femaleness.

In the first place, it's athletic. With the increasing emphasis on triple jumps for women as well as men since the 1980s, especially since the elimination of school figures from international competition in 1991, successful female skaters need to be superb athletes. Comparing females' jumping ability to males' may be counterproductive in that the males probably will continue to maintain a slight advantage in this area. But neither does it do skaters or spectators any favors when the media label females as *either* athletic *or* artistic, since doing so tends to belittle the very strong athletic ability of even the most "artistic" skaters who have made it high enough up the competitive hierarchy to attract media attention, as well as obscuring the very real artistry of a so-called "jumper" like Tonya Harding. And there could be more emphasis (in the choreography of women's programs as well as in the commentary) on the extreme skill and muscular effort required for moves like combination spins and complex footwork sequences, reminding viewers that the *movement* looks beautiful because of the work the skater puts into it, not just because her face and body type happen to fit socially agreed-upon standards of beauty.[16]

What would happen if connotative trappings of glamor were banned, with the skaters competing in simple leotards and tights or stretch pants, so that the competition as a whole would look more like a sporting event and less like a beauty contest or debutante ball? This would certainly allow skating to be taken seriously as a sport by male sporting standards. On the other hand, I do think something would be lost if the signifying element of costume were eliminated, something that makes figure skating more than just a sport, and which attracts viewers who otherwise ignore sporting contests in favor of more artistic (or rather, more meaning-oriented) forms of entertainment. At the same time skating has increased in athletic content while continuing to insist on the presentation of female skaters as objects of beauty, men's skating has evolved both athletically and artistically. Perhaps in an effort to avoid occupying the structurally feminized position of aesthetic object, male skaters of recent years have tended to demonstrate artistry by playing characters or by exploring the abstract expressive qualities of a simply clothed body in movement on the ice (notably Brian Boitano, Paul Wylie, and Mark Mitchell). The result is that while female skaters who are considered "artistic" usually achieve that label by submitting themselves to the status of objectified *work of art*, males achieve artistry by maintaining their subject position as *artists*, creators of the artistic expression that is the performance.

What I'd really like to see is more women claiming that position. And if sportscasters are going to comment on the artistic values of the performances, they should learn to distinguish between a pretty face or an attractive figure on the one hand (and why should this even be worth commenting on? we rarely hear about how good-looking male athletes are while they're out there landing triple axels or dunking baskets or hitting home runs), and on the other hand a female intelligence at work presenting herself, through the images she evokes with her body and movement. Although Harding at her best, when unburdened by criminal associations, offered many of these values, I'd like to close by commenting on some other encouraging performances from the 1994 season.

In the 1988 Olympic Winter Games at Calgary, Katarina Witt knew that her strongest competitors could do more difficult triple jumps than she could; what she had to offer in her freeskating program was artistry. She has explicitly stated that she used the role of Carmen to flirt with the audience; much of her program consisted of posing and making eyes at the audience, sometimes not even skating for several seconds at a time. For this she received high artistic marks from the judges, even if Elizabeth Manley did finish ahead of her in the free skate. Debi Thomas, the other gold medal favorite, faltered in this event and fell to third overall, behind Manley, while Witt's placements in the figures and technical program kept her first overall. The media played up her sex appeal, reporting that both U.S. actor Woody Harrelson and Italian skier Alberto Tomba wanted to date her. But Witt's holding onto gold through seduction rankled among those of us who prefer to see women achieve rewards on the basis of deeds rather than looks.

So I found Witt's performances in her 1994 return to Olympic competition after six years as a professional a welcome surprise.

In the first place, just for a female skater to be still in competitive form at twenty-eight is encouraging to see: No, women are not washed up as they leave youth behind. Wth her full, well-rounded woman's body Witt skates at least as well now as when she won her first Olympic gold in 1984 as a skinny teenager.

Elaine Zayak, also twenty-eight, returned to competition this year as well to finish fourth at the U.S. Nationals, although she did so after one year's retraining following three years off the ice entirely, unlike Witt's experience as a full-time professional skater. Neither woman expected gold medals; now that figures are gone, skaters in the nineties are required to master far more triple jumps than during the eighties. Ironically, although known as an artless jumper during her teens, Zayak now emerged as a complete, mature, aesthetic skater compared to her younger U.S. competitors.

Both Zayak and Witt proved that adult women can maintain their athleticism and continue to grow artistically. Experience does count. While Zayak's artistic triumph in '94 lay simply in proving that she could achieve the flow and gracefulness that had seemed to elude her in the past, Witt used her 1994 performances to demonstrate that as a woman and an artist she had something to say. She wasn't just there, as in the past, to look beautiful (despite Verne Lundquist's comment as she took the ice for her technical program in Norway that "she does have a radiance about her"), to be an aesthetic object; now, through her skating, she addressed the audience as a speaking subject.

Her technical program was set to sweeping, powerful music from the film *Robin Hood, Prince of Thieves*. Harding, who has often favored such sweeping, powerful movie music as a complement to her own strong style, used this same soundtrack for her (unsuccessful) 1993 free program, and several senior pairs used it for their free programs at the 1994 U.S. Nationals. But in her short program, Witt took the music's original context literally, taking on the character of Robin Hood. Her hair pulled back into a low queue, she is costumed as the legendary hero in a loose cream-colored shirt and thick black tights, topped by a suede jerkin that by hanging loose below the belted waist might by some stretch of the imagination qualify as a skirt but in context reads as a male rather than female garment. It certainly doesn't serve the function of modesty—it's the uniform opaqueness of her tights from waist to ankles that makes her appropriately covered up. The program begins with Katarina miming pulling back a bowstring before launching herself into a high-speed preparation for a high, fast triple toe loop-double toe loop combination. Throughout the program she skates strongly, with clean, stretched, undainty lines that cast her in a heroic, implicitly masculine mold. She includes gestures suggestive of combat, seeming to wield a broadsword two-handed above her head, and later to sheathe it again. Even when she curves one arm overhead in ballet fifth position, the pose is more reminiscent of a fencer holding the free hand out of the fray than a dancer framing her face. There's nothing in this program that a male skater would look effeminate performing (although a man who can skate this cleanly and this fast could probably also include a more difficult triple jump in the combination). The spiral sequence (as videotaped by CBS) emphasizes the noble thrust of Katarina's chest leading into the space rather than the extension of her legs (very straight, though not particularly high); even the typically feminine layback spins, which men generally are not flexible enough to perform, are devoid of frilly ornamentation. In the simple required layback, Katarina leaves her arms low behind her back, bent open at the elbows, emphasizing the strength as well as the curve of her back in holding the position, and the openness of her chest to the heavens. In the final combination spin, the briefly held layback position is canted more sideways than straight back and the arms are clasped together behind her back. Overall, the program connotes nobility and heroism, images that have traditionally been associated with masculinity. Here they are shown to fit just as comfortably on a female body, when not hampered by the traditional feminine accoutrements of skirts and curved wrists, which break up the straight lines that connote effective action.

For her free program, Katarina chose to skate to the song "Where Have All the Flowers Gone," which she collaborated in arranging with composer Pete Seeger, in a program honoring the people of Sarajevo, the now war-decimated city where she won her first Olympic gold ten years earlier. Although lyrics are forbidden in high-level skating competition, the music for the program begins with Witt's voice humming the melody, calling attention to the fact that with these four minutes on the ice, she is here less to submit herself to the judges' approval than to make a statement.

During the program, Katarina performs three triple jumps (triple toe loop in combination with a double near the beginning of the program and alone toward the end, and a triple loop on the landing of which she briefly puts her hand down on the ice), as well as a double axel and double flip, and two double salchows that were probably intended as triples. The program, however, is not designed to showcase difficult jumps; rather, the focus is on the skating as a whole, not just tricks, and maintains connections to the anti-war message framing the performance. The first section, to horns and snare drum, is skated strong and fast, with broad turns and the strong jump combination, ending with a flying camel spin with sharp changes of body position on the exit, followed by a backward pivot folded over at the waist to transition into the next passage. In this section, accompanied by a delicate piano melody, the arms are held loosely curved at the wrists and elbows and follow broad curving paths, as the body folds and unfolds about its center. This is the most "feminine" section—suggestive of grief over the losses in the Bosnian war—with its repeated downward focus and movements of bending from the waist, as in pain, or, more likely, because they are smooth and sustained, in sorrow. Next, martial rolls of a snare drum evoke images of marching and military drill in their dehumanizing aspect as Katarina swings fisted arms in opposition across her body, and especially as she executes crisp, precise footwork, replacing one foot neatly behind the other or turning along a straight line from front to back on one foot, the free leg often swung straight and high as in a goosestep (even once kicked forward above her head in a catch step), with the arms and torso held rigidly still. The final section of music is more upbeat and flowing, with what sounds like a military fife leading into warmer horns. With the second strong triple jump, extended spread eagle, in which Katarina slowly raises her arms, palms up, from beside her legs to an open V (and then strokes with her arms open and turned up), and the final series of spins finishing with both fists clasped together and reaching forward and upward as Katarina's gaze follows them, this ending seems to offer a message of hope for peace.

She wears a severe red lace skating dress with high neck, long sleeves, and longer-than-usual-for-freeskating skirt (covering the mid thigh in front, nearly knee-length in back), with beige tights and skates. The dress thus connotes "female skater" without any overtones of sexuality or glamor. In this program Katarina's body is presented not as an aestheticized object but as an instrument, under her conscious control, with which she comments metaphorically on a current political situation relevant to her participation in the Olympic games.

Finally, I'd like to offer Nicole Bobek's exhibition program, performed after she placed third in the 1994 U.S. National Championships, as a rare example of a female skater demonstrating a sense of humor and positioning herself as in control of the exchange of gazes between herself and the spectators. As in many post-competition exhibitions, the skating is a bit ragged (probably due to late parties the night before), but in this case the fact that the performance is not a seamless, unified whole is incorporated into its design. Dressed in what appears to be a two-piece skirted bathing costume (with, of course, flesh-colored fabric across the midriff and flesh colored tights), primarily in black sequins but with pink, blue, and silver stripes in an inverted triangle across the chest and forming a "belt" across the top of the trunks, Nicole skates to a medley of upbeat 1950s and '60s pop songs (and the theme song to *Hawaii 5-0*) by Jive Bunny and the Mix Masters, a deliberately disunified accompaniment. To the opening words "Come on, everybody, everybody, everybody," with arms extended forward and sideways she repeatedly curls her fingers up toward herself, inviting the audience to join her for a day at the beach, or (in reality) to watch her perform the series of tricks that make up a skating program.

Between tricks (starting with a double axel followed by an easy half jump with raised arms and exaggeratedly bent wrists for punctuation, and a sit spin combined with a Biellmann spin [see glossary]), she undulates her torso and hips in good-natured grooving to the music, and she smiles at the crowd, often wide eyed and wide mouthed and bobbing her head around, to let us know she knows she's being silly. When the lyrics exhort "Come on, let's twist again," she performs a number of variations of the Twist on skates. With bent knees and one hand raised to her brow as if to shade her eyes from the sun, she leans into a couple of brief spread eagles that look like she's riding a surfboard, somewhat off balance. Then she shoots both hands like guns at the audience in a gesture that seems to mean "I see you and I know you're watching me and saw that I didn't do that perfectly, but I'm still the one running this show." In a sitting position on one foot with the free leg stretched forward from behind the skating foot, she rides in a circle around a center defined by her hands on the ice, a kind of self-induced death spiral. From that position, she lies face up on the ice and pushes herself backward with her blades while circling her arms in alternation as if swimming the backstroke, extremely silly but in keeping with the mood of the piece. When she gets up she does a ragged double toe loop probably *intended* to read as a failed triple. This is followed by a half-turn back-to-front jump with both feet coming up toward her rear end while her hands come to either side of her head, as though she's having a tantrum at having botched the previous jump.

The next "trick" is Nicole's forward spiral, probably the best one around: she has the strength and flexibility to achieve, though not a full 180 degrees of extension, certainly close to it, and without holding up the free leg with one hand as Nancy Kerrigan does. For this program, she repeatedly bends and straightens her fists downward from her chest in time to the music as she holds the position, then circles her arms in a swimming motion as she exits the spiral. She begins a difficult footwork sequence, then reverts to simple, largely two-footed skating; as the lyrics ask "Is it a bird? Nooo! Is it a plane? Nooo!" she shakes her head and upraised hands at the audience to get them to join the fun. Then the music offers a repeated ("broken record") passage of "Great balls of fire" as just "great balls, great balls,..." to which Nicole performs a series of four split jumps, reminiscent of Scott Hamilton's and other male skaters' exhibition practice of getting the crowd to count how many they could do in a row. Nicole struts right up to the boards and shimmies in the face of whomever was sitting in the front row—again, an in-your-face connection to the crowd often seen from male skaters who playfully accept their positioning as sex objects through performance, but on their own terms; here that's given a particularly female turn. Finally, after an extended series of star turns, she kicks up and falls into a split on the ice that looks both showy and more painful than it probably really is.

The typical female skater presents herself seriously as there to be looked at for the perfection of her skating and of her beauty, looking at the spectators only to seduce their gaze back onto herself and submitting herself to their approval. Bobek, on the other hand, establishes control of the play of gazes between performer and spectators by deliberately acknowledging the intentional or unintentional flaws in her performance and by looking directly at the spectators to confront them with her awareness that they are looking at her. The way she presents certain cliched "sexy" or "feminine" moves, such as rolling her torso or curving her wrists, with a knowing smile, as a shared joke between herself and the audience, makes the seductive can-can of her competitive long program retrospectively seem to have been tongue in cheek, deliberately over the top, as if she played along with the conventions of feminine display accepted by the figure skating establishment in order to win a high enough competitive placement to qualify to perform in the exhibition.

I hope to see more of Nicole's subjectivity in competition programs, and that of anyone else who dares to escape the trap of conventionalized feminine artisticness to be instead a female artist/athlete. Strong, consistent triple jumps wouldn't hurt either.

< NOTES >

Thanks to Sally Banes, Nichole Gantshar, and Julia Ridgely for assistance with the preparation of this essay.

1 Still the figure skating world's term for females of any age.

2 Roland Barthes (1972). "Myth Today" in *Mythologies*. New York: Noonday, pp. 113–159.

3 Roland Barthes (1977). "The Third Meaning" in *Image, Music, Text*. New York: Hill & Wang.

4 For examples, see Abigail Feder, "A Radiant Smile from a Lovely Lady" (this volume); Ellyn Kestnbaum, "Masculinities on Ice: Figure Skating and Real Manhood," paper presented at the Popular Culture Association annual conference, Philadelphia, Pa., April 1995.

5 As of the 1994–95 season, the amount of jumping required of males and females in the short program is somewhat more even than in past years. Senior men are still required to include either two or three triple jumps; while senior ladies may still perform all doubles, they are now permitted to perform two triples rather than only one. Both men and ladies now do one flying spin, since the second flying spin previously required for men has been replaced by a change-foot camel or sitspin, instead of the layback spin for ladies. Ladies are still required to perform one spiral sequence and one step sequence while men perform two step sequences. (USFSA *1994–95 Rule Book,* Colorado Springs: USFSA, pp. 94–96.)

6 United States Figure Skating Association (1992). *1992–93 Rule Book.* Colorado Springs: USFSA, p. 107. USFSA rules conform with those established by the International Skating Union.

7 Henie finished eighth out of eight in that competition. It wasn't until 1927, after her school figure skills had a chance to improve and skating officials had a chance to get used to seeing women's legs and women performing the same athletic free skating moves as the men, that she won her first world championship.

8 USFSA *Rule Book,* p. 107.

9 The skirt also connotes a sense of the skating competition as a formal occasion, like a ball (until the 1970s men usually completed wearing jackets and ties). Certainly the rhinestones and sequins that adorn women's costumes are there to read as "jewels." It is these images that have continued to associate figure skating in the public imagination with an effete old-money upper class, despite the fact that very few serious skaters come from such backgrounds. But the implied association with this inaccessible social stratum may be part of skating's appeal for some skaters and fans. And for those fortunate few who manage to parlay international medals into lucrative professional skating careers, skating can in fact provide an entrée into the associated privileges new money can buy.

10 Laura Mulvey (1975). "Visual Pleasure and Narrative Cinema." Reprinted in *Feminisms: An Anthology of Literary Theory and Criticism.* Robyn R. Warhol and Diane Price Herndl, eds. New Brunswick: Rutgers University Press, 1991.

11 In both her 1994 Nationals and Olympics free skates, Tonya didn't fall, but "popped" the triple axel into a single, failing to pull in her arms and legs tightly to achieve the necessary rotations. Dick Button, in his live ABC commentary on the Nationals, stated that Tonya "elected to do a single," but the height and awkward body position of the jump show that it was not a conscious decision before takeoff to substitute a jump advanced skaters find quite simple, but an uncontrollable failure of nerve or muscular response in the crucial instant at or just following takeoff. As Scott Hamilton has explained elsewhere regarding the phenomenon of "popping," it's involuntary.

12 ABC telecast of 1994 U.S. National Championships.

13 See Abigail Feder. "A medalist of a Different Color." Paper presented at the American Theatre in Higher Education annual conference, Chicago, Ill., July 1994.

14 Christine Brennan. "New Women Bring Back Old Style: It's Art Over Athleticism" in *Washington Post* (January 25, 1993), p. C5.

15 It's the multi-revolution jumps that tend to be do-or-die propositions; being off by the slightest split-second in timing or angle of body position taking off, in the air, and landing can mean a fall. Falling is far less common in spins, glides, or stroking, although the combination of an awkwardly placed edge and a hole or bump in the ice certainly can bring a skater down in even the simplest of moves. More common small errors are a less than smooth stroke or a spin that travels over the ice rather than remaining centered in a single location.

16 As my friend Julia puts it, there is something sort of wonderful about the way Surya Bonaly seems to grunt when she skates. After all, triple jumps are hard work.

5

Fear of Falling

I have been following figure skating in a relatively informal but passionate way for years. By "informal" I mean that I have acquired a fair amount of knowledge about skaters, about the presentation of skating on television, and about controversies (concerning, say, judging); at the same time, I am a neophyte in that I still really can't tell the difference between a triple flip and a triple salchow. My limited knowledge hasn't prevented me from articulating firm opinions, and I have often found myself swept up by the frenzy of competition. For instance, during the famous 1988 Olympic showdown between Katarina Witt and Debi Thomas, popularly billed as the "dueling Carmens," I enthusiastically adopted the popular conception of Witt as villainess, as ice princess, and of Thomas as the earnest and forthright challenger (at the 1994 Olympics I was equally taken in by the image of Witt as a wise old timer). I've cheered for Brian Boitano. I was appalled that Isabelle and Paul Duchesnay, the brother and sister ice dancing pair who challenged many of the gender stereotypes of the sport, didn't get the gold. And so on.

When Nancy Kerrigan was attacked and the subsequent involvement of Tonya Harding was revealed, I consumed news of the event as enthusiastically as anyone I know. What interested me in particular about the Harding/Kerrigan event was how it foregrounded and exaggerated issues that have been present in the presentation of figure skating as a spectator sport for years. Abigail Feder's essay in this volume on the presentation of women's figure skating is a sobering reminder that in the one sport where women tend to be more visible than men, the price paid for such visibility is the excess of stereotypes of femininity. The fact that figure skating is virtually absent from such recent studies as Susan Cahn's *Coming On Strong* (1994) and Mariah Burton Nelson's *The Stronger Women Get, The More Men Love Football* (1994) suggests that the battle between "femininity" and "female strength" is not really being waged in any particularly ground-breaking ways on the ice.

Yet however much figure skating seems to be ruled by extremely conventional representations of femininity, I find that analysis of spectatorship vìs-a-vìs figure skating raises more complicated issues. Just as the supposedly universal and ubiquitous "male gaze" of the classical Hollywood cinema functions quite differently when examined through the lens of female spectators and female pleasures, so the spectacle of figure skating takes on a different look and set of expectations when viewed through the lens of female spectatorship.

Consider in this context one of the many peculiar devices employed in the NBC made-for-television movie *Tonya and Nancy: The Inside Story* (broadcast April 30, 1994). A series of fictionalized interviews with a range of commentators on the Harding/Kerrigan affair are featured in the telefilm. Taped rather than filmed (thus creating the illusion of authentic interviews), and featuring direct address to the camera in the style of talking heads documentaries, these interviews included television producers, a former skater, a 60s activist, and a skating judge. Two of the interviews included in the TV movie serve as appropriate images of the issues at stake in this essay, a very speculative exploration of female spectatorship in relationship to figure skating.

Two individuals, one female and one male, are identified as "supporters" of Harding and Kerrigan respectively. Both of these interviews occur in the last half hour of the teleplay. The Harding supporter appears after Tonya Harding is pictured at her practice rink wielding a camcorder and sporting a t-shirt that reads "no comment." The woman is middle-aged and she wears an "I Love Tonya" button. "It's just so unfair," she says angrily and passionately to the camera. She continues:

The way the judges have always treated her...and the media! That's why we started the fan club. Because the Nancy Kerrigans of the world get all the attention. And somebody like Tonya who's had to struggle all her life.... The Tonyas of this world just get pushed aside. It makes me sick.

The Kerrigan "supporter" appears a bit later, following images of Tonya and her husband Jeff Gillooly planning what they will say to the police. The Kerrigan supporter appears to be a bit younger than the Harding fan club organizer, but he is also middle-aged (and balding), wearing horn rimmed glasses, a button-down shirt, and a cardigan around his shoulders. His tone is also angry, though not quite as personally involved as the woman's. He says:

> Don't give me that bleeding heart crap about unhappy childhoods. I mean, what are we saying here? That because she comes from a dysfunctional family that she's supposed to grow up and marry a jerk and commit a crime? What ever happened to free will? I mean, look at Nancy. Now she sacrificed too. But she played by the rules. You get what you deserve.

While it might be appropriate to describe both of these "supporters" as passionate in their defenses of their heroines, there is no question that the Harding fan is more emotional and seems to have more at stake personally in her identification with the skater. The Harding fan even seems somewhat deranged, whereas the Kerrigan fan utters what was quickly becoming popular common wisdom concerning the paths of the two skaters. In addition, the contextualization of the interviews creates an odd juxtaposition between the female fan who reacts and the male fan who comments. It is, of course, no coincidence that the more deranged and excessive fan is female, while the male fan embodies cool reason and sarcastic restraint.

While the gender dichotomy of these two presentations of spectatorship does not surprise me, I find it a matter of some curiosity that both "supporters" are distinctly middle-aged. One suspects, perhaps, that the Harding/Kerrigan affair, as retold in this made-for-television movie, offers the possibility to middle-aged spectators to take sides and to act out fantasies and projections of the meanings of success and failure for the female skaters. Both fans are identified as "supporters," which suggests an investment stronger than everyday, run of the mill spectatorship. Yet the intensity of each "supporter's" defense of her/his favorite speaks to a particular quality of figure skating and its relationship to its viewers. For figure skating is notorious for its provocation of histrionics, from the outlandish and fluid standards of judging to the dramatic question that is raised every time a skater glides onto the ice: will she fall?

Falls are the unconscious of figure skating, the dangerous id that can emerge at any time and upset years of preparation and devotion. There is a hierarchy of falling in skating: There are near falls and real falls. When a skater's hand touches down after a jump or a landing is two-footed, then we are witnessing a near fall, the possible prelude to a real fall. Among the real falls, there are variations of degree, from awkward but recoverable stumbles onto the ice to splats in which the graceful, athletic body is out of control. A real fall is always potentially catastrophic, but it offers the opportunity to witness the gumption of the athlete in his or her recovery time. More than one fall signifies a crumbling of confidence.

The fear of falling is a factor in all figure skating, whether the competitors are male or female. Brian Boitano's performance at the 1994 Olympics was ultimately reducible to a single moment, repeated over and over again (as such moments always are), in which he fell during his short program. But I want to argue that the fear of falling has special significance for women skaters, and in particular for the relationship that exists between female spectators and female skaters. Perhaps more than any other spectator sport, women's figure skating relies on the precarious balance between athleticism and the display of grace, i.e., femininity. The fall shatters the balance, and in particular disrupts the performance, of femininity.

In addition to the anticipation of falling, figure skating offers a unique set of circumstances as a spectator sport. First, there is the visibility of women in the sport. Televised women's competition not only draws huge numbers of women viewers, but supposedly even more viewers than televised football games. Second, the visibility of "femininity" in figure skating is a proverbial knife that cuts both ways. For while femininity is an expectation for female skaters, it is also a spectre haunting men's figure skating. Throughout the history of the sport, male athletes have had to contend with the associations of figure skating with a gay sensibility, and televised coverage of the men's competition often wavers uncomfortably between a submerged acknowledgement of that sensibility and an affirmation of heterosexual and/or firmly "masculine" identities. Indeed, both of these were on display during the 1994 Olympic games in the men's competition. Elvis Stojko's much heralded innovative choreography based on the moves of martial arts (he has a black belt in karate) provided a stunning, if implicit contrast to the gold medalist Alexander Urmanov, whose style is much more classical (i.e., "feminine"). Stojko was referred to constantly as a new breed of figure skater, with the implication that he was bringing a more explicitly masculine presence to the sport.

The Tonya Harding/Nancy Kerrigan saga foregrounded virtually all of these elements particular to figure skating. As a sport in which women are so central, it comes as no surprise that the coverage of women's figure skating competition often relies on excessivly stereotypical views of women, from the good girl/bad girl dichotomy to variations on fairy-tales. During the Harding/Kerrigan affair, the two skaters became opposites even more rigidly defined than Katarina Witt and Debi Thomas in the 1988 Olympics. The tension between athleticism and artistry was polarized in the contrast between Harding (whose sturdy thighs were often commented upon in this context) and Kerrigan. Obviously, Kerrigan was designated the more "feminine" of the two skaters, with Harding's fondness for hunting, pool, and cigarettes interpreted as signs of, if not "masculine," then at the very least "unfeminine," behavior.[1]

If the anticipation of the fall is a particular feature of figure skating, then the Harding/Kerrigan affair foregrounded that feature in a very dramatic way. Prior to the National Championships in Detroit where Nancy Kerrigan was attacked, both skaters had particular histories of their relationship to the fall. Harding is best known for landing a triple axel jump in competition, but she is also known for failing to land that trademark. Kerrigan's relationship to falling was not focused on a particular jump, but served rather to emphasize the troubles she had had with the strain of competition. At the 1993 World Championships, Kerrigan was in first place entering the final stage of the competition, and she proceeded to stumble through her program (finishing in fifth place). The televised coverage of the event showed Kerrigan waiting for her scores, and the camera slowly zoomed in to capture the look of anguish on her face; Kerrigan uttered the words, "I'd like to die."

Even the attack on Kerrigan, and in particular the images of her screaming in pain that circulated widely, acquired some of the features associated with the fall. To be sure, Kerrigan was "felled" by a baton wielded by an attacker, not by her own inability to complete a jump, and she fell off, not on, the ice. But the image of a skater screaming immediately evokes the spectre of the fear that haunts skating. Kerrigan's screams of pain and rage may have been in response to an attack, but they are precisely the response one imagines to the fall.

It doesn't require too much imagination to see that the fear of falling in figure skating represents more than a failed jump. It represents confidence in the spotlight, or the lack thereof, and during the Harding/Kerrigan story, it represented a kind of moral gauge, particularly when Kerrigan completed her short and long programs "flawlessly" (to use her overused word). Falling becomes an indication of a variety of syndromes that are presumed to be particular obstacles to female athletes—poor self esteem, fear of success, terror of the spotlight. And in the most general and far-reaching sense, the fear of falling on the ice represents a discomfort with spectacle and public exposure in general. The significance of falling in this metaphoric sense during the entire Harding/Kerrigan affair did not just occur on the ice, in that both women are somewhat inarticulate off the ice. This is especially true of Harding, who had difficulty reading her prepared statement during the infamous news conference where she acknowledged that she knew that "people close to her" had participated in the attack, and who, when interviewed during the Olympics after it became obvious that she would not win a medal, attempted in vain to make Kerrigan's patriotism an issue.

Given how central female spectatorship has been in film, television, and mass culture studies of the last decade, it is useful to consider how and to what extent the female spectators identified in other forms of mass culture might relate to female spectators of figure skating. Studies such as Tania Modleski's analysis of soap operas and popular fiction (1984), or Janice Radway's examination of romance novels (1984), have put into question the supposedly simple, transparent ways in which women respond to these examples of mass culture. For while neither Modleski nor Radway question the strength of women's identifications, they do not assume that identification to be a simple matter of identifying with cultural ideals of femininity.

Figure skating offers a display of grace and femininity to which women in this culture are presumed to aspire; in this sense, figure skating offers a spectacle of identification. Indeed, one could go so far as to say that the presentation of figure skating keeps female athleticism within safe boundaries by emphasizing constantly the grace and the prettiness of skaters. But then there is the nagging question of the fall—and of the fact that what spectators actually see in watching figure skating is less an idealized spectacle of femininity than the potential acting out of the *failures* of femininity.

Very schematically, and following work on female spectatorship in film, the significance of falling in figure skating could be defined in two very different ways. Imagine yourself watching a favorite performer as she takes the ice. One of the mini-bios that often accompany televised coverage of ice skating has emphasized how much she has struggled to achieve perfection. As she takes the ice you are excited and nervous for her. She glides, she spins, she turns, and then she is ready to jump. She falls. You gasp. You blink. You hurt for her. You share her pain. You have identified with her so closely. Now imagine yourself watching another skater, one about whom you have some suspicions. As she glides confidently across the ice you find yourself a bit contemptuous of her. Who does she think she is? She completes her first triple combination and you begrudgingly join in the praise of the television commentators. But then she two foots a landing of a jump, and you find yourself becoming edgy and if truth be told, hopeful. On her next jump she falters and spills, legs akimbo, across the ice. You laugh.

Those familiar with recent film theory concerning spectatorship, and female spectatorship in particular, will recognize these two scenarios: in the first case there is an excess of identification, leaning towards a masochistic desire; in the second, there is distance from the image produced by identification with the imagined male spectator, and attendant sadistic pleasure in the falling apart of the image of femininity (Doane 1991: chapters 1, 2). In the first case there is imagined closeness to the skater; in the second, distance from her. For the purposes of this essay, the particular dynamics of cinematic identification as rendered through psychoanalysis are less signficant than the simultaneity of closeness and distance. The relationship of female spectatorship to figure skating is to be found in the particular way in which identification and distance intersect. The popular conception of Nancy Kerrigan and Tonya Harding was that spectators "identified" with Kerrigan and "distanced themselves" from Harding, that there was hope that Kerrigan would succeed and that Harding would fall. The news reporter who functioned as the narrator of *Tonya and Nancy: The Untold Story,* put it quite bluntly near the conclusion of the televised movie. Over an image of Tonya Harding, he says: "Imagine how it would feel to know that 100 million people want you to fall." And over a contrasting image of Nancy Kerrigan, he says: "Imagine how it would feel to know that if you fall you would fail 100 million people."

But if Harding and Kerrigan embodied an opposition between distance and closeness, between hoping she falls and fearing she'll fall, it is far more typical for those responses to exist simultaneously. There is nothing particularly new about this hypothesis concerning the simultaneity of closeness and distance; this is precisely what many feminist theorists have argued about the nature of women's responses to many different forms of mass culture, from Modleski's argument that the villainess in soap operas provides both an object of scorn and a projection of power to Radway's claim that women identify with romance novels because the male characters that inhabit them exhibit a utopian synthesis of male and female qualities. What *is* particular about spectatorship and figure skating is the significance of falling. Films, television programs and novels may have symbolic ruptures; ice skating performances have real ones, when the fragility of performance is amply on display. Few televised spectacles offer such consistent possibilities for disruption. And when a skater falls, the performance is shattered, perhaps momentarily, but often irreparably. Put another way, the significance of the fear of falling lies in a particular contract established between spectator and skater; the rupture of performance is immediate.

In addition, there is another quality particular to figure skating, and that is its association with the desires and dreams of adolescent and pre-adolescent girls. It is well known that figure skating has a particular following among adolescent and pre-adolescent girls. Of course adult women watch the sport as well, but I believe one of the major appeals of figure skating for adult women is the recapturing, recollecting, and revisioning of the experience of adolescence. It is easy to trivialize that recapturing as a kind of simple minded idealization of adolescent ideals, whereby the girl and the adult woman both fall into rhapsodized identification with the image of perfection, the object of all-adoring gazes. It is also easy to pathologize the recollection of adolescence, which is implicit in the interview with the female "supporter" of Tonya Harding in the television movie; indeed, it doesn't require too much imagination to see in her anger over the unfairness of Harding's treatment a projection of her own anger about herself. But given how central the fear of falling is in figure skating, I think it is too simple to attribute female spectatorship to the mimicry of patriarchal ideals of womanhood, whether on the part of an adolescent girl who identifies passionately with a figure skater or an adult woman who relives adolescence. Indeed, so much of the experience of watching figure skating involves the anticipation of or reaction to the fall, that one begins to suspect that part of the appeal of the sport for women viewers is less the exhibition of femininity than the exhibition of femininity as a performance fraught with danger and possibilities of failure.

It is useful in this context to look at a series of books about figure skating that are directed to an audience of adolescent and pre-adolescent girls. As narratives that extend the experience of watching figure skating, such books often function to mediate the fear of falling. In December 1993, the "Silver Blades" series, by Melissa Lowell, began publication. At the time of this writing, five books have appeared in the series. Silver Blades is the name of a skating club in Pennsylvania to which the four heroines of the series belong. Each volume focusses on a different skater and a particular issue she must confront, usually having to do with the pressures of competition. Throughout the books, falling is a major motif. The first book in the series, *Breaking the Ice* (1993), introduces Nikki Simon, whose family has just moved to Pennsylvania so that she can take advantage of the Silver Blades club. She tries out and is accepted into the club, and is introduced to the three girls who will become her co-heroines in the series—Jill Wong, Tori Carsen, and Danielle Panati. Each of the girls experiences the kinds of problems one might expect—fear of competition, conflicts between skating and a social life, and snottiness from other skaters. The character of Tori Carsen is particularly interesting in this respect. In the first book she seems to embody the ice princess, in that she attends a private school and plots to denigrate any skater by whom she feels threatened. Tori suffers from an overbearing mother (shades of Tonya Harding) who insists on attending all of her practice sessions. By the conclusion of the first book, Tori has apologized for her evil ways, and in the third book in the series, stage fright is shown from her point of view (she suffers a humiliating fall before her performance even begins). In other words, the series offers to its young readers not only the possibility to understand why an ice princess might act the way she does, but also the opportunity to see her change for the better.

In order to become successful performers, the girls must also learn to be successful spectators. This simultaneous process of spectatorship and performance is developed quite succinctly in the second book in the series, *In the Spotlight,* in which Danielle is chosen to be the soloist at the club's show. (Tori fully expected to be chosen.) Danielle has confidence problems that are multiplied by her fear of being overweight. In addition, she meets a boy she likes, and suffers the conflict between romance and dedication to skating. While all of Danielle's conflicts are resolved in a fairly predictable way, her success on opening night is prefigured by her ability to appreciate the feats of her fellow skaters. Potential ice princess Tori saves a panicking skater who falls out of formation, and pairs Nikki and Alex perform so well that Danielle is "awed by how well they skated together in such a short amount of time" (p. 128). When it is Danielle's turn to perform solo, she has so identified with the entire spectacle of the show, and with the other skaters, that she does (as one might suspect) a superb job ("The audience began to clap, and Danielle actually found herself smiling. This wasn't so bad, she told herself. In fact it was fun!" [p. 129]).

Of course skaters fall in the Silver Blades books, but when they do it is always a learning experience through which the girls focus, practice harder, and succeed. At the same time, their own progress and maturity is equated with their learning not to revel in the misfortunes—i.e., the falls—of other skaters. Everyone falls, the books suggest, but the results are never as catastrophic as they might seem. Falling and how one responds to it are measures of success and maturity in both performance and in spectatorship.

I imagine the young girls who read the Silver Blades book as acting out their own fantasies of being stars on the ice, certainly, but the books also function as primers on the art of watching skating. Girls are encouraged to be supportive of each other, to focus on their own performances, and not to gloat over the mistakes of others. In the first book of the series, when Tori claims that Nikki ran into her on the ice on purpose, the girls tell Tori that she has watched too many old movies. In that common retort is an interesting twist, for the Silver Blades books seek to rewrite Hollywood conventions of competition between women, arguing instead for an idealized community within which there is support and possibility beyond every fall. The imagined love and attention that comes with a successful performance is always available, as long as one combines performance and spectatorship in the right proportions. As fiction for young girls, the Silver Blades books are supposed to present role models and life lessons. I think the books also capture the fantasies that figure skating represents, not just for adolescent and pre-adolescent girls, but for adult women who seek, consciously or not, to re-enact those fantasies of performance.

The fantasies of performance are given a particularly interesting form in a film that, unlike the Silver Blades books, was marketed to appeal both to girls and to women. In the 1979 film *Ice Castles,* the rise and fall of a figure skater is quite literally charted by her relationship to the fear of falling. Lexie is from a small town in Iowa and is blessed with natural, raw talent; at a regional competition she is spotted by a prominent coach who assumes her training. Lexie is eager to follow her dreams of skating, yet she is awkward and ill at ease as an object of spectacle.

A crucial moment occurs in the film when Lexie is one of a small group of skaters profiled in a Christmas television special. One of the skaters, the French national champion, was reported to have suffered a nervous breakdown, but she is well enough to skate in the special. But when the French skater sees Lexie skate beautifully and flawlessly via a television monitor backstage, it is too much for her to bear. The French skater goes onto the ice and fails miserably, falling constantly. Lexie watches the monitor with the kind of distress that in melodrama signals much more than sympathy with the object of the look. Indeed, before too long Lexie herself will fall during an impromptu practice session following her discomfort at a party; what she suffers is not just momentary humiliation (as did the French skater) but permanent blindness.

Ice Castles is remarkably on target in the way it taps the emotion and drama of figure skating, for it is precisely the fear of falling that makes the experience of watching figure skating unique. More specifically, *Ice Castles* demonstrates the fear of falling and female spectatorship simultaneously. It is no coincidence that the two views that promote terror—terror on the part of the French skater that Lexie is too good, and terror on Lexie's part that the French skater falls so badly—are mediated by a television screen. Earlier in the film, we are told that part of Lexie's remarkable natural talent is her ability to watch skaters like Dorothy Hamill on television and imitate their moves perfectly. Lexie's dreams and fears are similarly mediated by a television screen, and in this sense she embodies not only a Cinderella story of a skater, but also a fable of female spectatorship.

The emphasis in both the Silver Blades books and *Ice Castles* on performance and spectatorship simultaneously, and of overcoming the fear of falling, suggests that the pleasures of watching figure skating for women involve not only identification with and anxiety about feminine ideals simultaneously, but also a certain satisfaction in witnessing possible spectacles of humiliation. Indeed, as much as the story of Harding and Kerrigan seemed to play on the desire to separate the bad girl and the good girl, and to see the bad girl fall and the good girl skate "flawlessly," the aftermath of the Olympic competition demonstrated how the appeal of figure skating lies in the very fluidity of the boundaries separating good girl and bad girl. For after Oksana Baiul won the gold medal, a new set of opposing pairs emerged. Baiul is an interesting study in contrasts, a young woman who skates with remarkable confidence (and with an equally remarkable persona) and who virtually always seems to be sobbing once she is off the ice. This contrast is also a variation on the fear of falling, but now in Baiul's case the question becomes when she will cry more than when she will fall. As is well known, Nancy Kerrigan complained loudly when she assumed (mistakenly) that Baiul was reapplying her makeup before the Olympic presentation ceremony, and suddenly it became common for Kerrigan to be criticized as a prima donna. During the exhibition of medal winners, Kerrigan stumbled and performed far from "flawlessly." My guess is that many female spectators were not only waiting for it to happen, but were secretly enjoying the spectacle of the fall. As much as women's figure skating may embody fantasies of perfect and idealized femininity, the fear of falling makes this a spectator sport in which the fall from grace is every bit, if not more, appealing than perfection.

< NOTES >

1 Interestingly, one of the peculiarities of this distinction between the more and the less feminine is that Harding was not only the more unfeminine but also the more obviously heterosexual of the two; in men's figure skating this would surely operate in the tension between gay and straight, but the operative distinction here is sexual/virginal.

< REFERENCES >

Cahn, Susan K. 1994. *Coming On Strong: Gender and Sexuality in Twentieth Century Women's Sport*. New York: The Free Press.

Doane, Mary Ann. 1991. *Femmes Fatales: Feminism, Film Theory, Psychoanalysis*. New York: Routledge.

Lowell, Melissa. 1993. *Silver Blades: Breaking the Ice*. New York: Parachute Press/Bantam Press.

———. (1993) *Silver Blades: In the Spotlight*. New York: Parachute Press/Bantam Press.

———. (1994) *Silver Blades: The Competition*. New York: Parachute Press/Bantam Press.

———. (1994) *Silver Blades: Going for the Gold*. New York: Parachute Press/Bantam Press.

———. (1994) *Silver Blades: The Perfect Pair*. New York: Parachute Press/Bantam Press.

———. (1994) *Silver Blades: Skating Camp*. New York: Parachute Press/Bantam Press.

Modleski, Tania. 1982. *Loving With a Vengeance: Mass-Produced Fantasies for Women*. New York: Methuen.

Nelson, Mariah Burton. 1994. *The Stronger Women Get, The More Men Love Football: Sexism and the American Culture of Sports*. New York: Harcourt Brace & Company.

Radway, Janice. 1984. *Reading the Romance: Women, Patriarchy, and Popular Literature*. Chapel Hill: University of North Carolina Press.

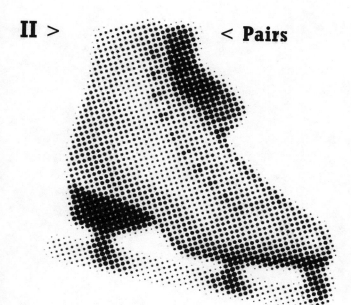

 **< Marjorie Garber**

Viktor Petrenko's
Mother-in-Law

On the day that Tonya Harding accepted a plea bargain from Oregon state prosecutors for her part in the assault on Nancy Kerrigan, the *New York Times* reported that more American journalism students want to be "public relations spokespersons" than print reporters or editors. What the *Times* called the "widespread interest in a career in image-making among young people," fostered by the on-camera appearances of glamorous presidential "mouthpiece" George Stephanopoulos, "uber-publicist" Pat Kingsley (who represents Tom Cruise), and Warren Cowan, the Hollywood press agent "befriended by clients from Rita Hayworth to Sylvester Stallone,"[1] has apparently displaced the allure of investigative reporting á là Woodward and Bernstein, and the frantic, adrenaline-pumping rush to meet deadlines in newsrooms from *Front Page* to *Mary Tyler Moore*.

It seemed no mere coincidence that the Tonya saga, which reporters now saw as coming to an inconclusive conclusion, should intersect with the story of hopeful young publicists on the make for a mike. "Now we will never know," began George Vecsey's column on the sports page of the *Times*.[2] "What the agreement did not include—and now might never be known for certain," lamented the front page account, "is the full extent of her knowledge of the Jan. 6 attack." And again, "while the unknowable might lack the scope and urgency of other celebrated but unresolved crimes, the extent of Miss Harding's role had remained the single burning question"[3]—a question the plea bargain rendered moot, and therefore mute. The "frenetic media coverage" that marked the Harding/Kerrigan case had become tautologous. Celebrity begat celebrity, notoriety begat notoriety, and in the latter days of the long-running *cause célèbre* the media began, inevitably, to feed upon themselves, analyzing, dissecting, and spin-doctoring all the surfaces and edges.

Was Nancy really nice, or really nasty? Was Tonya really nasty, or really nice? The more the public quested for answers, the more they got—we got—representations: Nancy's coaches; Nancy's parents; Nancy's physical therapist; Nancy's skating pal, Paul Wylie, Olympic silver-medalist turned (guess what) television reporter, who would later dismiss Oksana Baiul's gold-medal winning performance as "vamping for the judges." We also got *Tonya*'s coach, so carefully coiffed, so carefully spoken, so unlike her unruly charge, a woman who seemed, as a friend of mine said, always to be wishing to be Nancy's coach, Tonya's lawyers, and Tonya herself, defiantly if awkwardly camcording the reporters who were camcording her—not to mention the officials at various figure skating and Olympic committee "venues," as they say when the games begin, each of which offered "prepared statements" carefully prepared to say nothing. What was chiefly fascinating to me was how much money, apparently, went into the maintaining of the US Figure Skating Association's offices; in my innocence I had imagined a mimeograph machine and a mailing list, not a setup out of "L.A. Law." Amateur is a word that has clearly changed its meaning over time.

I live in the greater Boston area, the region that Nancy Kerrigan calls home, not far from her family house at Stoneham or, indeed, her practice rink on Cape Cod. As you can imagine, I grew impatient with the nightly visitations to the driveway in Stoneham and the Tony Kent Arena in Dennis—not as impatient as our local TV sports reporter, however, who clearly regarded figure skating as something other than a real sport, and contrived to be absent from the set on the long-awaited day of the Olympic competition.

Nancy, it turned out, had been seeing a "sports psychologist" to bolster her self-confidence since her catastrophic fifth place finish in a recent competition. Dan Jansen's sports psychologist made him write "I love the fifteen hundred" over and over again like some latter-day Dr. Coué ("every day in every way I am getting better and better") or Norman Vincent

Peale, or indeed like Miss Schieman, my basilisk-eyed third-grade teacher. Nancy's sports psychologist seemed to have turned her into the Barbie-doll of ego-ideal. "I was flawless," she told reporters over and over again after her Olympic performance. "I'm really proud of myself." "I skated great." Leaving aside the matter of troublesome adverbs and adjectives, has no one ever told her that these are things *other people say about you*, not things you say about yourself?

I don't really know what a sports psychologist is, or does, but my guess is that he or she frames sentences like these and gets the client to utter them. And, with luck, come to believe them. But like "I love the fifteen-hundred," these are ego-building sentences, mental calisthenics, auto-didacticisms, designed to be said to oneself under one's breath—not spoken out loud to an interlocutor. "I was flawless," like "I am dead," is an infelicitous utterance. It is in fact the comic solecism of a child, or, alternatively, the ventriloquized response of an automaton. When the real Nancy spoke, with a lip curled by disappointment at coming in second to Baiul ("come on—she's just gonna cry and mess up her makeup all over again") or the embarrassment of an over-age teenager pushed by her mother to wear her Olympic medal in the uncool embrace of Mickey Mouse ("this is so corny") the actual diction of an actual, and rather unsophisticated, person made the weird displacement of "I'm really proud of myself" even more disconcerting. It was as if, despite all the endless media interviews, we had never heard Nancy Kerrigan's voice before.

As for Tonya, her progress from "frankly I see dollar signs" to "I want to kick her butt" to "I just want the chance to represent my country" is recognizable as a shorthand version of the frontier spirit and the American way. Rockefeller, Kennedy, so many of our great patriotic dynasties have followed this well-trodden path of sanitization (and sanctification) through public service. But of course they were men. And the progress took more than one generation, not the milliseconds that pass for time in the electronic age. Too bad for Tonya that she was the bad girl, not the good girl. As any reader of fiction knows, though, the two are often twins, exchangeable doubles.

What struck me most about the media coverage of the Olympic games, was, I have to say, not the Nancy/Tonya saga, with which I was by that time (together with much of the nation) thoroughly bored, but rather the coy way in which issues of sexuality were elided when they did not coincide with mainstream family values. Here I am thinking, of course, of the way in which the *male* figure skaters were covered, or covered-up. Nancy had a doting family, all the stronger for being ex-working-class.

She also had Paul Wylie, clearly identified as "just a friend," and, somewhere offstage, some men she had dated. Tonya, of course, despite her trucker style, foul mouth, and triceps, had the egregious Jeff Gillooly, her once, twice, and who knows, perhaps future, husband. What about Brian Boitano? Or Scott Davis, the "American champion," as former champ (and gold medalist) Scott Hamilton kept calling him? They had press photos (Davis's, with lowered gaze and piercing blue eyes, was an over-the-top classic) and press clippings, but no visible significant others.

Boitano, an extremely articulate, frank and likable interviewee, pushed his baseball cap back over his clearly receding hairline (the contrast with his rugged mane in Calgary was, on the videotape replay, striking) and offered an endearing and rueful commentary on topics like aging, celebrity, and the pleasurable challenges of returning to competition. One of my gay male friends said he was "such a flamer it seemed like he ought to melt the ice." But we got no up-close-and-personal on Boitano, or, indeed, on any of the other male figure skaters except ice-dancing star Christopher Dean, who was congratulated on his impending marriage (his second; a former wife was among the judges for another skating event). And, of course, Viktor Petrenko, whose mother-in-law was the Ukrainian coach who had, at his urging, also taken on the training of the sixteen-year old Oksana Baiul.

Ah, Viktor Petrenko's mother-in-law…behind her loomed the unseen presence of Viktor's wife. Thus his rescue of Baiul, an extremely touching and appealing story, was spared even the merest hint of anything other than altruism by the audience's awareness of his marriage. Petrenko seemed like a genuinely nice guy (we also heard an account of his generosity to an injured American woman skater, taken to an under-equipped local hospital and provided by Petrenko with clean sheets and needles). He lives now, it seems, in Las Vegas, and his ease in border-crossing (he deftly translated for Baiul in her televised interviews, speaking English and Ukrainian in turn) made him available as an "American" hero of sorts, especially because Petrenko, like Boitano, quickly dropped out of medal competition, becoming part of the "pathos of the older skater" narrative that came effortlessly to replace the "return of the superstars" plot broadcast journalists had expected. But it was Petrenko's mother-in-law, Galina Zmievskaya, that deft grace note of heterosexuality, who carried the day.

Consider the ways in which family structures—certain family structures—were insistently stressed in the course of CBS's Olympic coverage, and, for that matter, in the coverage of print journalists as well.

There were Dan Jansen's blond wife and child, the latter named after the sister he lost to cancer just before an earlier Olympic competition. The photo-op of Jansen skating his victory lap (he loved the fifteen-hundred, the fifteen-hundred loved him) with a little flag in one hand and little Jane Jansen in his arms will surely come to replace the flag-draped US hockey star looking for his father at Lake Placid as an image of prototypical Americana. And Jansen and his wife Robin did seem wholesome, unpretentious, at least in contrast to Kerrigan, unprogrammed if not completely unrehearsed. There were more Jansen siblings, too, it turned out, home in Wisconsin toasting Dan's victory in beer. And then there was Bonnie Blair, five times a medalist, wearing the faint praise of "America's little sister" (a phrase one columnist astutely deconstructed as meaning more perky than conventionally beautiful), whose mother and the rest of the "Blair bunch," some fifty strong, sat in the stands and waved and sang. Bonnie Blair was part of the Norman Rockwell painting, even if she had to be Sis rather than Betty or Veronica. The journalist wrote that Blair had been cheated of the spotlight by Kerrigan and the Kerrigan story, and he was right. But the media allowed her to be a daughter. At least.

Not so the preponderance of the male figure skaters, who had no visible parents, no partners, no children—in short, no (televised) lives at all.

As I watched the Tonya/Nancy soap opera and reexperienced, as I do every four years, the American obsession with Olympic figure skating, I was struck by how very heterosexual it sets itself up to be. In pairs skating the woman is little and light, the man big and strong. He lifts her over his head and she depends entirely upon his strength and sureness. When a woman isn't little, the judges sometimes take off points; she's too heavy to lift with effortless ease. This was true of one skating pair from Russia (we had their story, too, including her weight loss—"she's a big girl" said Scott Hamilton during a particularly stressful lift) and also of Torville and Dean, the runaway favorites in ice dancing who came in a much-disputed third. Someone suggested to me that the judges didn't like the gender-bending in Jane Torville and Christopher Dean's program. She appeared to lift him at some points; at others she skated behind her partner and held his waist in her hands, rather than the other way around. Something about Torville and Dean didn't strike the judges right. Maybe they seemed to be having too good a time.

Watching the Olympics, I imagined a future Olympic event. Now that American-Gladiator-style sport stunts like "moguls" and "aerials" have been added to the competition, and, it appears, the old Scottish game of curling is on the way, the idea of new events seems less heretical than it once did. I doubt that the ancient Greeks did much luge or bobsledding, anyway. So what I wanted to suggest was same-sex pairs skating. Two men, two women, anything goes. Not a radical suggestion, you would think. Tennis has "ladies' doubles " and "men's doubles," as well as "mixed doubles." Is a "double" different from a "pair"? Why do we assume that pairs skating has to be one man and one woman?

For the same reason, it seems, that the judges didn't appreciate Elvis Stojko's leather-and-studs techno-rock. My favorite new phrase from the Olympic broadcast was Eric Heiden's strategy for moving faster around the speed-skating oval: "get a draft off your pair," he said. That's the way to do it. In the slip stream, carried along by the strength of your opponent who is also your confederate. "Get a draft off your pair."

But the pairs in speed skating are conceived as rivals, not partners—and especially not erotic partners. The problem with pairs figure skating is the cultural story of heterosexual romance. Or, to put it another way, the problem of the same-sex skating pair is the "problem" of homosexuality.

Same-sex pairs skating turned out, of course, to be an idea whose time had already come. Less than six months after the Games came the other Games, the Gay Games—some ten thousand athletes from 43 countries competing in dozens of events and awarded a total of some 5,500 medals—including pairs skating. Same-sex pairs. But not without a struggle.

In Montreal, professional skaters Jean-Pierre Martin and Mark Hird, who are friends but not lovers, encountered resistance when they practiced at L'Ampithéatre Bell, a Montreal rink where Martin works as a special-events consultant. "We did some side-by-side jumps and stands, then Mark lifted me a couple of times, and we left," said Hird, "No big deal." But it was. The next day Martin's boss reported that "people had complained about Mark and me skating together and that we'd been seen kissing," Martin explained, "Which is completely untrue." The rink, said the manager, was not a place for "the gay lifestyle." The pair—if they wanted to be a pair—were told to find another practice space.[4]

Instead, they told the press and mobilized the community, asking not only for practice time but for the same kind of "display window space" that L'Amphithéatre Bell provides to male-female couples: a place where they can show photographs of themselves and lists of their sponsors.

Notice that the rink owner had no other way of understanding the phenomenon of these men skating together than as a romance. They had "been seen kissing" by spectators—even though they hadn't kissed, and weren't lovers. One man had lifted the other ("No big deal") and the

Same sex pairs take the ice at the 1994 Gay Games in New York City (photo by Tracey Litt, Impact Visuals)

Martin and Hird in training (photo by David Blair)

verdict was: another invasion of family territory by "the gay lifestyle." Something had gone awry in the notion of the pair. Without the official sanction of a "display window space," the two male skaters were thought to have made a spectacle of themselves.

As they had with Nancy and Tonya, members of the media began to follow Martin and Hird, but in this case at their own direct invitation. When the two men showed up at a new practice rink for the first time they brought with them television cameramen from a local affiliate of the Canadian Broadcasting Corporation. "We were received quite warmly," said Hird with a smile. Before long L'Amphithéatre Bell, weighing its options, had offered them free training time—and a display window of their own.

What is a pair, anyway? Is it a dyad of "opposites" or of similitudes? Discussing a famous "pair of shoes" in a series of paintings by Van Gogh, philosopher Jacques Derrida repeatedly poses the question. "What is a pair?"[5] he asks. "What is a pair in this case?"[6] Does the concept of the pair assume complementarity, a correspondence of supposed opposites (male/female, left/right) within a normative system of likeness: a pair of shoes, a pair of gloves, a pair of heterosexuals? A pair is supposed to be "useful."[7] "You reassure yourself with the pair"[8] says Derrida—with the idea of pairing. A "pair" completes the set, leaves no excess, no supplement, no fetish. "If the double doesn't make a pair," it is perhaps because "the pair is the condition of the symbolic correspondence. There is no symbolic contract in the case of a double which does not form a pair. Which would not be one (selfsame) thing in two, but a two in identity."[9]

A double which does not make a pair—which would not be one selfsame thing, but a two in identity. Is this the problem posed by the same-sex dyad, a problem that is conceptual and philosophical as well as political and "moral"? The stake of the pair, its parity or pairedness, lies in part in what it does not foster: "The pair inhibits at least, if it does not prevent, the 'fetishizing' movement; it rivets things to use, to 'normal' use.... It is perhaps in order to exclude the question of a certain uselessness, or of a certain perverse usage,"[10] that art critics have tended to insist, or to assume, that Van Gogh's two shoes make a "pair." But "what is a pair in this case?" And in the case of the same-sex skaters? What rules of pairing do they fail to abide by, what "reassurance" do they refuse to give?

Pair: "Two persons or animals of opposite sexes"; "a man and a woman united by love or marriage; an engaged or married couple"; "two partners in a dance"; "a mated pair of animals"; "two separate things of a kind that are associated or coupled in use, usually corresponding to each other as right and left (less frequently as upper and under)"; something "composed of two corresponding parts, which are not used separately, and consequently are named only in the plural" (like scissors, bellows, spectacles, balances, stocks—or trousers); or simply, "a set of two"—all definitions sanctioned by the *Oxford English Dictionary.* What is a "pair" in the figure skating rink? If your answer is "two partners in a dance," you have (perhaps mercifully) forgotten the phenomenon of "ice dancing," a separate Olympic event that mimics the ballroom style. Pairs skating, by contrast, is supposed to be athletic, gymnastic, a sport as well as an art. The skaters strive to attain the condition of the penultimate definition I have given here, a single entity (tool, instrument, garment) made up of two parts that function "as one."

Let us again ask Derrida's question: "What is a pair in this case?"

Long before the Gay Games of summer, in the thick of the tabloid turmoil surrounding the Winter Games, another same-sex skating pair was to be seen in a prominently placed "display window." In fact, it was none other than Nancy and Tonya. In the midst of the controversy, *New York Newsday* published on its front page an image described by its rival newspaper, the *New York Times,* as "an image that many people across the country were waiting for: Tonya Harding and Nancy Kerrigan skating together." The image was a composite, as a printed caption clearly indicated: "Tonya Harding...and Nancy Kerrigan appear to skate together," it said, and a subheadline in larger print read "Tonya, Nancy to Meet at Practice." Nonetheless the *Newsday* picture was declared "the ultimate journalistic sin" by the acting dean of Columbia University's School of Journalism. *Newsday*'s editors, it turns out, had been divided as to whether the fact of the photo's composite nature was clear or not; the next day when one "picked up the paper on [his] front porch," he told the *Times,* "'I said, Uh-oh, it looked very real.'"

"Uh-oh, it looked very real" could also be seen as the Montreal rink manager's concern when confronted with two male skaters—and gay male skaters at that—doing their side-by-side jumps and stands, then one lifting the other in the Amphithéatre Bell. *Tinker* Bell? Was this pair really a *pair*? And if so, what did it say about the fairy-tale romance of figure skating? Many medal winners in the pairs events have been, or have become, husband and wife. The audience, and maybe even the judges, like the idea that the romance is "real." In a time when image-making is the career goal of America's journalism students, and an association of amateur athletes maintains a headquarters more luxurious than that of many for-profits, was heterosexuality a bottom-line issue, a desirable corporate asset? What was *figure skating's* "ultimate sin"?

Where the composite photograph of Nancy and Tonya brought together through illusionistic technology two female skaters who wished to stay as far apart from one another as possible, the Montreal episode sought to separate two male skaters—can we call them gay blades?—whose co-presence on the ice threatened to look very real.

Yet perhaps the media's insistence on differentiating between Nancy and Tonya—nasty or nice? sweetheart or bitch?—plays into our culture's apparently limitless fascination with keeping even the most "independent" women dichotomized, and therefore in their place. Virgin and whore, daughter and loner, butch and femme. Perhaps Nancy and Tonya *were* a pair, after all, to everyone but each other.

< NOTES >

1 Trip Gabriel. "Public Relations Has Potent Image." *New York Times*. March 17, 1994. B1, B5.

2 George Vecsey. "Harding's Guilty Pleas Anticlimactic." *New York Times*. March 17, 1994. B11.

3 Michael Janofsky. "Harding Sets Plea Bargain In Conspiracy." *New York Times*. March 17, 1994. A1.

4 Robert L. Pela. "Gays on Ice." *The Advocate*. May 31, 1994. 48–49.

5 Jacques Derrida. 1987. *The Truth in Painting*. Chicago: University of Chicago Press. 259.

6 Derrida, 261.

7 Here Derrida quotes Heidegger's *The Origin of the Work of Art* on the question of "usefulness," the utensil, and the "product." Derrida, 261.

8 Derrida, 265.

9 Derrida, 283.

10 Derrida, 332–33.

7

< Robyn Wiegman
and Lynda Zwinger

Tonya's Bad Boot,
or, Go Figure

We want to begin with two stories, both about the Olympics:

1. A woman neither of us knows worked last year for the Gay Games, a homosexual version of the Olympics, but one whose relationship to the "real" Olympics had to be legally decided. The Olympic committee, as some of you know, secured trademark control over the use of the word "Olympics" and hence the organizers of the identity-based sports extravaganza chose "Games" to accompany "Gay" as the alternative to the forbidden word. "Olympics" now legally stands against the fall into sexual sin and disgrace, officially protected from the homosexual, that bitter fruit.

2. When a woman we do know made a reference to the Gay Games to one of her students, a college javelin thrower, the athlete uproariously laughed. Had the Olympics, for this athlete, never been anything else? Its campy love of spectacle, its obsession with bodies and power, not to mention Dick Button: in these contexts, it is certainly possible to think of the Olympics as a queer enterprise. (And if you know anything about the history of women's sports in the U.S., you know that financial backing, organizational formations, struggles for equal entitlement, spectatorship,

indeed performance itself have all been greatly attended to and enhanced by the efforts of lesbians.)

But you also know, as do we, that the athlete's laughter most likely ran in a different direction, one that we might understand as simultaneously defensive and condemnatory, on the whole symptomatic of a range of opinion and disavowal that informs the world of women's sports and the various cultural rhetorics through which the athletic female body has been and continues to be sexually subjected. We want to suggest that this disavowal is more pervasive in the realm of women's than men's sports, not because the homosexual is any less threatening in the former arena, but precisely because of the way women's bodies bear the cultural script of heterosexuality both as a material form and as a formulation of social bonds. In men's sports, as we all know, the relationship between cultural definitions of masculinity—of the male body articulated as the site of strength and power—and heterosexuality is remarkably consistent. That is, most men's sports, as cultural rhetoric and specular display, demonstrate a fluidity or compatibility between masculinity, the male body, and heterosexual codes of sexual desire.

4-MAY-1994   13:39   NEWMAIL

R: It seems to me that this relationship could be tagged, nicely enough, as one of homovisuality—where what one sees is of a piece (more or less) with what one expects to see, the visual narratives being here homogeneous with the hetero/gender codes. While our preliminary idea in writing this essay was to explain what was meant by "heterovisuality," the homovisuality of men's sports is its other side. Thus, in one of the ironies that word-play often provides, it is the _hetero_visual that connotes the way heterosexuality works though an insistence on sameness, cramming heterodox materials into some kind of homogeneous, normative shape. L.

Press RETURN for more...

This is the case no matter how homoerotically charged that athletic display may be, since the homosocial circuit of desire and power that governs masculine bonds is motivated, as Eve Kosofsky Sedgwick suggests, by its dichotomous relationship with—its structural antithesis to—the overtly homosexual. It is for this reason that Sedgwick reads male bonds as decisively privileged within and in fact constitutive of the heterosexual itself.

In women's sports, on the other hand, the heterosexual inscribes a decided disjunction, at times a quite evident and deep conflict, between the athletic female body, cultural norms of femininity (think, for instance, of rugby), and accepted forms of female social bonds. We understand this disjunction as arising in part from the active / passive split that traditionally governs the visual scenarios in which the female body appears—what feminist film theory has defined as the implicitly masculine structure of the gaze. It is hardly a surprise to recognize that the female body, muscled and in motion, perhaps (gasp) sweating or (double gasp) not at all conscious of, perhaps not even self-conscious about the buoyancy of her breasts—such a female body violates the classic visual paradigm in which the female body is defined by and articulated as the locus of heterosexual masculine desire. Or perhaps it is most accurate to say that such a female body threatens to violate this paradigm, threatens to dismantle the heterosexualized femininity in which women's bodies (we like the double meaning here) are cast.[1]

At the most obvious level of analysis, the threat of the athletic female body to traditional notions of femininity is contained by the rhetoric of sport itself—by the way female athletes are routinely described in the language of the aesthetic and its (evil) twin, the sexual fetish. Mass popularity (or to be more accurate, consumer appeal) is often contingent on the athlete's ability to signify along a trajectory of "elegance," "grace," and "beauty," and it is decidedly necessary to mask the power of a well-trained body with a variety of feminine behaviors, motherhood (or desire for it) often being the privileged one.

6-MAY-1994   10:21   NEWMAIL
R: I disagree with this, profoundly so; though it is accurate in my opinion to say that a certain sentimentalized de-biologized/de-bodied maternal narrative can sometimes be stuffed into the "femininity" rubric. Mostly, though, motherhood is just exactly like the athletic female body in terms of the anxiety about femininity, about muscles and strength, that it inspires. L.

L: Yes, yes, motherhood is hardly an unathletic activity, but in its narrativization as sentimental and disembodied, it has come to function in the realm of the televisual as the means for the female athlete to reclaim a normative "femininity" which subsequently extends her commodity value. Remember Mary Decker and Flo Jo? R.
Press RETURN for more...

To be devoid of the traditional markers of femininity (and these markers are as often behavioral as physical, though they are conveniently subsumed to the latter) is to be an unnatural body, and this unnaturalness is most often conflated with homosexuality and its popular referent for women, masculinity. Two overt examples come to mind here. The vilification of

Bev Francis in *Pumping Iron II: The Women* where the fear of muscularity outstripping femininity culminated in the most well developed body losing the competition to, quote, softer and more feminine forms. And two, the horror expressed by the U.S. infomedia about the so-called masculine bodies of East German swimmers and runners in Olympic coverage in the 1970s. In both of these cases, a heterosexualized rhetoric of sport served as a policing mechanism for institutionalizing specific gendered and sexual significations for the athletic female form, thereby protecting that form (the ones that could be glossed as feminine, that is) from the taint of homosexuality.

Connected to this kind of fetishistic attention to the particularities of women's bodies is the way that the conflict raised by the specter of the female athlete speaks to and within cultural formations of female bonding. After all, women's sports fail to elicit, in ways we often don't stop to think about, the kind of popular rhetoric of homosociality that attends men's sports.[2] What accounts for this absence? Why is the rhetoric of the homosocial as defiantly denied in women's sports as it is celebrated in men's? And how does the cultural prohibition against the homosocial in women's sports affect the way the media in 1994 received, produced, and pondered the now infamous ice fight? To consider these questions—and to link them to our broader conversation about the heterovisuality that governs the world of women's sports—we want to return to Sedgwick, to a passage in *Between Men* in which she claims a continuity of organization and sentiment between female homosocial and female homosexual bonds that does not describe, she says, relationships among men. Such an analysis is part of what we understand as the problem of bad booties. Or what could be called, in another register, to hell with Cinderella.

Between Women

At the outset of the work we might now point to as the birth of queer theory, Eve Sedgwick moves quickly to an explanation of her study's rather singular focus on men. Much has been made subsequently about the political significance of such a focus, with its seeming evacuation of lesbians and questions of lesbian sexuality; we raise this issue here to situate Sedgwick's reading historically, within the terrain of feminism itself. We must quote at length:

> [I]n a society where men and women differ in their access to power, there will be important gender differences...in the structure and constitution of sexuality.

For instance, the diacritical opposition between the "homosocial" and the "homosexual" seems to be much less thorough and dichotomous for women...than for men. At this particular historical moment, an intelligible continuum of aims, emotions, and valuations links lesbianism with other forms of women's attention to women: the bond of mother and daughter... the bond of sister and sister, women's friendship, "networking," and the active struggles of feminism. The continuum is crisscrossed with deep discontinuities—with much homophobia, with conflicts of race and class—but its intelligibility seems now a matter of simple common sense. However agonistic the politics, however conflicted the feelings, it seems at this moment to make an obvious kind of sense to say that women in our society who love women, women who teach, study, nurture, suckle, write about, march for, vote for, give jobs to, or otherwise promote the interests of other women, are pursuing congruent and closely related activities....

The apparent simplicity—the unity—of the continuum between "women loving women" and "women promoting the interests of women," extending over the erotic, social, familial, economic, and political realms, would not be so striking if it were not in strong contrast to the arrangement among males... (2–3)

For Sedgwick, the relationship between homosociality and homosexuality is structurally different depending on gender: whereas for men, the homosocial (or what she glosses as "men promoting the interests of men") is opposed to the homosexual ("men loving men"), "the adjective 'homosocial' as applied to women's bonds...need not be pointedly dichotomized as against 'homosexual'; it can intelligibly denominate the entire continuum" (3).

What constitutes the "simple common sense" that leads Sedgwick to this assertion? After all, Camile Paglia and Katie Roiphe might love, teach, study, nurture, suckle, write about, march for, vote for, give jobs to, or in their minds promote the interests of women without doing so according to what many of us in 1995 might consider a feminist, womanist, lesbian, or otherwise anti-patriarchal political agenda. This is not, clearly, the common sense of U.S. popular culture, where female homosexuality, while often suggested, is repeatedly contained by featuring female bonds within narrative scenarios contingent on familiar (and familial) heterosexual roles and presumptions (the bond of mother and daughter, for instance, sister and sister, various women's friendships, women's social organizations). No, Sedgwick's "common sense" must be understood as arising from feminism, where its assumed continuity of aims, emotions, and valuations between female homosexual and homosocial bonds bizarrely promotes Sedgwick's turn to male homosocial formations as the seemingly more immediate and politically salient locus for describing the constitutive force of heterosexual prescriptions and homophobic alliances.

In other words, Sedgwick's commitment to feminism underlies her definitive turn toward male homosociality and in this, she reiterates the following chain of assumptions characteristic of early 80s feminism:

1. that the totality of "women's interests" can be defined from within the logic and political horizon of feminism (in other words, that feminism always defines the parameters in which we understand what constitutes the interests of women);

2. that these interests ultimately reside under the sign of "woman" (that is, that the political interests of women can always be understood as being about "women");

3. that feminism can guarantee that both "women" and the notion of "women's interests" can be disentangled from complicity with patriarchy and its historical privileging of men; that "women's interests," in short, never benefit or promote men;

4. and hence that all women's bonds are interest based—sexual and otherwise—and can be theoretically placed under the same cultural umbrella.

By accepting feminism's ultimate investment in understanding itself as outside of and in opposition to patriarchy, *Between Men* exchanges a critique of the heterosexualized practices that attend female bonds (inside and beyond feminism) for a homosocial continuum that comes to stand as the antithetical example to the homophobic injunctions of heterosexuality that discontinuously condition relations among men.

This is not to say that Sedgwick should have read erotic and social bonds among women as equally discontinuous to those among men. For us, Sedgwick has no debt to lesbians to settle, because she is completely right that there are differences between male and female homosocial structures—differences arising from the force and asymmetries of gender and power that cannot be dismissed. But instead of inflecting feminism's investment in a homosocial/homosexual continuum as the broader cultural commonsense, we might reflect on how it is the threat of this continuum (and not, as the case may be for men, its more obvious and radical disjunction) that engenders various deeply homophobic practices that condition both women's relationships with one another and the highly sexualized representation of female bodies themselves.

This is, as you are beginning to suspect, a lengthy introduction to the second part of our paper, which will finally, we promise, not only take you onto the ice, but strand you there in the clotted mess of heterosexual social norms and visual narratives wherein female bonds are so elegantly undone. But first a few more preliminaries in our pre-game show. Sport, we hope you will assume, is a symptomatic site of the anxieties that attend our culture's understanding of female homosociality. It demonstrates how the potential continuity between female homosociality and female homosexuality is disavowed through an intense insistence on a heterosexualized femininity, on one hand, and through the cultivation of individual narratives of performance and personality on the other. Nowhere are these two aspects more deeply etched than in the world of women's figure skating, that premiere sport of the Winter Olympics. Here, the athletic female body strains under the regime of aestheticized female beauty, negotiating a narrow space of acceptance between muscular strength on one hand and the "grace" and "loveliness" of a thin, fashion-ready and heterosexualized body on the other. Such negotiations are importantly about the individual female body: this is, in too many respects, a beauty pageant on ice, a conflation of the talent and bathing suit competitions. And it is well worth noting that success in these realms is often measured by one's ability to be miniaturized: to serve, for instance, as Nancy Kerrigan enthusiastically has, as Mattel's prototype for a children's doll.

For the little girls who will love that doll, who will comb its hair, apply its makeup, suckle and nurture it, and of course be driven—in passions of alienation and anxiety—to destroy it, the ideological basis of female bonding is perhaps too altogether clear. It congeals around fixations early attached to and constitutive of feminine desires, most pointedly those in which femininity is decisively individualized through an insistent visual focus on female bodies and their minute cultivations. These fixations do not bode well for homosocial bonds that might disrupt the heterosexual convictions of patriarchal organization, and certainly they do not serve as precursors to modes of social bonding that might culminate in women's team sports. All of this is common sense perhaps, but it only begins to explain why Tonya Harding was driven to mistake her skate for a miniature glass shoe.

28-APRIL-1994 16:16   NEWMAIL
L: The thing about the heterovisual that I am realizing is that there are two registers in which it operates within television—and it is in fact to television that it needs to be tied: as both an element in understanding the way various narrative genres come together AND as the structure of the apparatus as a whole, as a commercial enterprise and assemblage of

images that cohere under an ideology of compulsory heterosexuality. To really discuss this is a different paper, of course, but what's interesting about t and n is how their narratives play out in the first sense of the heterovisual—in the way ideologies shape the telling of the story, in the codes of media logic, in the way the female body is always heterovisually framed. R.

R: I am thinking that your notion of the heterovisual explains WHY the t and n story is A Story, and why it is written like it is: the heterovisual IS the grounding and invisible logic which makes it imperative that Nancy's body be the good one. Unequivocally. The tv/commercial commodity that is the most visually-pleasing (allegedly) of all women's sports, that is, must be grounded in a body that can be heterovisually positioned in both screen and print narrative, and the narrative that is selling most stuff these days is the one where the family story guarantees a certain het-fem virtue and visual presence. In this sense, it is definitely, indeed definitively tied to the visual. L.

Press RETURN for more...

Go Figure

The rhetoric of sport thus has a lot of cultural work to do. It must mask the power of a well-trained body with a variety of feminine behaviors; it must contain the threat that such a body poses to the heterosexualized femininity that strives endlessly—one might even say valiantly—to imprison it. While all female bodies are no doubt poised betwixt and between "the language of the aesthetic and its twin, the sexual fetish," female athletes are most poignantly and visibly so. These particular bodies, presented to us as visual commodities first and narrativized commodities second, are the fertile proving ground for our modest proposal that it is finally a rampant heterovisuality that provides the codes through which the female body is simultaneously dressed up and exposed.

Figure skating offers a nicely liminal locus for the rhetorics we are investigating. It is a sport which displays the feminine body as feminine; in this it is not unlike the art of ballet, which might well deserve consideration under the rubric of athletics given the kind of training it requires. But of course, analogies between skating and ballet tend to twist the other way: it is skating's ideological heritage as the great grand-daughter of ballet that underlies the sport's incessant attention to femininity and to the graceful and elegant fashioning of the female body as an aesthetic. In "The Legs of the Countess," Abigail Solomon-Godeau discusses the ideology of idealized femininity that adheres to ballet as an artistic form, drawing attention in particular to the historical developments of the early nineteenth century:

All considerations of the nineteenth-century ballet stress that it produced the
most highly articulated and aestheticized expression of idealized femininity.
With the development of pointe in the second decade of the century, the
ballerina became an etherealized vision of sublimity. Her airy weightlessness,
embodied in the darting, floating movement of her body en pointe, is the
emblem of a femininity purged of earthly dross and carnality.... the ballerina
is a figure of another, more rarefied world. At the same time, this new primacy
of the ballerina signals, in Lynn Garafola's description, the historical
movement in which "femininity itself becomes the ideology of the ballet,
indeed the very definition of the art."

This spiritualized representation of the ballerina as the incarnation of an
idealized femininity is, of course, ballet's own representation of itself to itself....
(Solomon-Godeau, 285–86)

Like ballet, women's figure skating has depended on femininity as both
vehicle and aesthetic goal. But within the past six years it has become
increasingly difficult (though by no means impossible) to pretend that the
rhetoric of artistic expression covers the whole arena, as women's figure
skating has been evolving into what is routinely called a more "athletic"
sport. As this summary, gleaned from one of the many make-a-book-quick/
make-a-quick-buck supermarket narratives about Nancy/Tonya, suggests:

In the long program—four minutes for the women, four and a half for the
men—judges look for variety of jumps as well as quantity.... Each type of
jump involves landing and taking off on different edges of narrow, concave
blades. Each one is a different, learned skill, but only experts can tell the
difference between most jumps.... Six years ago, at the Calgary Olympics,
most women were attempting only three triples. Now, to be competitive, top
women must attempt five or six triples. (Coffey and Bondy, 125)

The sport/art of women's figure skating has strained hard to assimilate
this new, or rather newly visible, hybrid body—the body dedicated to the
grace that depends on strong hard muscles. Concomitant with this development, the "genteel world" (this is a phrase used by nearly all commentators) of figure skating has become increasingly insistent about its
standards of grace, beauty, and elegance—qualities that are seen as increasingly at risk when set against the remarkable physical accomplishments
so arduously earned by some of the younger aspirants to gold and glory.
Into this increasingly unruly set of schooled figures, the Nancy/Tonya cat-
fight burst gloriously and compellingly, becoming a main attraction even for

those who, like one of us, hadn't paid much attention to the graceful sport of women's figure skating. But that was before....

The Whack Heard 'round the World

The visible syntax of sport is routinely supported and supplemented by other cultural discourse repositories—*People* magazine, *Inside Edition*, *Eye to Eye*, CBS Olympic coverage, supermarket books quickly cobbled together, even fancy academic theorizing. All have found in the 1994 Winter Olympics a story that seems to lead, however messily or contradictorily, to gold. Nancy Kerrigan and Kristi Yamaguchi fed our national appetite for victory and at the same time kept our images of femininity safe: they were nice girls and good friends too—nothing weird like those East Germans or the women in the speed skating lanes. Take Randi Reisfeld's (*The Kerrigan Courage: Nancy's Story*) word for it:

> When Kristi said she really wished Nancy the best, she meant it. When Nancy said she was prepared to be happy if Kristi won and she lost, she meant that sincerely.... Nancy has a philosophy about rivalries anyway, outside of her relationship with Kristi. "We're all there for the same thing. You go out there and you skate and then someone else goes out there and skates. We're all there to do our best. The rest is up to the judges. It's not competing head-on with somebody, you know?" (75–76)

As factual assertion, this is ludicrous: a skater's relative ranking depends as much on the others' mistakes as it does on her own merits in this rarefied level of competition. Something else is being performed here, some other cultural work is at hand: what anxiety has been put on ice?

There is something about women competing that brings them, in the context of the heterovisual and its policing of female social bonds, into anxious, because intimate, view. (If male rivalries are vehicles of/masks for homoerotic investment, what horrible vision does this conjure when the muscled bodies are women?) Familial narratives perfectly chill such homophobic panic, remaking athletes into the good girls we love to ogle. Consider, for instance, the media-ized version of the Kerrigan family, with its sweet narrative attention to the (eponymously) "legally blind" Brenda and her elegant, dutiful daughter. The take on this mother-daughter pair is epitomized most painfully we think by the photo of Nancy applying her mother's makeup. This image nicely anticipates the course of play that will ensue when little girls receive their new Nancy dolls (is it sinister to conjure the corresponding activities for those lucky tots who get our fantasy toy, the Tonya Harding Action Figure, instead?).

The lengths to which the makers of myth are driven to bridge contradictions in the familial narrative can be riotously funny too: here's one quite valiant writer striving to recoup the Basic Blue Collar Family narrative (scripted by fifties' family sitcoms) in the teeth of the quite large amounts of money the skater was already raking in: "But even now, when the money from Campbell's Soup and Reebok is starting to flow, the Kerrigans still pitch in, ironing their daughter's fancy dresses: Brenda, barely able to see, wields the iron, Dan guides her on where to place it" (Duffy, 56). Another approach is simply to metaphorize them both into one sum-lump: "Her close family has always been her mainstay, the lump of gold Harding never had" (Duffy, 56). These are only small pieces of the overarching sentimental nuclear family background narrative of the Ice Princess who just naturally grew from the mulch and topsoil of the dominant ideology's favorite hetero-alibis:

> Before Detroit, Nancy had already captured the hearts of America with her story—her legally blind mother, Brenda; her welder father, Dan, who worked two jobs so she could skate; her working-class background; and her grace going for the gold,' says CBS's Connie Chung [whose show did weekly updates on Kerrigan's recovery].... (A Kerrigan interview brought the show its highest ratings ever.) (Kellogg, 16)

9-JUN-1994   6:37   NEWMAIL
R: Don't we need to explain more fully the way that the rhetoric of sport is contingent on the narrative of the nuclear family and the heterosexualizing of the daughter? Is it all as obvious as our conversation seems to think? L.

L: It's too familiar not to be obvious. Besides, to get into it with extreme specificity in this case would necessitate a whole new section, one that looked at how, before the whack hit the fan, we were treated to a completely different "Nancy." The media that was suspicious about her looks as a sign of her (presumed upper-) classedness transformed her into the determined good daughter of a protective father, complete with blue-collar roots, and it was this image that was crystallized and finalized by the oft-repeated picture of daddy carrying her out of the arena. The hetero-sentimental- feminizing narrative has to look effortless and natural, and it has to involve daddy to work best.[3] R.

Press RETURN for more....

Beauties and Booties

But these nice ice girls who love their mothers and have high school chumlike relationships with their closest rivals are serious athletes who could deck the prince as easily as waltz off with him, who don't need fairy godmothers to dress them for the ball because they have their own gold (American Express cards), who are in the game for bottom lines never acknowledged in the how-to-be-a-nice-girl handbooks (magazines, television, movies, Connie Chung interviews). It's a precarious kind of disavowal we are engaged in when we see only the image and not the business. And of course it is the unmasking of this disavowal by a noncomplying player that has pretty soundly rattled nearly everyone on and near the ice.

That noncompliant one had been rattling cover stories for some time before the assault on Kerrigan. She is "'trailer trash'" (Orlean, 51), "an outsider in the world of ice princesses...an in-your-face, asthmatic divorcee from a broken family" (Kellogg, 10), who makes it impossible to forget that her legs, with their "blocky muscles" (Orlean, 48), give the lie to many of the sport's genteel pretensions and alibis. No Nancy-ish "swan on ice" (another ubiquitous phrase), this is a skater of whom Brian Boitano remarked: "'She jumps like a male skater.... There's an incredible strength and control in her jumping'" (Swift, 63). Her coach has said: "'She should be on the front line of a football team'" (Swift, 63). A representative Tonya Harding fan club member says simply, "'She's a stud'" (Orlean, 52). This "'abused child spanked by her mother with a hairbrush'" (Orlean, 51) was the first American woman to land a triple axel in competition, and she had a mouth as unlike Nancy Kerrigan's (at least the Kerrigan Randi Reisfeld interviewed) as possible: Tonya Harding. "During the Olympics, most athletes focus on the thrill of competition. Not Harding, who told *Primetime*'s Diane Sawyer, 'I have a job I've been doing for 20 years, and I want my paycheck'" (Kellogg, 12).

Discursively constructed to represent purified heterovisualized femininity, figure skaters are not supposed to talk like this. Contradictorily instructed to be athletic and artistic, strong and graceful, figure skaters aren't supposed to look like this either. In order to conform to the heterovisual requirements of their chosen job, their bodies must invisibly be trained and constructed in ways decidedly unfeminine: Nancy hides this; Tonya doesn't, not in the body nor in narrative/life. Curiously the explanation for the difference between them, a difference which so nicely maps onto and covers over the schizophrenic and impossible to reconcile claims of the sport and its self-narrative, grounds itself in the body—Tonya's athletic body is too athletic, and her aesthetic body is fraught with the perils of late 20th century heterovisuality:

> "We're just like the Cleaver family," said Diane Braverman, Harding's on-again, off-again coach. The happy veneer was not deep. Harding remained fragile on many topics, very sensitive about her weight problems. By normal [hah] standards she was a slim, athletic woman, a blue-eyed beauty. In the world of figure skating, which rivals ballet in its low-body-fat demands, Harding bordered on obese. For the nationals she had clearly lost some weight, but Harding would not say how much or how she had gone about it. She was clearly embarrassed.... (Coffey and Bondy, 59)

Further, and maybe worse, her mother (no Brenda Kerrigan she)—the body which produced hers—has lived in trailers and has believed too heartily and often in the institution of marriage and nuclear familyhood. Harding's body, with its frequently referred to weight shifts (Kerrigan's had them too, but Harding's ups and downs are more focused on), is as unreliable as is her mouth as organ of representation of all that an ice princess, which is to say the ultimate avatar of heterovisual desirability, is required to be. The sport may have moved, that is, away from compulsory figures but it moved to, well, compulsory figures.

And so we have a most convenient geometry for depositing the ambivalences and contradictions we need to disavow to get on with the business of disavowal: two women, both Olympic quality figure skaters, different physical "types," apparently heterosexual or at least on offer as such, both of working class extraction, each in some ways the skating mirror image of the other, one pretty much by now inscribed in the national myth repository as bad and the other as good. Or, in the words of *Time* magazine, what we have here is "Kerrigan, the goddess of good.... Harding, the consort of thugs" (Carlson, 58). Is it a surprise that the good aligns with the ethereal, elegant heterovisual femininity and the bad with the nasty effluvium of muscles and training and unladylike behaviors like car racing and elk hunting? The adjective of choice for Kerrigan is "elegant"—it is the single most commonly spoken and written descriptor. For Harding, it is rather harder to single one out, as the adjectival buffet is more varied, but "hardscrabble" is certainly right up there. What is clear, however, is that the descriptions of Kerrigan focus on her body and move out from there to her life; of Harding, from her life to her body. This is, admittedly, a purely subjective and as yet unquantified impression. But it certainly makes sense from a heterovisual point of view: Kerrigan's visible presence is the one chosen, in the script we have seen unfolding, the story made of the crime and its aftermath, to represent the Right—that is, the Straight—Stuff.

The quantifiable skills—jumps without ice contact, leaps without pratfalls—are set over against the more subjective, but apparently at least allegedly utterly visible (heterovisible?), unquantifiable qualities of "musicality," "grace," and, surprise, "elegance." Guess which column we ("we") like the best? The quantifiable athletic accomplishments emphasize the body—not the merely visual body, but rather the trained, accomplished, strenuously working body, the sweating, not perspiring, body; the unquantifiable, the "artistic" body is one that in motion helps us forget all the gritty details of life in musculature and skeletons and the squishier unmentionables. Is it an entire accident that facing the final page of *TV Guide*'s "As the Rink Turns" is a full page ad for Kotex maxi pads that will not embarrass their wearers or wearers' beholders by "shifting and moving and just not protecting like they're supposed to" (Kellogg, 13)? Oksana Baiul, chest thrust out, arm flung back, legs graphically leading up to that fateful V seems to be on the brink of gracefully sailing smack into the final line of the ad: "Finally, a maxi that really stays in place so it really protects. Kotex Understands" (Kellogg, 13).

The Tonya and Nancy story shows and tells itself in the realm of the fetish and the operational field of the mechanisms and sustaining fictions of disavowal; so too the elaborate cultural narrative that is heterovisual femininity, which is to say the femininity pressed into service by a heterosexuality which both stipulates and denies its desires for certain contradictory visual traces of strength and beauty in the allegedly feminine body. The Harding/Kerrigan pairing produced by the narrative machine of print and televisual narrative displays for our delectation and horrified frisson the extent to which heterosexuality is an institutional and nervous, anxious, precarious insistence.

And among the detritus that stays with us after all those weeks of CBS gazing and *People* weekly reading are several instances of a curious juxtaposition. This ice princess soap opera, this saga of Pretty Mean Skaters, this true life thriller, this Basic Icerink, this Bladegunner plot, keeps getting linked, visually more often than any other way, with the Lorena Bobbitt story. For instance, the *Maclean's* January 24, 1994 cover features, over the title of the magazine, this teaser: "The Skating Scandal and the Bobbitt Trial." On each side, we find inset headshots of Tonya Harding and Lorena Bobbitt, both smiling. We find ourselves mulling that cover image over as we return again to the stunningly mean-spirited *Newsweek* piece from 1992:

We know it in sport as the slugger vs. the boxer. Or the front runner and the closer. The volleyer and the baseliner. And, best of all: the athlete and the artist. At the ladies' figure skating, the North Star of the Olympics, that is precisely what we had. Indeed, we had it on two levels: Midori Ito, athlete, vs. Kristi Yamaguchi, artist, for the gold; and Tonya Harding, athlete, vs. Nancy Kerrigan, artist, for the bronze.... barely into their original programs, on their first jumps, both the athletes, Ito and Harding, fell. And there they were, one after another, down on their rear ends, scrambling to get up, hoping somehow to outrun the white shavings that marked their bottoms and their ignominy. (Deford and Starr, 50)

Might the extraordinary and even virulent fascination with which we have watched this ice opera unfold have something to do with yet another kind of fetish operation?

The gold around the winner's neck is of course a mere metonymy for the rest of the gelt accumulated by media and by the individual skater if she is a good enough girl. It is impossible to over-emphasize that final requirement. The femininity story is a profitable one; the athletic prowess of an Olympic quality skater is worth far less money without it. The truth is that Harding never was, even pre-whack, much of an endorsement property; she was known to be too loudmouthed, too badly behaved, too unladylike. Kerrigan, on the other hand, was well ensconced in that end of the business long before this year's circus increased her earning potential exponentially. As Kellogg attests: "Whether or not she gets the Olympic gold, experts estimate that her brave demeanor and Katharine Hepburn good looks could earn her $10 to $25 million in endorsements. At last count, she was sorting through more than 50 TV-movie offers" (8).[4]

Coda

As dizzying as a triple axel is this tangle of interlocked and interlocking hetero-normalizing stories. At its base, we find the seen female body, the scene of the heterovisual plot. Time now to brush the white shavings off and get to the end of the story. The spectacle that is women's figure skating is a drama about the confusing mix that is the female body—the athletic and artistic, the muscular and passive, the jumping and gliding female body. Punctuated by what became ubiquitous sight bites—Tonya dashing after the tow truck, Nancy sailing the ice with one leg reaching for heaven—this melodrama parsed the transgressive hybridity of un-narrativized representative bodies back into recognizable heterovisual codes. The individual bodies, in other words, have been put in their places:

the long lanky body of Nancy Kerrigan has been figured as feminine (read: elegant, innocent, wounded, virginal); the body with hips, thighs, and muscles as female (read: lower-classed, sexualized, powerful, bad). Virtually all the infotainment products emphasize this split, which is itself an artifact of the operations of the heterovisual apparatus. (Long lanky Nancy is, in real life, for instance, a mere five feet four inches).

Here is a particularly compact representative sample:

> Compare these rivals. Both women come from working-class backgrounds. Harding is a powerful skater with a mighty jump. Just as impressive to a connoisseur is the forceful way she strokes along—almost into—the ice. It's sheer, thrilling athleticism. But Harding's body is not ideal; she has thick thighs and forearms. Also, she is not musical. Kerrigan is—and a good deal else. She is a good jumper when not plagued by nerves. Her balance of skills is the strongest among women skaters, and she performs with an undulating, pleasing lyricism. To complete the picture, she is lovely to look at, with a lean musculature, sculpted features. (Duffy, 55)

This evil-twinning paradigm is an operation common enough in narratives which are grounded in hetero-ideologies and the stories we make of them. We can find a parallel setup in another set of stories—theoretical stories grounded in the visual register, the register wherein women's bodies and genders are persuaded, coerced, bribed, and policed into heterosexual femininity, or at the very least, the appearance of it. That femininity is a masquerade, a performance, is by now a critical commonplace; what we want to emphasize is that this performance requires a certain set of visual relations and tropes.

In order to maintain the various fictions of gender, not only must the masculine be continually divided and separated from the feminine, but the feminine, in equally strenuous ways, must be kept apart from the (grossly, muscularly) female. This operation is crucially maintained in and by the field we are calling the heterovisual—the field, that is, of the seen and sited body, and of the technologies that pursue, in a kind of incessant commodified framing, that body. Tonya Harding is coded, when all is said and done, as the heterosexual sexual female who refuses femininity and thus takes all kinds of spectacular pratfalls. Her marital difficulties, her familial soap opera, her naughty wedding night video—these are offered as both cause and result of her refusal to be a nice, feminine girl. This positioning is further buttressed by the media insistence on her mouthiness—especially about gold and money, or more accurately, about Olympic gold as money—as well as by her very ungirlish interest in things coded as masculine: visible body strength, pool sharking, elk and deer shooting, drag racing, pickup trucks. And Nancy Kerrigan, concomitantly, virtually loses her body to the narrative tropes of a virginal if not asexual femininity.

9-APR-1994   16:34   **NEWMAIL**

R: It's not right, then, to say that when it comes to the cultural injunction against same sex bonds, masculine relations incite more homophobic panic. Even women in our culture who are heterosexual (or who think they are) are much more precariously so than they ever want to know. "Athletic" female bodies deeply trouble them too (and not just the heterosexual boys on behalf of the captive population of het girls in their midst/mitts). Which is why, and this is probably what you are saying more elegantly (oops—a Nancy Kerrigan descriptor, sorry), femininity is so incredibly rigidified and prescribed and intensely demanded, especially visually, in women's figure skating—because the kind of athleticism that can signify against the normative heterosexual can exist in a fairly normal ("""""normal""""") looking feminine body too. L.

L: But at least such bodies aren't together on the ice. No pairs for the heterovisually contested. R.

L/R: Is that why it took two [heterogeneously coded?] gals to figure all this out? R/L. Press RETURN for more....

< **NOTES** >

1 This is not to suggest, however, that the definitions of "heterosexualized femininity" do not shift historically. After all, one might argue that under the forces of contemporary commodification, the relationship between the athletic body and cultural forms of femininity is a negotiated one: models have slimmed down in order to pump up, and athletic clothing is, along with dieting, one of the fastest growing consumer markets in the U.S.

2 It is not surprising in this context to consider that women's skating garners in the U.S. the largest television audience of all women's sports, though it is perhaps more telling to consider how unavailable to mass media audiences is anything resembling women's team sports. For instance, it was just this year that the final four games of women's college basketball were covered by a major television network.

3 For a fuller discussion of these connections see Zwinger.

4 Kerrigan is not the only one making out like a bandit. Consider, for instance, the network bonanza:

Indeed, the added expenditures for interviews seems to have translated into some ratings growth, particularly for *Hard Copy*. In the early overnight metered markets corresponding to the February sweeps period (NSI, Feb. 3–28), *Hard Copy*'s 7.7 rating, 15 share marked a 2 share-point gain (up 15 percent) from the show's year-ago sweeps average in the metered markets. *Inside Edition* posted a 7.1/15 during the same period, 1 share point (7 percent) ahead from its February 1993 average. *A Current Affair* was also up 8 percent, with a 7.4/13 in the overnights. (Freeman, 15)

A rating or share spike of only 1 or 2 percent during the critical November and February sweeps periods can bring an extra $5 million to $15 million in revenues, says one tabloid producer. (Freeman, 15)

CBS recorded the eighth-most-viewed telecast in TV history with the airing of the first round of women's figure skating from the winter Olympics in Lillehammer, Norway. [It was] the highest-rated Wednesday night for any network in television history.... [and] the largest household audience in history. (Coe, 16)

With Olympic Gold meaning millions to networks and performers alike (Dorothy Hamill recently bought the Ice Capades [Kellogg, 12]), it is no wonder that so many are so eager for these athletes/artists to fall smack on their bottom lines. To paraphrase those venerable artists of the heterovisual, ZZ Top: they got legs, and they know how to use them.

< REFERENCES >

Carlson, Margaret. "Public Eye: Now for the Skate-Off." *Time*. 21 Feb. 1994: 58.

Coe, Steve. "Olympics Sweeps Prime Time." *Broadcasting & Cable*. 28 Feb. 1994: 16.

Coffey, Frank and Joe Layden. *Thin Ice: The Complete, Uncensored Story of Tonya Harding, America's Bad Girl of Skating*. New York: Pinnacle Books, 1994.

Coffey, Wayne and Filip Bondy. *Dreams of Gold: The Nancy Kerrigan Story*. New York: St. Martin's Paperbacks, 1994.

Deford, Frank and Mark Starr. "American Beauty." *Newsweek*. 2 Mar. 1992: 50–52.

Duffy, Martha. "With Blades Drawn." *Time*. 21 Feb. 1994: 53–58.

Freeman, Michael. "Tabloid TV's Holiday on Ice." *Mediaweek*. 7 Mar. 1994: 14–15.

Haight, Abby and J.E. Vader and the Staff of The Oregonian. *Fire on Ice: The*

Exclusive Inside Story of Tonya Harding. New York: Time Books, 1994.

Kellogg, Mary Alice. "As the Rink Turns." *TV Guide*. 12 Feb. 1994: 8–14.

Orlean, Susan. "Popular Chronicles: Figures in the Mall." *The New Yorker*. 21 Feb. 1994: 48–63.

Reisfeld, Randi. *The Kerrigan Courage: Nancy's Story*. New York: Ballantine, 1994.

Sedgwick, Eve Kosofsky. *Between Men: English Literature and Male Homosocial Desire*. New York: Columbia University Press, 1985.

Smolowe, Jill. "Tarnished Victory." *Time*. 24 Jan. 1994: 50–54.

Solomon-Godeau, Abigail. "The Legs of the Countess." In *Fetishism as Cultural Discourse*. Eds. Emily Apter and William Pietz. Ithaca, N.Y.: Cornell University Press, 1993: 266–306.

Swift, E.M. "Not Your Average Ice Queen." *Sports Illustrated*. 13 Jan. 1993: 54–63.

Zwinger, Lynda. *Daughters, Fathers, and the Novel: The Sentimental Romance of Heterosexuality*. Madison: University of Wisconsin Press, 1991.

8

< Diane Raymond

Feminists on Thin Ice
Re-Fusing Dualism in the Narrative of Nancy and Tonya

"Sisterhood Was Powerful" reads the title of a recent *Newsweek* article.[1] The feature could have been yet another angle on the Nancy Kerrigan/Tonya Harding controversy but instead was an examination of the current struggle between what *Newsweek* author Laura Shapiro and a number of others are calling "difference" (or "gender") feminism and "equity" (or "power") feminism. These two positions are being characterized both by their proponents and by press reports as the two major contenders for hegemony in current feminist discourse. While it might not be obvious at first glance, parallels exist between the skirmishes between Kerrigan and Harding and within feminsm, and they are worth exploring for a number of insights they offer.

First, these two stories are stories of Difference writ large, but the difference(s) invoked are not rooted in any *a priori*, inherent heterogeneity but rather are constructed (though not necessarily consciously) to serve an agenda. In the same way that the press sought to exaggerate and reinforce whatever differences existed between Kerrigan and Harding, media portrayals of the current "war" within feminism have managed to gloss over the shared concerns and goals of these theoretical perspectives. Second, the notion of difference as these portrayals depict it is not difference read as innocent or neutral but rather as threat. Like that *Newsweek* article which warns of threats to "sisterhood" and to feminism, accounts of Nancy and Tonya included more modest warnings about the danger to ice skating, to women's athletics, and to the Olympics; others more dramatically deployed the story as metaphor for the demise of sports in general or, in some cases, of western civilization itself. Third, implicit in all these treatments is the assumption that difference is constituted by polarities; indeed, accounts of the contested terrain within feminism (like the accounts of Kerrigan and Harding's contest) ignore a number of alternative competitors and perspectives, including those of women of color. Simplicity seems to come in pairs, no more and no less; gone are ambiguity, intersection, complexity. Finally, these stories revel in the carnivalesque aspects of their subjects, even as they (or at least the more sophisticated of them) reflect self-consciously on our obsession with such spectacle. Indeed, despite at least thirty years of dynamic and visionary work in feminist theory and practice, such activity—like women's figure skating, the third most watched sport in this country—was largely ignored by the mainstream press until these bitter rivalries gained ascendency. This new attention has done little to enhance our understanding or even to create interest in alternatives; instead, the emphasis on spectacle has decontextualized and trivialized its subjects.

Lest these complaints be read as yet another simple-minded and banal example of media-bashing, let me make clear that the participants themselves—skaters and feminists—have eagerly engaged in their own sound-bite wars. While the names of Harding and Kerrigan have more popular currency than those of the embattled feminists I have in mind, the amount of air time and print space the present controversy has garnered—from *Esquire* to *Newsweek*, from tiny local newspapers to the *New York Times*—is noteworthy nonetheless. As equity feminists, Katie Roiphe, Camille Paglia, Naomi Wolf, and Christina Hoff Sommers (despite *their* differences) have taken on difference feminists Catherine Mackinnon, Andrea Dworkin, Shulamith Firestone, and Susan Douglas (Sommers also includes here Carol Gilligan and a number of others who share very little except her label "gender feminist") and created sparks less bright but similar to those generated by "Skategate." Indeed, equity feminists have published a spate of new books written for mainstream audiences of women who have given up on feminism. These works—many of them long on passion and short on argument—explore what is wrong with "the movement" and try to rescue feminism from the difference feminists who, according to equity feminists, have perverted the "real" meaning of feminism and are responsible for alienating women from its fold. Their analyses tend not only to assume that there should be one monolithic movement but also to elide real differences within each so-called camp. In addition, popular talk shows have featured feminist luminaries like the telegenic Wolf, Roiphe, and Paglia, who try to sell this new[2] brand of feminism.

If feminists themselves are guilty of such oversimplification, one can hardly fault the press for selling it to the public in that form. Indeed, this material would not sell did it not touch some chord in each of us. Popular culture, like all culture, is a set of signifying practices, and no narrative would be compelling unless its meaning(s) resonated with some buried aspect of our cultural unconscious. *Newsweek* columnist Meg Greenfield's slightly hyperbolic words try to account for the popular fascination with Nancy and Tonya: "This particular saga touches much that is important and a bit that is downright primal in our lives, and…it also provides some insights into the state of our peculiar contemporary universe."[3] Clearly, deep and abiding myths about women and women's nature(s) operated to keep mainstream audiences fascinated with every detail of the continuing saga. The Harding/Kerrigan competition plays to girls' dreams of becoming figure skaters and to "residual memories of the fairy tales and girls' books and comics and movies" where women "were allowed a little mischief."[4] In a sport characterized perhaps primarily by the fact that one does not face one's opponents directly, the story of these women managed to wed them so thoroughly that it became virtually impossible to speak or write of one without the other, linked forever by a ubiquitous hyphen.

Like the Nancy Kerrigan/Tonya Harding story, the internal division within feminism is a media sensation, yet another version of the favored cat fight. Indeed, I shall later argue, difference here is *sexualized* difference and these narratives offer us the opportunity to be voyeurs and mark these contests not only as a struggle for moral and political ascendency but also as erotically charged. The deep divide within feminism, like the deep divide between Harding and Kerrigan, is a socially constructed one which plays off myths and ideologies about gender, sexuality, power, and knowledge. These stories come to us in pairs, but they are not simply about pairs but rather about oppositional and, we would believe, mutually exclusive pairs. Even for a culture deeply committed to binary thinking, this is strong stuff. Such binary thinking has a long and distinguished history in western philosophical thinking, beginning perhaps with Socrates himself.

Though it would be inaccurate to fully credit (or blame) Socrates and his most famous student Plato with the invention of dualism,[5] one cannot understate the importance for Western thought of the Socratic dualism which is grounded in the distinction between mind and body. Its legacy in Judaeo-Christianity is but one example of the powerful and pervasive impact of that doctrine even on those who in the final analysis reject specific or general aspects of those views. While the distinction between mind and body may very well be the most familiar and most seemingly incontrovertible, Socrates' ideological system is not only grounded in other, perhaps even more fundamental dualisms (notably, the distinction pivotal to Athenian "democracy," namely that between free citizen and slave) but also gives birth to a virtually limitless set of binary oppositional pairings. Indeed, popular as well as scholarly modes of thinking are rife with seldom-questioned and familiar pairings as common as they are "black and white" and "all or nothing." The fact that logicians label such fallacious thinking "bifurcation" has done little to rehabilitate consciousness. And postmodern theory's complaints about such oppositional thinking have not even begun to transform the actual practice.

In this essay I want to interrogate dualism as a metaphysical and epistemological theory and to lay bare the normative consequences it entails. My treatment here will be necessarily rather cursory not only because of space constraints but also because critiques of dualism are now fairly routine, thanks to feminist and other radical theory and postmodernism. My goal is to use my distillation of those critiques to explore a dangerous and nearly ineradicable tendency within feminist theory to be seduced by dualism, even in spite of feminism's rejection of much of traditional "masculinist" thinking. The story of Nancy Kerrigan and Tonya Harding is particularly useful in this context as it not only exemplifies the problematic implications of contemporary feminism's current practical and ideological impasse but also can inform feminist theory's more recent debate. Finally, I suggest that the narrative embedded in the recent fascination with Nancy Kerrigan and Tonya Harding reveals a useful insight into the popular imagination's construction of feminism and perhaps hints at strategies to transform those perceptions.[6]

Dualistic Thought

Moments before Socrates is to drink the poisonous hemlock, his student Crito asks him how he would like to be buried. Socrates' answer ("Any way you like...that is, if you can catch me and I don't skip through your fingers"[7]), goes beyond merely chastising Crito for his failure to understand fully the implications of the proofs for the immortality of the soul which are the body of the text and the focus of their prison conversation; he is also making clear his commitment to the view that his death is only the death of his body, not that of the *essential* Socrates: "You must keep up your spirits and say that it is only my body that you are burying; and you can bury *it* as you please, in whatever way you think is most proper."[8] His only instruction is the paradoxical one that his students offer "a cock to Asclepius," the god of healing; clearly, for Socrates, death is a cure for life. This dualistic ideology conceives of the body as a prison, not only the source of moral error (which Christianity will seize on as *sin*) but also of intellectual error. It is the body (in sense perception) that allows us to desire that which we ought not to desire, or overdo that which should be done in moderation; it is the body that misleads us into thinking that mirages truly exist, to confuse a magician's tricks with reality, to mistake or misjudge based on temporary and fleeting material inconstancies. Soul (or mind) is what we truly are, and, for Socrates, everything in this world of "shadows" has in another perfect world a corresponding "form" which is essentially what that thing is.

I will not rehearse all of the critiques of Platonic forms, critiques deployed as early as Aristotle. While virtually no one accepts this master narrative as a description of reality, the power of the Socratic story lies not in its dubious metaphysical framework, but rather, as I have suggested earlier, in its pervasive cultural currency. Rather than rehash the standard attacks, then, I shall examine some of the implications of the dualism itself.

A dualism like the Socratic one described above is not simply a positing of differing realities but is rather a hierarchical vision of reality. Indeed, though I shall not argue for this here, it seems likely that every dualism implies a hierarchical ordering of the differing entities, where one side is valorized over against the other. Thus, it is clear even from the brief description of Socrates' argument, that soul or mind is essentially *self*; and body or matter is shadow, prison, source of error. For philosophers who have traditionally sought certainty, the body is a stumbling block—given how much the material world changes[9] and how inconstant is the body (illness and drunkenness tend to be favorite examples of philosophers, but aging is clearly another); philosophers have been obsessed with a need to recover some permanent substratum that did not change, was universal, and could not die or be destroyed. Descartes (1596–1650), in the modern era, succumbed similarly to this temptation when he posited two absolutely irremediably distinct entities—mind and body—and then was forced to make the absurd claim that the pineal gland served as the nexus for their interaction. During this same era, philosophers like Locke (1632–1704) and scientists like Galileo (1564–1642) posited primary and secondary qualities where primary qualities are those which are "utterly inseparable from" the object under consideration and secondary qualities are those which are "in truth nothing in the objects themselves," but rather are produced in the perceiving subject.[10] Accidents or secondary qualities, then, are viewed as inessential add-ons, characteristics of a thing that are *not* what the thing truly is; and how could Nothingness/the Not be worthy of philosophical investigation?

But whether such thinking takes the form of a Socratic or Cartesian world view or the primary and secondary qualities of the early scientific revolution or appears as Berkeley's ideas or Hegel's Geist,[11] each system doggedly insists on the priority of some aspect of reality over some other. Mind, then, is superior to body, and one can easily see how other evaluations fall out from dualism. But key for my purposes here is one particular pair, namely the binary division between male and female.

Dualism and Gender

One need not leap very far conceptually to grasp how the poles of gender emerge from mind/body dualism. Woman seems inescapably *em*bodied because of obvious biological processes like menstruation, pregnancy, and breastfeeding. The "somatophobia" described by Elizabeth Spelman[12] as characteristic of western philosophy has, in the perceived link between women and nature, entailed and justified fear and hatred of women as well as, as her argument so effectively demonstrates, racism. Further, the dichotomous arrangement of accident and essence makes gender, race, age, sexuality and so forth addenda to one's "true self." Yet the essential substratum that seems to remain looks suspiciously like a white, heterosexual man.[13]

Little in western philosophy until very recently dealt with bodily existence. Even the *death* of the body has rarely captured philosophical interest except in the form of the profound denial which leads one almost immediately to posit—like Socrates—the existence of an immortal soul, which, in the popular imagination, seems to possess all of the desired virtues of the body and none of its dreaded vices; even Socrates, as he imagines his own death, pictures himself doing that which he loves best "in a state of heavenly happiness," philosophizing with other souls whose bodies have died long before. Other sorts of references to the body, when they do occur, are generally references to errors of sense perception that make concrete why one must not trust the body. The following well-known passage from Descartes' *Meditations* considers the certainty of one common "corporeal object," namely a ball of wax:

Let us begin by considering the most common things, those which we believe
we understand the most directly, namely, the bodies we touch and see. I am
not speaking of bodies in general, but of one body in particular. Let us take,
for example, this piece of wax which has just been taken from the hive; it has
not yet lost the sweetness of the honey it contained; it still retains something
of the smell of the flowers from which it was gathered; its colour, shape and
size, are apparent; it is hard, cold, it is tangible; and if you tap it, it will emit
a sound. So, all the things by which a body can be known distinctly are to be
found together in this one.[14]

And yet he then moves from this vivid and compelling image to show why,
as the wax is placed near a flame, the senses cannot be responsible for
revealing to us the true nature of the wax:

[W]hat remained of its taste is dispelled, the smell disappears, its colour
changes, it loses its shape, it grows bigger, becomes liquid, warms up, one can
hardly touch it, and although one taps it, it will no longer make any sound.
Does the same wax remain after this change? One must admit that it does
remain, and no one can deny it. What, then, was it that I knew in this piece of
wax with such distinctness? Certainly it could be nothing of all the things
which I perceived by means of the senses, for everything which fell under taste,
smell, sight, touch or hearing, is changed, and yet the same wax remains.[15]

Finally, Descartes argues, it is "understanding alone," that is, an act of
pure intellect, which has conceived what is the wax. In so doing, he
manages paradoxically to restore the trustworthiness of perception by
transcending sense perception entirely:

[T]he perception of it, or the action by which one perceives it, is not an act
of sight, or touch, or of imagination, and has never been, although it seemed
so hitherto, but only an intuition of the mind, which may be imperfect and
confused, as it was formerly, or else clear and distinct, as it is at present
according as my attention directs itself more or less to the elements which it
contains and of which it is composed.[16]

Attention, then, is key to understanding the true nature of corporeal
objects; yet, ironically, it may very well be the body that subverts the
intellect's "clear and distinct" perceptions.

Passages like those above are easy to find in western philosophy and
could be multiplied almost without end. And while differing and at times

contradictory outcomes flow from various philosophers' somatophobia, all share a reluctance to take seriously human embodiment, to consider embodiment as a possible site of knowledge. And in adopting such skepticism about the body, philosophers have participated in and reinforced the repression of more general cultural fears about corporality, change, decay, and death. Members of marginalized groups—women, people of color, and gays and lesbians, for example—become psychic representations of *nothing but* embodiment; in a patriarchal system which normalizes the white, heterosexual male, that "person" must be de-raced and de-sexed in order to function as form or standard-bearer. Anything deviant, then, is a disturbing reminder of the realm of physicality and must therefore be distanced. It is no coincidence that these target group members are vilified with references to the body, to sex, and to nature. Hitler's massive campaign of anti-Semitism, for example, described Jews as dirty, as like animals, as child molesters, and Jewish women in particular as sexually insatiable. Many of the same vicious stereotypes are levelled at gays and lesbians in today's homophobic imaginary.

Sherry Ortner's classic essay, "Is Female to Male as Nature is to Culture?" discusses what she believes to be a cross-cultural equation of femaleness with nature.[17] Even those feminists who yearn nostalgically for a kinder, gentler prehistorical matriarchy implicitly adopt this framework via their claim that such social systems valued nature (in particular fertility) and therefore valued women's "essential" nature. African-Americans—whether as slaves in the antebellum United States or as citizens in a racist system—are often portrayed as closer to nature, more animal-like (or more child-like), more embodied (think about white patriarchal fears about sexually well-endowed African-American men). Such an ideology cuts at least two ways: while white hegemony may no doubt envy black "naturalness" and racism becomes (like sexism) a complicated form of reaction-formation, the sense that bodily immanence traps one and limits one's potential is not so far from the Socratic notion that the body is a prison. And thus *white* basketball star Larry Byrd becomes the "thinking man's athlete."

But another dualism operates within the dualism of male and female, a dualistic framework which structures our shared understandings of what it means to be a woman. This dualism between "good girl" and "bad girl" (played out in an almost endless variety of cultural icons like Mary and Eve) abandons even any pretense of the allegedly separate but equal philosophy of other binarisms. Here women (and this dualism has served to police other marginalized groups as well) in patriarchal systems are seduced (or blackmailed) into being "good" with offers of reward (marriage, children, economic security, protection from violence, Mother's Day, etc.) and threatened with the losses that follow if they transgress (lesbian bashing, loss of children, economic dependence, general denigration by the culture, etc.). While some argue that this "double standard" has evaporated with women's broader participation in the work force and greater reproductive autonomy, I would maintain that, while the terms of the discourse have changed and some "exceptions" are occasionally permitted, one should not confuse the greater blurring of the borders with their disappearance. Here Foucault's reminder that power is not always overtly coercive and obvious is apt; indeed, power must mask itself in order to be tolerated, and the greater subtlety of these new regimes of power may only mean that the power is less easy to name and therefore less easy to resist: "Its success is proportional to its ability to hide its own mechanism."[18] Recent backlash in the form of heightened violence against women and children, new ordinances against gays and lesbians, the popularity of scholarly anti-feminist tracts, and the wide-reaching rejection of feminist "heroines" (e.g. Anita Hill) suggest that patriarchal culture cannot tolerate limitless "exceptions." These exceptions seem either soon co-opted, tokenized, or suppressed. Indeed, there is a certain irony in the latest version of the good girl/bad girl split in that today's "good girl" seems—at least according to some of the popular media—to be one who might have been "bad" by earlier standards, that is, one who enjoys sex with men. I'll be returning to this point in the next section of this essay.

It is crucial to understand one other aspect of dualistic thinking not yet discussed, that is the unacknowledged, unconscious interdependence of the two sides of the division. Sartre, for example, points out in his *Anti-Semite and Jew*[19] that the anti-Semite needs the Jew; if the Jew did not exist, he would have to be invented. Similarly, masters must have slaves or they cannot be masters; homophobes need homosexuals. Likewise, men must have women in order for them to be men; this analysis suggests that masculinity must rebel against femininity and all that it represents. The fragility of binary divisions means that each pole is threatened by any sign of rapprochement and so depends on distance and negation to assert its "own" identity. In part, this analysis explains the vehemence of the cultural responses to those who transgress boundaries; the homophobe, for example, sees a subversiveness in gay and lesbian life that the growing numbers of assimilationist gays and lesbians reject.

Feminism and Dualism

Every theory is a product of multiple, intersecting, unstable social conditions, and feminist theory is no exception. Both so-called "first wave" and "second wave" feminists[20] accommodated (to their perceived ideological advantage) dualistic thinking about women's "nature." While nineteenth century liberals like John Stuart Mill and Harriet Taylor suggested that women could be (more or less) just like men where opportunities are truly equal, others (for whom the contemporary label "cultural feminist" may work best) valorized women's differences from men. Where liberals clearly preferred maleness as a universal standard for thinking and practice (though they were generally careful to mask the preference with terms like "humanity"), cultural feminists adopted the dominant ideology of the "angel in the home," arguing that women's heightened moral sensibility would bring a new civility to the realms of politics, economics, and education. Both liberals and cultural feminists assumed without question the dualisms embedded in the western philosophical tradition, namely between self and other, mind and matter, autonomy and dependence, public and private, and nature and culture. But where liberals sought to expand club membership to include women by expanding women's range of choices, cultural feminists wanted to acknowledge and maintain gender differences as they valorized femininity and the female realm of domesticity. Neither offered a deep critique of gender, with cultural feminists explicitly adopting a gendered model and liberals careful not to deny the possibility of "natural" differences between men and women. Rather than confront the inegalitarian nature of the family, most feminists maintained that women could be better companions of men and mothers of children if allowed to develop autonomously. In this light, it comes as no surprise that early suffragists abandoned—both ideologically and practically—their African-American "sisters" rather than scrutinize the ways in which dominant stereotypes privilege white women over women of color.

In the mid-twentieth century Simone de Beauvoir's *The Second Sex* inaugurated the second wave. But this text is structured around yet another polarity, namely that between immanence and transcendence. Despite the breadth of her often radical critique of patriarchy, Beauvoir cannot resist the philosophical traditions (particularly Cartesianism) in which she is steeped. As immanence, as embodiment, women, for Beauvoir, cannot be autonomous agents. Indeed, her descriptions of menstruation and pregnancy are nightmare scenarios more in keeping with a rabid antifeminist agenda than the overthrow of patriarchy. Women's lives, and she is scrupulously careful to insist that they are socially constructed, are lives of waiting, of living vicariously, and therefore inauthentically (or, in the existentialist jargon favored by her and Sartre, in bad faith). Despite her insistence that women are made, not born, her distaste for women's bodies and her powerful identification with men and traditional male values subvert her commitment to the possibility of full liberation. Though she seems to want to dismantle gender, her dualism traps her: women must strive for agency, for transcendence, but—because women's bodies perpetually call us back to immanence—women must somehow become men. Thus, women's and not men's bodies continue to be problematized.

Since the late 1970s most feminists have given up the search for biological or cross-cultural determinants of behavior. But the tendency to totalize and to essentialize gender and gender differences continues. Presupposing an essentializing dualism, many feminists have been led to ask, "what *is* women's nature?" And given the limitations of binarisms, the range of possible answers is also quite limited: women can be like men (and hence must explain or try to ignore the obvious physical differences between men and women) or different from men (and articulate not only what form those differences take but also position those differences in a normative framework).

Indebted to Beauvoir, second wave feminists struggled with their embarrassment over women's embodiment and—even as they fought for reproductive rights and challenged cultural stereotypes about women— failed to challenge deeply held dualisms and so failed to develop strategies that might have been more transformative. Radicals like Shulamith Firestone read Beauvoir quite literally and saw women's bodies as the enemy; given that, as she claimed, women's reproductive capacities are the source of male oppression, women must employ developing technologies to separate reproduction from women's bodies. Liberals, like their nineteenth century counterparts, seemed to wish away women's bodies in their attempts to urge "equality." For liberals, women were just like men who occasionally needed contraceptives, abortions, and child care. Indeed, liberal thinkers seemed fairly comfortable with traditional gendered distinctions but merely asserted that the privileged categories that fall out from "maleness" need not exclude women, or at least need not exclude all women. Radical feminists' separatist policies polarized lesbians and heterosexual women and were impracticably "utopian" even for most lesbians. Cultural feminists, like their nineteenth century counterparts, embraced male/female binarism but either simply reversed the normative agenda by valorizing what they saw as women's deeper and closer ties with nature and children, greater moral sensibility, and more connected relational modes or proposed a separate but equal framework for social relations. Little attention is paid to the possible origins of these different voices,[21] and even less to how power differences may reinforce these dynamics.

This very crudely sketched outline of feminist theories is not meant to exhaust the theories, nor is it intended as thorough analysis; and in the last twenty or so years feminism—influenced to a great extent by postmodern theory—has been interrogating its own essentialist, binaristic assumptions. Feminist standpoint theory, emerging in postmodern feminism and in the writings of women of color like bell hooks and Patricia Hill Collins, has embraced subjectivity and context, rejected transcendent notions of truth and justice, and demanded that theory attend to differences among women—that we learn "from the margins." Feminist critique has turned inward, no doubt a healthy reaction to its history of gender essentialism and blindness to shifting and multiple identities. As Susan Bordo has put it:

> Where once the prime objects of academic feminist critique were the phallocentric narratives of our male-dominated disciplines, now feminist criticism has turned to its own narratives, finding them reductionist, totalizing, inadequately nuanced, valorizing of gender difference, unconsciously racist, and elitist. It seems possible to discern what may be a new drift within feminism, a new skepticism about the use of gender as an analytical category.[22]

Much recent discussion has centered on the possibility of a social theory built on an acknowledgement of diversity and an analysis of gender oppression in the absence of universalized, transcendent, *a priori* standards. And much work remains now that the critical and deconstructive projects of postmodern feminism are largely completed: "feminist scholarship has remained insufficiently attentive to the theoretical prerequisites of dealing with diversity, despite the widespread commitment to accepting it politically."[23] But this search within academic feminism for a theoretical basis for multiplicity has been relegated to the wings while polarized and highly publicized debates between so-called "victim" or "difference" feminism and "power" or "equity" feminism are spotlighted on center stage. Feminists in these two camps—and ironically even combined they probably do not constitute anything close to a majority of feminist theorists at work today—have so dominated the debate over feminism that mainstream audiences may assume that no alternatives exist. Sadly, though some of the issues so central to feminist organizing continue to be discussed, much of the current debate has centered around ownership of feminism; further, when concrete issues do move to center stage, those issues seem to focus on sex and sexuality (e.g. pornography, date rape, and so forth) rather than economic issues. Though I would never claim that women of color are not concerned with sexuality, the lack of attention to economic issues marginalizes those women already marginalized both in the feminist movement and in the dominant culture.

But sexuality and women battling over sexuality titillate. Whether it is Andrea Dworkin claiming that the penis is inherently a weapon or Betty Friedan maintaining that feminism's problem is its "obsession with rape" which, she argues, "is a kind of wallowing in that victim state, that impotent rage, that sterile polarization,"[24] the sexualized approach to feminism revisits but inverts the dichotomy of good girls and bad girls, where in this case good girls are attractive, like men and sex, and enjoy feeling powerful; bad girls, in contrast, are unattractive (read: lesbian), dislike sex, and "seem instead to celebrate their vulnerability."[25] Even *Esquire* magazine featured the new breed of what they called "do me" feminists who "are embracing sex (and men!);"[26] they quote approvingly Naomi Wolff who avers that "we need sluts for the revolution" (p. 52). These feminists are able to reassure men who "fear that women will cut off sex when they achieve economic parity.... This worry sprouts from the underlying male fear that a lot of women don't really like sex just for itself" (p. 56).[27]

Despite the tradition in the United States of compassion for the downtrodden, this country's ideology of rugged self-reliance and succeeding against adversity (another embedded dualism) has promoted an impatience with difference feminism, conceiving of it as man-hating, whining and old-fashioned in an era which has convinced itself that racial and sexual barriers no longer exist. And equity feminists who insist that the problem with feminism is that "we're told we'll be raped, sexually harassed, treated unequally at work" and that message would "if we listened, ...leave us feeling hopeless" (p. 52) resonate not only with women who have political and personal alliances with men but also with women who are politically and psychically exhausted in a context where no broad-based movement exists which might challenge on-going sexist oppression. Further, equity feminism's emphasis on personal *will* to achieve one's goals resonates with a culture that glorifies individualism and individualized effort. But equity feminism's caricature of academic and activist feminism, its isolationism and individualism, and its defusing of women's anger in favor of what is claimed to be "power" misses (deliberately?) the empowering message of second wave feminism that "the personal is political" and of using anger to create agency and social change. Katie Roiphe, for example, seems just plain wrong in her stubborn insistence that "Take Back the Night" marches (note the exceedingly non-wimpy slogan!) promote victimization and engender fear in women. Ironically, while patriarchal ideology has promoted the notion of woman as victim (requiring male protection), it is uncomfortable with women proclaiming their own victimization. Clearly, the difference is that patriarchal culture sees women as victimized by their *essential* nature which is submissive and weak; in contrast, difference feminists see women victimized *by men*. But difference feminism is ultimately flawed because it acccepts an essentialized gender binarism, frequently arguing that maleness itself is the source of violence.

Nancy and Tonya: Feminism Under Seige

Dualism, as I have argued, depends on polarized thinking, and so must insist on and emphasize the differences between the members of the pair. While one could fairly easily recite similarities in Kerrigan's and Harding's lives and experiences, few reports bothered to mention them, making much instead, for example, of Tonya's endorsement of Nike and Nancy's of Reebok; forgotten was the fact that both are *sneakers*. But remember here that one dilemma for all dualists is finding an explanation for the possibility of interaction between the members of the oppositional pair. That is, once one has polarized the opposing entities, one must provide some sensible theoretical basis for their dialogue. Yet to assert and acknowledge their interdependence would be to challenge the very basis of the binarism. So efforts to bring the sides together inevitably seem absurd; given how deeply drawn is the chasm between them, efforts to marry them are doomed because they are self-defeating. So Descartes had to maintain that the pineal gland at the base of the neck is where mind-body conversation occurs; did we not possess a pineal gland or were its function better understood in Descartes' time, he would have had to stumble on some other gateway.

Similarly, with respect to gender, the extremes must be reconciled. The cliché "opposites attract" seems coined precisely to explain how—in a world bifurcated by gender—two members of what seem almost to be different species can be expected to share a life together or even want to. Followers of the Nancy and Tonya story wanted some sort of showdown between the two, even as Kerrigan insisted that she would keep her distance and most people acknowledged that it was unlikely Harding would be good enough in competition to pose a genuine threat to Kerrigan. Further, the very presence of a number of other competing skaters seemed an awkward reminder that even the world of skating was bigger than these two combatants; these multiple perspectives seemed to force a shift in focus and to threaten the ground of the dualism. The *New York Post*'s doctoring of its cover photo to suggest an on-the-ice confrontation between Harding and Kerrigan functioned, absurdly, like Descartes' pineal gland to contrive a relationship between the two. Before Harding's involvement in the attack on Kerrigan was known, *Time*'s (January 24, 1994) cover photo pictured the two seated together; later, when this was no longer appropriate for obvious reasons, the February 21 cover foregrounded Nancy Kerrigan in color and placed a large image of Harding's face in the background. The grainy, black and white image of Harding made her seem particularly ominous, but it also kept them conjoined.

Dualisms make for captivating reading and easy thinking; they admit of no ambiguity, no complexity. A number of dualisms operating both explicitly and implicitly during the media blitz over Skategate surface easily. In particular, one sees almost immediately how the furor over Nancy Kerrigan and Tonya Harding exemplifies in glorious narrative detail the good girl/bad girl dualism discussed above. Nancy was described as Snow White, graceful, artistic, and elegant; in contrast, Tonya was the wicked witch who was at best athletic (note that this term has also been applied to two other figure skaters, Midori Ito and Surya Bonaly, both women of color), at worst trashy. Pictures of the two almost always recalled for us Nancy's "skill" and "grace" and Tonya's "awkwardness;" photographs of Harding frequently showed her falling or making a mistake of some kind.

Despite similarities in their class backgrounds, Nancy played like a high class counterpart to Tonya's working class interests in bowling and playing pool. Kerrigan was the "goddess of good," Harding the "consort of thugs."[28] Kerrigan was constantly referred to as a "lady." Her coach, for example, described her as a "polite young lady" and, when asked about Kerrigan's brief conversation with Harding when they met at the Olympics, she noted: "Nancy is a very strong-minded person...and very level-headed. We don't have to coach Nancy as to what to talk about. She thinks and feels the right things. She always has."[29] Frequent references were made to Tonya's thighs, her dyed hair (an *un*natural blonde), and her clothes. Nancy has a coach, Tonya a "mentor *du jour*." The following quote describing Tonya's outfit at the Olympics was not unusually venomous during the height of the attention: "Tonya is wearing a blue USOC sweatshirt over black tights. She looks ready for touch football.

Nancy looks like she's going to meet the queen."[30] The same commentator goes on to describe the skating outfit revealed after Tonya removed her sweatshirt: she's wearing a "flowery one-piece outfit that looks as if it came from the remainder table at Almy's going-out-of-business sale."[31] Another reporter described the skating costume she wore for her last program as "more a trapeze artist's pink creation."[32]

Indeed, Tonya came to epitomize embodiment, and the intense vilification she received from press and public alike suggests deep somatophobia as well as misogyny. Despite our alleged modern rejection of old-fashioned standards of propriety for women, descriptions of Tonya, emphasizing her smoking, her painted fingernails, and her poor fashion sense read like Victorian renderings of the "fallen woman." The fascination with Tonya's legs and her weight (referred to by one commentator as "thick thighs and forearms"[33]), the constant belittling references to her dyed hair, her asthma, her crying—who could forget Tonya's flesh, her corporality? Tonya, we were told, had posed for topless photographs. Tonya admitted that she wanted to win the gold medal for the money: "to be perfectly honest what I'm really thinking about is dollar signs."

Nancy, in contrast, transcended even her knee injury to win the silver medal—nothing distracted from her performance. Her ability to discipline her body *and* mind contrasted with Tonya's "antics" and Harding was frequently pictured as inconsistent (she was skewered, for example, with the fact that she first insisted on Gillooly's innocence and then admitted that he had probably been involved), out of control, and irresponsible. Nancy, we were told, epitomized the American values of family, discipline, niceness, and self-reliance; thus, Tonya had to symbolize everything wrong with contemporary culture. Even Tonya's history of spousal abuse did not soften the criticisms; in some ways, it served to make her seem more hapless, to mark her off from the other contestants. Indeed, Harding is the only married woman ever to free skate in the Olympics and her marital history may have been too painful a reminder of reality for the rarified "ice princess world of women's figure skating."[34]

The venom directed at Tonya by the popular press and mainstream audiences is in keeping with wider cultural responses to women's misdeeds. Given our discomfort with nuance and ambiguity, coupled with polarized stereotypical thinking about gender, reactions to "bad girls" often seem disproportionate to their actual deeds. Such a hyperbolic response may offer a measure of psychological security: if we can identify the single, errant female, we can police her conduct and even benefit by using her example to control other women; analyzing guilt and innocence in, say, Bosnia or

Rwanda, does not lend itself to such facile moral bimodal approaches and leads to moral exhaustion and a sense of being overwhelmed. So "bad girls"—even as they have very little *real* power in patriarchal systems—are touted as powerful and dangerous even as the system demonstrates its ability to control them and restore order; Tonya's threatened lawsuit, then, is seen as undermining the legitimacy of the entire Olympics committee and her behavior was portrayed, as I argue above, as dangerous not simply to the one other competitor whom she injured, but to sports, to the spirit of the Olympics, and even to morality more broadly construed. Such "empowering" of individual women is all the more ironic given the contrast with recent press treatments of O.J. Simpson, whose crime, if he is guilty, is certainly far more heinous than Harding's; not only have press reports underlined the "fundamental American belief" of innocent before proven guilty; they have also deflected blame *away from* Simpson to condemn the American public for investing too much and unrealistically in sports "heroes."

Ultimately, a number of factors led to the satisfaction of revenge and catharsis: Harding, everyone seemed to agree, was never really in contention; she was stripped of an earlier medal and her membership in the World Figure Skating Association; and she was finally humiliated with an offer to move to the world of professional wrestling. Further, however, even when women do commit horrific acts, their acts are trivialized in a forest of *ad feminam* attacks which serve to control any real threat. So Imelda Marcos, for example, is never mentioned without a reference to her hundreds of pairs of shoes.

Yet even within the morality play in which Nancy epitomizes innocence and goodness and Tonya guilt and corruption, these bipolar categories are never stable. Indeed, one must remember that the poles which distinguish some women from other women (which seem not to exist in a comparable way for men) must coexist with categories which distinguish one gender from the other. Thus, though it is true that good girls exist in relation to bad girls, those good girls must be subsumed in some way by patriarchal gender categories. This tension means that subordinate categories have a tendency toward destablization, meltdown. So good girls will not remain good girls. Rather, they cannot help but become the scapegoats of cultural reassessment, saturation, and, ultimately, ennui. Astute commentators hinted at this dynamic; one noted, for example, the growing phenomenon of "exasperated boredom with and even suspicion of Harding's competitor, the good girl Nancy Kerrigan."[35]

But those commentators who noticed the shift tended to blame it on our suspicion of innocence and our barely concealed love of villainy. Such cynicism no doubt plays a role here, particularly at this moment in our cultural history when talk show hosts urge audiences to determine innocence and guilt through applause, when backlash against incest survivors once again casts doubt on innocence, juries free the Menendez brothers, and crowds of spectators scream "Free the Juice": "Nice people are not the ones who engage our minds, or, to some extent, even our sympathy. Boring, we say. Bring on the troublemaker."[36] But what commentators failed to note is how innocence is frequently tied to gender—the notion of virginity, for example, is virtually synonymous with innocence and seems not even to apply to men.

Women who are innocent are desired but they are also caught in a well known double bind: as objects of desire, they can remain unapproachable and risk being seen as frigid or eventually lose their appeal; or they can meet the desire with their own desire and risk falling off their pedestals. Given that these categories are unstable, the innocent's position is temporary and her shift inevitable. Or, as Audre Lorde has noted:

> On the one hand, the superficially erotic has been encouraged as a sign of female inferiority; on the other hand, women have been made to suffer and to feel both contemptible and suspect by virtue of its existence.[37]

Nancy Kerrigan was the consummate "ice princess" but—despite her acknowledged ability to stand up to competitive pressure—she simply wasn't interesting enough as a good girl. Her repartee with reporters was sweet but boring, and her disastrous appearance on *Saturday Night Live* made clear that, even with the occasional self-parodying comment, her talents lay on the ice. Olympics commentators noted that her final performance was flawless but lacked the passion and creative energy of Oksana Baiul. Mainstream audiences began to see her as a money-making self-promoter whose disparaging remarks about Disney World (and, worse, Mickey Mouse) suggested an ungrateful biting of the hand that feeds her. Her perceived "whining" at not receiving the gold medal and her caustic comments about orphan and war survivor Baiul—Kerrigan clearly did not have sole ownership of victimhood status!—were the final nail in her cultural coffin.

But what I am suggesting here is that even if Kerrigan had not committed the faux pas outlined above, her fall from grace would have occurred nonetheless. The good girl cannot remain good in a game which is constructed to be dependent on constant shifts in meaning. Even the comment cited above that Nancy looks as if she is going to meet the queen may be hinting that Kerrigan is becoming too big for her tutu. And, if I am right that dualisms are interdependent, then, in part, we lost interest in Nancy as Tonya faded from the limelight. Indeed, more recent reports of their (individualized) exploits are now relegated to the back pages of newspapers.

What might our polarized feminist views contribute to our understanding of the story of Kerrigan and Harding? When one begins to flesh out the implications of these perspectives, the limitations of dualism become even clearer. Victim feminism, with its focus on the ways in which women are oppressed under patriarchy, would seem, at least initially, to see Kerrigan as the obvious victim of a physical assault intended to destroy her chances for success. In this sense, victim/difference feminism would hold the same view as the popular common sense position. And yet it seems particularly odd to frame Kerrigan as a victim, given her performance at the Olympics, the numbers of adoring fans, and her multimillion dollar advertising contracts. Further, for difference feminism, there must be more here, for all women—regardless of other differences—are oppressed by virtue of their gender. Thus, one has to see Harding as a victim as well; indeed, if we are to take women's "voices" seriously, one must give credence to the fact that Harding herself claimed victim status, not only in her history of spousal abuse but also in her claim to have been manipulated by Jeff Gillooly. This perspective is consistent with difference feminism's tendency to essentialize gender differences and to frame masculinity as violent and domineering.

But mainstream media and general observers were unwilling to see both Harding and Kerrigan as victims; for in a binary framework, if there is one victim there must be an obvious persecutor, and that was Harding. Harding's critics condemned her even more vehemently for her attempt to secure victim status for herself: "You're asking people to feel sorry for you. In your own mind, you seem to be convinced that you are somehow as much a victim as Nancy Kerrigan. Don't you see how insidious that is? How dangerous?"[38] Meg Greenfield more moderately suggested that one problem with today's psyche is that the American rags-to-riches story of overcoming obstacles to achieve success has been replaced with the notion that early deprivation exists everywhere and—worse, she says,—"we pronounce early hardship or even less than an idealized, Norman Rockwell-style family-life reason to expect and accept all manner of moral shortcoming."[39] Even generally sympathetic Brent Staples of the *New York Times* accused Harding of exploiting the "rhetoric of victimhood" and he explicitly made the connection to feminism that I have been deploying when he positioned Harding's framing of her victimization on a spectrum along with product liability suits and "ultra-radical feminism." But perhaps the most stunning rejection of the "victim" label came recently from the sister of brutally murdered Nicole Simpson: "my sister," she said, "was no victim."

I do not want to suggest here that the fact that the American public has lost patience with victim narratives means that victim feminism is wrong. But, oddly, if one adopts the perspective of victim/difference feminism, and assumes that both Harding and Kerrigan are victims (because all women are by definition), then it seems impossible to ascribe responsibility to either party; further, it seems absurd and unproductive to suggest that both are victims but that one is more a victim than the other. A spectrum of victimization continues to essentialize femaleness as victimized. In addition, victim feminism is hard pressed to account for Kerrigan's *success* in not only surviving her injury but going on to incredible competitive and financial glory. Is she nothing but a dupe of advertisers who will now use her to sell their products and of the ideology of competition and ambition at which she was so successful; if so, Kerrigan's "choices" have no more substance or agency to them than do Harding's. Indeed, the only difference, from the victim feminism point of view, would seem to be that Kerrigan is guilty of false consciousness in a way that Harding, who admits being manipulated and controlled by the men in her life, is not. Thus, in treating women as essentialized Women who all share (equally?) in gender oppression, the difference feminist cannot offer a sensible account of women's agency (at least until patriarchy crumbles) and grossly oversimplifies women's complex relationships not only with men but also with other women.

At the same time, the power feminist seems trapped as well. Though Kerrigan's success story would seem to epitomize the power/"do me" feminist ideal, this too is overly simplistic and permits any number of possible readings of the narrative. While Naomi Wolf suggests that power feminism has respectable roots in the early women's suffrage convention at Seneca Falls, she fails to acknowledge that at the heart of power feminism is the desire not to transform culture but rather to be able to participate in that culture alongside men. Indeed, the term 'radical' nowadays lumps together incredibly disparate philosophies of feminism and feminist spokespeople almost solely on the basis of their refusal to accept the rules of the game; understanding this fact is the only way to make sense of a group that includes maternal feminists, ecofeminists, radical feminists, cultural feminists, lesbian separatists, socialist and Marxist feminists, antipornography feminists, postmodern feminists, psychoanalytic feminists, and women of color feminists (though it is far more likely that this last group will be ignored in the categorizing). So, given one understanding of power feminism, both Nancy and Tonya are power feminists who seek to compete and, most importantly, to win. Indeed, Tonya's willingness to stretch the rules to accomplish that goal suggests a masculinist model of victory at all costs. Her initial lack of remorse and insistence on "kicking butt" at the Olympics seem more in keeping with traditional male norms surrounding the competitive ethos; and her willingness to challenge the Olympics Committee with a lawsuit makes clear that she does not let herself be pushed around. But where patriarchal culture might be willing to tolerate men who adopt the Vince Lombardi "nice guys finish last" ideology, women who attempt to do so (or are even perceived as attempting to do so) cannot be accommodated. So Tonya's credentials as a power feminst might be suspect given that she broke rules which are held to apply to all. Yet where do equity/power feminists find these rules? If the notion of equity implies that we are where we need to be (that is, past historical barriers) and that we can now participate alongside men, given that the rules were created in a patriarchal system (and that power feminists reject notions of an alternative female culture), aren't we left with men's games? So, for example, on this model it is quite apt for the National Rifle Assocation to appropriate power feminism in its new marketing strategies to increase gun sales among women by urging women to "refuse to be a victim." Further, given that equity feminists adopt gender-blindness, they will refuse to see these games as men's games and so will not, indeed *cannot* logically, acknowledge the presence of different standards for women *within those games* based on gender. This blindness is particularly ironic given that women's figure skating is generally acknowledged to be art as well as athletics and that the standards for judging tend to be "subjective."

Power feminists, like power non-feminists, cannot articulate or justify any coherent basis for limits on conduct. Given the principle of egoism that underlies this view, one is hard pressed to explain what is wrong with Harding's actions (even if she *is* guilty) other than the fact that she got caught and lost it all; but perhaps power feminism should admire her nerve and her willingness to risk it all for her ambition rather than fault her for her failed effort. And, after all, few of us (even with their increasing popularity) can claim to have had a made-for-television movie created about us. The power feminist urges women to "go for it" as if the only thing holding anyone back is personal will; but this decontextualized analysis of agency cannot account either for mitigated responsibility or for psychosocial factors influencing behavior. So, not surprisingly, equity feminism's flaws mirror difference feminism's: where the former ignores gender socialization in the interests of agency and action, the latter essentializes gender to the extent that agency ceases to exist.

What can we learn from all this? We have seen that dualistic frameworks impose limits on thinking, and that the dualisms which now plague feminism hinder it from moving forward in a theoretical and an activist sense. Further, we have seen that gender dualisms impose limits on what women can be; to bifurcate our options in this way is not to offer much of an option at all. As long as theory and practice remain confined in dualisms, even attempts to break free of this framework will be reinterpreted and reassimilated through the lens of binarism.

Postmodern theory, with its emphasis on multiplicity and heterogeneity, is especially useful here; but postmodern theory without an analysis of gender identity and an historical understanding of oppression will fail as social theory. Postmodern theory is instructive in its insistence that we ground our narratives in the contexts and specificities of people's lives; this notion implies that we must resist the tendency to oversimplify and challenge ourselves to embrace moral and intellectual ambiguity, not to wallow in confusion and ethical paralysis but rather to invite multiple perspectives and a constant rereading of texts. Dominant culture does not ignore diversity but promotes it so as to define it narrowly and reductively through stereotypes; by replacing those binaristic stereotypes with richer and more multiple notions of meaning, we not only acknowledge that we must bring the margins to the center (as feminists and postmodern theorists have argued) but also that the center is implicated in the margins.

The saga of Nancy and Tonya helps to illustrate not only what is wrong with dualisms but also where feminists might productively intervene in popular culture. Obviously, my use of the story suggests that feminists must enter popular debates and work toward the construction of more ambiguous, more multiple meanings of current dramas. This task implies not only that feminist theorists must move outside the sheltered ivory towers of academia but also that we must learn to communicate more accessibly. In part, this normative agenda raises questions about marketing: if we expect to move the current debate between equity feminists and difference feminists past its present impasse, then we must not only reject the assumption that difference and equality constitute an opposition; we must also learn to sell nuance and complexity, to market a richer, more diverse, more inclusive feminism that does not betray women at the margins, that is not afraid to acknowledge the existence of oppression, that deploys anger to transform culture, and that re-envisions power in new, non-essentialized ways. In short, we need to move beyond the static and polarized models which confine Nancy Kerrigan and Tonya Harding.

< NOTES >

Special thanks to Masato Aoki for helping me to think through these ideas; to Marie McHugh and Laura Rattner for supplying me with countless articles on this story; and to Joanna Knowles for her moral support.

1 Laura Shapiro, "Sisterhood Was Powerful." *Newsweek*, June 20, 1994, pp. 68–70.

2 Though I brand equity/power feminism "new," Wolf claims that her version of feminism has its political and intellectual roots in the Seneca Falls convention of 1848.

3 Meg Greenfield, "Moral Icecapades." *Newsweek*, February 28, 1994, p. 70.

4 Ibid.

5 For example, while some pre-Socratics (e.g. Thales [624 B.C.?–545?]) were monists who simply disagreed about what element constitutes the world, others like Pythagoras (570 B.C.?–some time after 520?) were unabashed binaristic thinkers; for Pythagoras, for example, ultimate principles are the limited and the unlimited, which are equated with good and evil and which generate a host of other moral and physical pairings based on opposition. Indeed, late antiquity regarded Plato as a "neo-Pythagorean" and tended to confuse their ideas, particularly those relating to the immortality of the soul. Finally, Eastern thought which precedes Greek philosophy by many centuries is rife with binarisms. To explore such connections is far beyond the scope of this essay.

6 It will soon be obvious in this essay that my deployment of the term "feminism" may refer to a number of different and not always consistent social realities. At times it will refer to past and present feminist scholarship and theory, which, given its relatively esoteric subject matter, its highly technical discourse, and its small circulation, is generally not known to non-academics and probably not known to non-feminist academics. Second, it may refer to feminist activism and practice, which while it may overlap with the former, often (and sadly, in my opinion) does not. Third, it may refer to popular presentations of feminism, as seen, for example, in *Ms.* magazine, in occasional media favorites like Camille Paglia, or in current debates over issues central to feminism like abortion. Finally (but certainly not exhaustively), it may refer to popular (mis)perceptions of feminism which emanate from untold, hard-to-pin-down locations. In cases where my context does not make clear which

sense of feminism is operative, I shall do my best to clarify.

7 *Phaedo*, trans. Hugh Tredennick, 115C.

8 *Ibid.* my emphasis.

9 Some in fact have argued that Socrates' intellectual mission was to create a philosophy that might respond to the pre-Socratic Heraclitus' maxim that "all is flux," or, more popularly, "one can never step into the same river twice."

10 John Locke, *Essay Concerning Human Understanding* in *From Descartes to Locke*, ed. T.V. Smith and Marjorie Grene, Chicago: University of Chicago Press, 1940, p. 366, 367.

11 Note here that the latter two are generally described as monists, yet their monism relies nonetheless on a dualistic rejection of and distancing from the material world and lived experience.

12 Elizabeth V. Spelman, "The Erasure of Black Women." *Quest*, V, 4, 1985, pp. 36–62.

13 This tension is clearly at work in Socrates' world of forms where souls *do* seem to be gendered, though Socrates' own premises would seem to undermine that outcome. This speaks more to Socrates' own privileged position in Greek society than to any necessary gendering in the world of forms; though without gender, a soul might seem difficult to describe, it certainly does not seem conceptually impossible. What this dilemma does suggest, however, is how the detachment of so-called "accidental" qualities leaves little if anything worth retaining behind.

14 Rene Descartes, *Meditations*. trans. F.E. Sutcliffe. New York: Penguin Books, 1988, p. 108.

15 Ibid.

16 Descartes, p. 110.

17 Sherry B. Ortner, "Is Female to Male as Nature is to Culture?", in *Women, Culture, and Society*, ed. Michelle Zimbalist Rosaldo and Louise Lamphere. Stanford: Stanford University Press, 1974. Feminist research since this article was published suggests that Ortner overgeneralized her findings; but my argument does not depend on the universality she alleges. Further, I do not mean my argument to imply any essentialism in the equation of maleness with mind or culture or even of dualism itself. Nothing in consciousness, unconsciousness, or lived experience requires such an *a priori* ordering.

18 Michel Foucault, *The History of Sexuality*, trans. Robert Hurley. New York: Vintage Books, 1980, p. 86.

19 trans. George J. Becker (New York: Grove Press, 1962). Particularly interesting for my purposes here is Sartre's contention that anti-Semitism is a form of Manichaeism, another dualistic view in which "no reconciliation

is conceivable; one of them [good or evil] must triumph and the other be annihilated" (p. 41).

20 The jury is still out on the "third wave" of twenty-something feminists.

21 Such thinking comes out of Carol Gilligan's seminal work, *In a Different Voice*, whose careful insistence on socialization as the probable origin of these differences has been ignored or deemphasized in cultural feminist writing which is profoundly essentialist. Ecofeminism is also tied to this branch of feminist theory (Cambridge: Harvard University Press, 1982).

22 Susan Bordo, "Feminism, Postmodernism, and Gender-Skepticism," in *Feminism/Postmodernism*, ed. Linda Nicholson. New York: Routledge, 1990, p. 135. I should note here that Bordo, Linda Alcoff, Collins, and others are "difference feminists" in a *different* sense, that is, they want an analysis of gender in the context of multiple, shifting, non-essentialized identities. All are influenced in their thinking by postmodernism, though they disagree about the extent to which postmodern theory can inform feminism. I will continue to use the term "difference feminism" to refer to Mackinnon et al., who see sexism/gender oppression as the primary form of oppression and who tend to essentialize sexuality.

23 Nancy Fraser and Linda Nicholson, "Social Criticism without Philosophy," in *Feminism/Postmodernism*, ed. Linda Nicholson. New York: Routledge, 1990, p. 33.

24 Betty Friedan, *The Second Stage*. New York: Summit Books, 1981, p. 362.

25 Katie Roiphe, *The Morning After: Sex, Fear, and Feminism on Campus*. Boston: Little, Brown and Co., 1993, pp. 43–44.

26 Tad Friend, "Goddess, Riot Grrrl, Philosopher-Queen, Lipstick Lesbian, Warrior, Tatooed Love Child, Sack Artist, Leader of Men," *Esquire*, February 1994, pp. 47–56.

27 Not surprisingly, the media are often inconsistent in their assessment of the threat feminism poses to men. Witness, for example, the hysteria in the press over Lorena Bobbitt who, it was widely claimed, signified universal women's (feminists'?) rage against men and the omnipresent threat of reprisal.

28 Margaret Carlson, "Now for the Skate-Off." *Time*, February 21, 1994, p. 58.

29 John Powers, "The Gang's all Here." *Boston Globe*, February 18, 1994, p. 49.

30 Bob Ryan, "Media Don't Need to Practice Overkill." *Boston Globe*, February 18, 1994, p. 52.

31 Ibid.

32 Michael Madden, "For Harding, It's a Case of Unanswered Prayers." *Boston Globe*, February 24, 1994, p. 35.

33 Martha Duffy, "With Blades Drawn." *Time*, February 21, 1994, p. 55.

34 Kate Rounds, "Follies: Reflections on a Sport out of Whack." *Ms.* IV, 6, May/June 1994, pp. 27–33.

35 Meg Greenfield, "Moral Icecapades." *Newsweek*, February 28, 1994, p. 70.p. 70.

36 Ibid.

37 Audre Lorde, *Sister Outsider*. New York: Crossing Press, p. 53.

38 Dave Nyhan, "Dr. Dave's Tonic for Tonya." *Boston Globe*, February 13, 1994, p. 73. Though the jury is still out literally and figuratively on the O.J. Simpson case, compare the Nyhan statement with the following comment by a bystander moments before Simpson was arrested: "You love this person…. You love this person no matter what. Even if he did do it—I don't condone killing a person, don't condone taking a life—I would support him. He's a victim, too, because, '*What brings a person to the point that they strike another person?*'" [B. Drummond Ayres, Jr., "Crowd, with Disbelief, Still Cheers for the Juice." *New York Times*, June 19, 1994, p. 21. My emphasis.]

39 Greenfield, p. 70.

9

The Glass Slipper

Cinderella, the most popular of all the fairy tales, describes the dark curse of female competition and envy. It tells us that women must not compete with one another, for aggression will only defeat the aggressor and ensure that the victim will triumph. The winner must be a complex mixture of strength and weakness—she must be *disadvantaged* (Cinderella is young, orphaned and mistreated) but in possession of certain inherent qualities which assure her eventual triumph. She must be hard-working (Cinderella toils and scrubs) but the qualities through which she triumphs are not a matter of willpower, but rather her natural attributes of primarily beauty, and also goodness. The Prince falls in love with Cinderella because she is the most beautiful girl at the ball. The slipper competition which ensues is really no competition at all, although it has the form of one, because the slipper was made for Cinderella: only her foot will fit into it. The other sisters try in vain, and in the Grimm version, at the urging of their mother, one actually cuts off her toe and the other her heel, but the Prince discovers the fit is not natural, the shoe is oozing blood, and rejects them.

What a strange, punishing tale! Competition is a natural emotion, sibling rivalry a universal phenomenon. And Cinderella really *does* possess qualities her stepsisters lack; she is the proverbial prettier younger sister. But Cinderella is a story about women and in women envy is construed as a damning emotion. Thus the step-sisters' resentment is portrayed as so exaggerated and they are figured as so cruel to Cinderella as to preclude any reader identification with them. In different versions of the story, they come to different horrible fates, but in the majority their punishment is absolute: they have their eyes pecked out by birds, or are forced to dance in heated iron slippers until they drop dead of exhaustion. This same narrative of the poison of female jealousy is repeated in Snow White and Sleeping Beauty—two of the other most popular fairy tales, although these focus on mother-daughter competition. In all three tales, however, a man is needed to intervene and save the heroine from potentially fatal aggression by a larger, older, and uglier woman.

Competition, in men, is treated quite differently in literature. Competition is a universally condoned rite of passage in the development of the male ego. The fairy-tale hero runs a race or enters a contest or undergoes a challenge in order to prove his mettle. The terms of the competition are straightforward: the strongest or swiftest or tallest wins. Competition brings with it only the possibility of success with no spectre of retalitory punishment. The hero's strength does not need to be masked in ashes.

Everything about the position of women has changed since the ninth century when the earliest version of the text surfaced, but Cinderella remains as popular in the twentieth century as ever before. The myths of femininity continue to speak to us through the bridge of centuries, across thousands of cultures, in voices whose power endures.

The dreamy, kitschy world of figure skating aspires to create a fairy-tale land. Young girls in glittering costumes compete to be chosen Ice Princess. The Ice Princess embodies the same uneasy mixture of beauty and toil as Cinderella. While skating is a sport—usually, the occasion for the most democratic of competitions—it is a peculiar kind of sport, where "artistry," is weighed with technique and a pleasing arm or well-proportioned thigh is as much part of what it means to skate well, as executing a proper landing. In skating, ideals of femininity are actually *part of the terms of the competition.* "Image is everything," one coach told *The San Francisco Examiner:*

> Judges regularly call the parents and coaches of a skater to suggest that she wear more pink, or grow her hair back long or see a dermatologist to clear up patches of teenage acne. One judge reportedly told one top skater to get a

nose job because the girl's nose was "distracting." A skater who rebuffs a judge's suggestions risks repercussions come competition time. (3/27/94)

The Ice Princess of the skating world, prior to the 1994 Olympics, was Nancy Kerrigan. Although Kristi Yamaguchi had won the 1990 Olympics, and Kerrigan was only a bronze medalist, she had already far outgrossed her with eleven million dollars worth of endorsement contracts. Her coach, Evy Scotvold admitted, "It's a packaging process, very much so. You're trying to become a princess of the ice.... You try to make sure they know they have to behave, they have to have good manners and they have to be well-dressed. They know they will be watched on and off the ice" *(San Francisco Examiner, 3/27/94)*.

Nancy's Reebok ads perhaps best capture the particular combination of effort and effortlessness, will and grace that skating celebrates. The ads show her falling, alone, and then the girlish sound of her voice says pluckily that the best thing she's learned is how to get up again. The possibly masculine message of self-determination is intercut with two traditional icons of femininity: a rose, fragile and ornamental, and a ballerina on a jewelry box, twirling unreflectively, perfect and mechanized, devoid of will.

Long before the Lillehammer Olympics, Tonya Harding had been pegged as a step-sister. Although her skating was technically strong, her inherent attributes were all wrong. Her look was too muscular, her costumes too risqué, her behavior too aggressive. At one tournament points were actually deducted for a "trampy" costume; a reporter quipped she looked like a hooker. At another, her dress came undone as she skated. All of these qualities are reflected in a style of skating which was deemed too "athletic," for athleticism, in skating, is poised against feminity. As Jirina Ribbins, a figure skating expert quoted in the *New York Times*, explains: "If Tonya skates to perfection and anyone else skates to perfection, Tonya loses because her style is not the style they are looking for. Tonya is athletic, not elegant and lyrical the way judges like it. Everyone is looking for the next Sonja Henie" (2/23/94).

Whenever you have two women competing in a field, the media tend to link them together, like Chris Evert and Martina Navratilova, as if they are jealous sisters, competing in a beauty contest. But the Tonya/Nancy spectacle was really born *when a narrative developed which confirmed the women's respective positions in the tale*—when the bad sister took malicious action toward the good sister. Although Nancy was pretty and perfect and perfectly suited to being Cinderella, *she didn't become her until she was victimized.* Without Cinderella's victimization, the spectator may identify with the step-sisters and be jealous of Cinderella's goodness and beauty. (It is interesting to think of the ways in which Tonya could be seen as disadvantaged—as having internalized values which cripple her. If Nancy represents the solid working class from which it is possible to rise, Tonya can be seen to represent the permanent underclass, the cycle of poverty. The fairy-tale heroine's handicaps, however, must all be *external;* within herself the heroine must remain pure and unaffected).

The videotape of the attack was played again and again on the nightly news: Nancy, in virginal white lace, carried to safety in the strong hands of her loving father, crumpled and crying "Why me?"; Nancy's sobbing face on the cover of *Newsweek.* (The seduction of sorrow is a gendered phenomena; a crying man—say Dan Jansen at his sister's funeral—would never adorn a national magazine both because the public would not enjoy seeing this kind of masculine vulnerability and because showing it would be considered disrespectful of the man. Images of broken men are usually reserved for Rwandan peasants—or gay men with AIDS.) It was through this event that Nancy's popularity blossomed. As *The Daily Telegraph* describes it, "Her new celebrity as victim has brought the reward her skating never quite has: fame, with its attendant multi-million dollar advertising and media deals" (2/19/94).

Had Kerrigan been attacked by a bad man, as it initially appeared she was, the story would have been dramatic, but commonplace. The extraordinary public fascination lay in the revelation that *behind the bad man lies a jealous woman—a wicked step-sister, a rival.* In part the story was received with such relish because it appeared to be a blow to feminism: the note of triumphant salaciousness is most evident in male journalists' coverage. But it was not just men who were compelled by the story: women were equally responsive.

In Bruno Bettleheim's reading, Cinderella is an enactment of the Oedipal drama, in which the girl becomes convinced that a jealous older woman— her mother—is preventing her from achieving her heart's desires. Thus, for women, the revelation about Tonya may tap into the deep-seated, repressed suspicion towards other woman and ring true to them. This suspicion is something which feminism, with its emphasis on female bonding and solidarity, may have encouraged women to further repress. The Tonya/Nancy story may have been greeted with the relief of a psychological truth finally given a story through which it can be understood and played out—the same function, in fact, that Bettleheim argues fairy tales always fulfill.

With uncensored glee, the media swiftly transformed the events into a fairy tale. A moral reading was embraced. It was: "A tale of good and evil, of noble struggle and ruthless skullduggery...one of those profound revelations of human nature through the metaphor of sport..."(*Daily Telegraph* 2/29/94). There was "a beautiful princess and a stepsister, a fable worthy of the Brothers Grimm, set in the fairy-tale snows of Lillehammer" (*Montreal Gazette* 3/6/94). "The regal, graceful, endorsement rich Kerrigan," is posed against "the shrill inelegant Tonya...a classic good vs. evil, Snow White on blades vs. the surly ice witch" (*Los Angeles Times* 3/6/94).

There is pleasure in understanding life through familiar, deeply felt narratives, and Cinderella has endured because, in addition to containing elements which conform to a sexist ideology, it also contains psychological truth. There are thousands of versions of Cinderella: the tale exists in many cultures. We are accustomed to thinking of Cinderella as a western saga, but the earliest versions come from the East (hence the emphasis on small feet shod in slippers). As well as dealing with Oedipal entanglements and sibling rivalry, the figure of Cinderella provides a point of universal identification. In childhood, we all experienced ourselves as young and weak, vulnerable to harm, our merits unrecognized. These kinds of feelings are obviously common to men and women, but tend to be relegated to the myths of femininity. Cinderella provides a narrative of a successful coming of age whereby the young are able to triumph over the obstacles poised by powerful elders against their development.

The narrative of the fairy tale is deeply embedded in our consciousness; it structures as well as reflects our perception of reality. In the media's description and the public response, one sees the transformation of the events to fit Cinderella. One also sees, at points, the players' conforming—consciously or unconsciously—to their appointed roles. But mysteriously, a striking number of elements in the Tonya/Nancy saga *do* conform to the fairy tale, both broadly and in uncanny particular. It is perhaps the addition of this third element—that of the uncanny correspondence—which makes the spectacle so unique. In the following points one sees the complex interplay between the three dynamics.

The Beautiful Becomes the Good, the Bad, the Ugly

Although Tonya's physique had always been compared unfavorably to Nancy's, after the attack it was as if her body had suddenly become public property and everyone had license to discuss it in minute detail. News reports described Tonya's thickened forearms, her displeasingly large thighs. Ordinarily, bald sexism surfaces indirectly in mainstream media, but with the fairy tale collapsing of elements, now that Tonya had been shown to be Bad, it was permitted to say she was Ugly. John Head writes in the *Atlanta Journal and Constitution*:

> I had spent weeks railing against the people who attacked Harding's looks, the ones who called her the ugly duckling to Kerrigan's swan. 'Stop talking about appearance and look at athletic ability,' I said, But my first thought when Tonya came onto the ice to skate her short program in Lillehammer was, 'Good grief girl. Who did your makeup? Ringling Brothers?' (3/7/94, p. 18)

Needless to say, a male athlete who misbehaved—say Mike Tyson— would never also be condemned as ugly. It just wouldn't be considered relevant.

Conversely the good, the beautiful and the talented are collapsed in Nancy. Note how even her own father is unable to distinguish between praise of her skating and praise of her appearance, as in this interview with the *Cleveland Plain Dealer*, "Nancy...was a picture of beauty. I don't think she could have skated any better" (2/24/94, p. 1D) Or this reporter's melding of Nancy's victimization, looks, Olympic performance, hair style, and obedience to elders, "She has been brave, and she had been classically beautiful. Kerrigan landed almost everything Friday night. She did what she was told. She could not have been much better. Every finger, every hair was in place" (*St. Louis Post-Dispatch*, 2/26/94). The *Boston Globe* ran a feature on the public interest in the story in which patrons were interviewed at a restaurant:

> At the long-awaited showdown between Harding and Kerrigan...many of the Depot's Olympic-watching patrons were discussing issues that had little to do with skating, or even with the infamous attack on Kerrigan's knee. Mike Differ, 24, wanted to know where Harding got such muscular triceps, 'Wow. She's Schwarzenegger on skates.' ... 'Nancy is the lady,' said a waitress at the Depot. 'She was unbelievable out there; what a goddess.' ... 'That Las Vegas glitter look has got to go,' says Taylor, 31, a manager at a Cambridge furniture store. 'She (Tonya) looks like she wants to be a showgirl.' (2/24/94, p. 23)

The equation of disparate characteristics is a key characteristic of fairy tales so that when the story begins "there was a beautiful girl who had two ugly step-sisters" the reader can be assured of what will follow (although the story never begins "once there was a handome boy"). It is striking that physical appearance as a defining characteristic of women, which colors all other characteristics, has continued—in spite of feminism—from fairy-tale time to the present. The wedding of Tonya and Nancy's looks with their behaviors and performances is the first signal the fairy-tale lens has been adopted.

Age/Sexual Status

Cinderella's step-sisters are of necessity "older" than she is. This is a recurrent pattern in fairy tales: the heroine, if not an only child, like Snow White, is frequently figured as the youngest. Age here stands for sexuality: the older ones may be tainted by the spectre of sexual experience, disqualifying them from heroine purity.

Although Nancy was engaged at one point, her fiancé rarely appeared in the press. Instead she is figured as a daughter, flanked by her tall, protective brothers and father. She is never portrayed as having a social life; her routine is frequently described as "monastic." Tonya's love life, by contrast, is in everyone's face. While Nancy's most memorable skating costume is a virginal white, Tonya's costumes display her breasts. The video of her wedding night, with its wedding gown strip-tease, later peddled to *Penthouse* by her ex-husband, became a trope for Tonya's aggressive assault on some of the dearest myths of femininity.

Moreover, these events are set against a background of increasing sexual conservatism in skating, as a number of prominent male skaters died of AIDS, compromising skating's image as wholesome middle-American family fun. There was thus increased pressure on the women to maintain figure skating's white-bread image. *Dreams of Gold*, by Wayne Coffey and Filip Bondy, an overnight paperback about Kerrigan, explains:

> There was great concern about spooking potential sponsors on the issue [of AIDS]. One USFSA member estimated that the association had lost about half a million in endorsements since the problem became a subject of the national press.... The figure-skating world actually policed itself on the sexual front. Scoring marks became subjective, prudish weapons.... Once these same judges had enforced economic and political ideologies,... now a greater moral struggle was at hand.... Under these circumstances the USFSA was infinitely more comfortable with Kerrigan than it would have been with her chief rival, Tonya Harding Gillooly. (St. Martin's Press, 1994, p. 54–57)

Decades after the sexual revolution, a second key characteristic of the fairy tale—the sexual ideology by which virgin maidenhood is linked to virtue and sexuality to ruin—is evident in full force in the perception of the two women.

Competitiveness

The fairy-tale heroine is hard-working, but not ambitious for anything to come of her work, or competitive with others to get it. While Nancy has been practicing skating the better part of each day for most of her life and her family has mortgaged their house in order for her to do so, when asked what the goal of all this effort is, Nancy demurs. "I just want to do my best," she insists. And she wants the same for all the other skaters.

Tonya Harding, on the other hand, is up front about her desires: she wants to win the gold and beat Kerrigan. Mary Jo Melone, in "Competing Values in Women's Athletics," asserted: "Harding would have been 'terrible Tonya' even without the attack on Kerrigan because Tonya doesn't hide her competitiveness. Kerrigan was always Cinderella at the ball, satisfying every dumb-dumb cliché about femininity, because she was always flashing that sweet, frozen smile"(*St. Petersburg Times* 3/3/94). But the more consistent mainstream opinion, voiced by CBS News anchors Bill Kurtis and Linda MacLennon, echoes the ideology of the fairy-tale that competitiveness is incompatible with female virtue: "Tonya Harding off the ice is no Cinderella as she has stated she wants to kick Nancy Kerrigan's butt competing in the Olympics." (CBS News, WBBM, Chicago 1/12/94)

Strength/Weakness

The fairy-tale narrative depends on a reversal of fortune whereby the strong are brought down and the weak rise, the struggling are rewarded and the secure toppled. By the time the 1994 Olympics approached, Tonya's career was past its peak and in decline. She had already landed the historical triple axle; at the 1991 Nationals she stood on the podium, triumphing over Yamaguchi and Kerrigan.

Nancy's position, on the other hand, had been that of a long and patient struggle. At twenty-four she had already been skating for many years, but she was a nervous, uneven performer, a perpetual runner-up type. After a particularly disastrous competition, she began to see a sports psychologist with whom she uncovered her fear of success (it is easy, in our culture, to understand why she might be confused. A woman who knows what she wants and pursues it, in a straightforward fashion, like speed-skater Bonnie Blair, does not generate the same kind of public interest and adulation—for she is not, in short, a Cinderella). Photo upon photo of competitions show Nancy standing, on the second or third tier of the podium, smiling her beautiful smile and looking up at the winner, waiting for her day in the light. It was a time America wanted to see arrive.

Willingness To Take Malicious Action

Cinderella's reversal of fortune turns upon an inner weakness in the character of the step-sister by which she condemns herself. The stepsister is defined by an inner desperation which causes her to resort to malicious action—action which, because of the moral law of the fairy-tale, is inevitably unsuccessful.

Tonya Harding's tragedy is that she bought into the terms of the tale and became convinced that *another woman* stood between her and the gold medal. Self-determination is not one of the myths of feminity, but in reality Tonya's obstacles were primarily her own: sufficient practice and consistent performance. When she became the only American women ever to land the triple axle in a competition (and one of only two women in the world to do so) she proved she had the capacity to be the best woman skater in the world. Were she to land the triple axle again and make no other mistakes—regardless of artistic bias—she could win the gold. If not, she would inevitably lose to the other highly ranked contenders, Oksana Baiul and Surya Bonaly. The only thing eliminating Nancy actually did was guarantee that she would place first in the Nationals—a competition she had already won in 1991.

Moreover, the attack itself was executed with the bumbling self-destructiveness of the schemes of the wicked—a conspiracy doomed to failure. Tonya chose as her associates people likely to betray her (it is interesting that Jeff Gillooly had threatened to break Tonya's legs and "end her career"—thus the attack on Nancy can actually be seen as a displacement of the threat of male violence on to her nearest female rival).

At the time of the attack, Nancy stepped fully into her role as Cinderella. Graphically victimized, her steadfast sweetness in the face of hardship was nationally broadcast. In spite of the press's goading, she responded to the attack only with silence. When asked how she felt about Tonya attending the Olympics with her, she maintained that she only hoped everyone would do their best. She knows, she said, how much it takes to get there. The desire for revenge—a compromising unfeminine emotion—was left entirely in the hands of the public.

The Mother

Why did Tonya choose to take on the role of step-sister? Consciously, she obviously hoped to get away with the attack so she would never be revealed to the public as malicious. But why would she wish to adopt that identity in her own self-image and her image to her husband? And to take on the inevitable risk of exposure and Nancy's consequential martyrdom?

The fairy tale contains a central psychological explanation for the difference between the step-sister and Cinderella and that is the character of the mother. Behind the bad step-sister lurks an active demon mother; behind Cinderella a saintly passive maternal figure. The bad mother is the underlying cause of the daughter's mistaken hopeless ambition: she eggs her on, conveying the message that her worth depends on achieving an external goal—to be Queen—and that she must therefore do anything in order to get it. When the step-sister tells her mother that the slipper does not fit, the mother urges her to cut off part of her foot; when you become Queen, she says, you won't need to walk anymore.

The fairy-tale heroine's mother, on the other hand, provides her with the positive internal image which is the source of her goodness and (with fairy-tale confusion) beauty. The heroine must rely on this internalized image for her mother is physically absent, thus setting up the narrative by leaving her daughter externally vulnerable to physical harm but internally equipped with the spiritual means to combat it (in the modern version—originating with Perrault—the protectorate spirit of the dead mother is available to Cinderella in the form of the fairy godmother; in the Grimm version it is a bird which comes from a tree which grows from her dead mother's grave which gives her aid. In other cultures it takes other animal forms; in the Chinese Cinderella it takes the form of a special fish).

These aspects of the fairy tale seem to contain some measure of psychological truth. While obviously far from predictive, the offspring of mothers who provide unconditional love are generally better equipped for happiness and success in life. Children whose mothers convey the message that external achievement is the only way out of a negative home environment often flounder and end up recreating that same chaotic environment in their own lives.

These ideas certainly appear to dovetail with the respective family histories of Tonya and Nancy. A waitress who was married six times, Lavona Hardy provided a home which was economically and emotionally unstable. Lavona gave Tonya the message that the only salvation—riches and fame—could be found through her skating. From infancy, she thrust skating upon the girl. When she was pregnant she told a friend that if she had a daughter, she was to be a skater (she later revised her story to make skating Tonya's initiative). Tonya was abused when she failed to perform and allegedly sexually abused, as well, by a step-brother.

By contrast, Brenda Kerrigan appears kindly, supportive and incapacitated. She provides spiritual sustenance, but must leave her daughter alone in the rink. Her mother's blindness is a crucial part of Nancy's image: "Before the attack, Kerrigan was perhaps best known for the fact that her mother, Brenda, is legally blind and peers closely at a television monitor for a glimpse of her daughter's elegant form" (the *Atlanta Journal and Constitution*, 3/13/94). Like Cinderella, Nancy is left alone in the eyes of the audience.

The Glass Slipper

The one detail anyone who has ever read Cinderella remembers is the glass slipper (or in the Grimm version, gold). It is such a striking image: the shoe which has no flexibility, which will accommodate none but one (in Bettleheim's reading the glass slipper is the vagina, by extension of which the slipper competition is the search for the appropriate sexual partner). Crucial to the description of the glass slipper is the idea that it is tiny: to fit it one must possess the *smallest* foot.

In most individual sports, the winner is the one who *exceeds* the existing record—who throws the javelin farther, or gets down the track faster. No ideal exists: the winner must be better than the other contestants, and if she is to make history, break all previous records. Thus the standard is always shifting. But figure skating is more about delicacy and constraint than freedom and invention. Its slipper is small indeed: each move is designed with a rigid ideal in mind. Above all, the winner is the one who makes *no mistakes*. Barely perceptible deviations from the standard cause points to be deducted. Most of the skater's program consists of required moves. Like the images of femininity, the menu of choices is extremely limited. Moreover, the skater must make her moves appear to be natural and graceful; the step-sisters are betrayed when the blood oozes from the slipper. And of course there can only be one winner, one Princess chosen.

The fulfillment of the fairy-tale in its particulars is extraordinary: at the Olympics a broken lace prevented Tonya from taking the ice on time, and when she did, she fell and had to begin again. At the ball of her life—the definitive never-to-be-repeated moment—the shoe did not fit. Exposed as a step-sister, the audience against her, she lost confidence and foundered.

The correspondences between skating and Cinderella cannot be fully accounted for by audience interpretation or the character's participation in this interpretation. Skating really *does* rest on putting on a white well-fitted slipper and performing an activity that looks a great deal like dancing at a competition reminiscent of a ball. Since Cinderella is the preeminent coming of age tale, the coincidental likeness between the objects of skating and the symbols in Cinderella may evoke subconscious associations which help explain why skating, more than any other sport, is so fraught with the ideology of femininity.

The Ball

Like the ball in which Cinderella appeared three times, the 1994 Winter Olympics took place over a series of nights. Opening night of the women's technical program drew a billion viewers worldwide and a hundred million in the US—the highest ratings ever for an Olympic broadcast. America—Prince Charming, the male spectator—watched as Tonya, heavy with the knowledge of the audience's contempt, picked a low unlucky number and fulfilled her role as the unworthy contender. Nancy picked a high lucky number (in fairy-tales to be lucky is the same as to be good and deserving of good luck) and floated flawlessly through. When asked about her expectations for the final evening, Nancy was coy, but admitted she was "happy the judges have chosen to rank (her) number one." The gold medal appeared nearly hers.

On the final night, dressed like Cinderella in a costume of golden threads, Nancy appeared shining and confident. The media is ecstatic; the tale is properly concluding. The *San Francisco Chronicle* says: "Kerrigan's beautiful performance—coming after Harding's glum unsteady show—restored order and balance to the sport. It also proved that a clear conscience and the goodwill of the entire world count for something..." (9/24/95). The *Irish Times* writes: "Few tears, No Blood as Snow White beats Poison Dwarf. Beauty Crushes The Beast." And the Swiss Tabloid *Blick* echoes: "Ice witch Tonya Harding was already penalized even before the ice fairy entered the stadium." Even in Tonya's hometown paper, *The Oregonian*, the headlines read: "Morality Play Follows Script: Harding 10th, Kerrigan 1st."

But Cinderella is not about two sisters; it is about three. Three is the magical number of fairy tales and it is the final night, at the final hour, in which the unexpected takes place. Oksana Baiul enters.

"An enchanting 16-year-old orphan from Ukraine" (the *Washington Post*, 3/13/94), Oksana is eight years younger than Nancy, a lithe, half-starved looking child-woman. Her costume and style of skating are even more feminine than Nancy's: she skates to Swan Lake in pink. Orphaned at twelve, she slept in the skating rink until her coach finally took her in. She comes from Eastern Europe, a land of desolation and hardship, whence many fairy-tales originated. She is the true outsider to the skating establishment since, as an unknown, she became, at sixeen, the youngest World Champion since Sonja Henie. Her tale is more touching: "How could Kerrigan compete with the fresh tale of an orphaned Ukraine girl?", asks the Kerrigan biography *Dreams of Gold*. "Baiul's life history rivals Kerrigan's for sympathy and sentiment.... Kerrigan's...mother, Brenda, is legally blind.... Baiul's mother died of cancer when she was twelve, leaving her an orphan. Her father had abandoned them when she was three" (the *Atlanta Journal and Constitution*, 3/13/94).

In addition to her other Cinderella qualities, by a truly literary twist of fate, Oksana becomes *more injured* than Kerrigan in a collision with another woman skater immediately preceding the competition. With no time to recover, she skates her gold medal performance on painkillers. Following her spectacular performance, instead of rejoicing she returns to her coach's arms and sobs desolately while a billion people watch. "Baiul was tired, she was in pain. She was crying for her mother again, who died three years ago of cancer.... This was going to be a split decision.... How could anybody decide?" (*St. Louis Post-Dispatch*, 2/26/94, p. 1C). But the decision was made and it came down for Baiul. "Baiul listened to her skates and to her heart. Kerrigan listened to her coaches, her practice sessions, and to her agent.... A championship should be more than part of a package. It was more than that for Baiul. There were tears from Baiul, as always, as they waited forever for somebody to find the Ukrainian national anthem, 'The Ukraine has not Perished'"(*Phoenix Gazette*, 2/26/94).

As if at the stroke of twelve, as soon as the vote for Oksana came in, Nancy began to reveal her true nature as the second sister, with her oft-detailed sulkiness and catty remarks. "Because of comments she has made about her competitors, Olympic judges and her new benefactor, Mickey Mouse, Kerrigan has gone from being America's sweetheart to an ungrateful vixen with a tongue sharper than the blades on her skates," writes the *Houston Chronicle* (3/6/94). A slew of other press appeared along the lines of the Associated Press story headlines (March 94): "Kerrigan may be tarnishing her golden image." The slightly acerbic remarks of Nancy's—obviously stemming from a disappointment she was precluded from expressing straightforwardly—were enough to thoroughly condemn her in the eyes of the public. For, as in the fairy-tale, one is either the true Princess or not the true Princess and the revelation of character is decided forever through a few chosen signs.

Today, while Nancy has retreated from public life, Oksana is planning to move to Connecticut. A new million dollar skating rink is being constructed in which she can train. How do we understand Oksana's crowning? Oksana fulfilled the Cinderella fantasy the best; her appeal was therefore the deepest. Perhaps she was also a better skater. But, as always with life and narrative—reality and the constructs of reality—the two are impossible to fully entangle. One judge gave Oksana one-tenth of a mark higher scores for artistic merit. Another had given Nancy the higher mark for technical merit. In the final round, however, in situations of otherwise equal merit, artistry is held to weigh more heavily than technique. That in order to make judgments in the face of ambiguity we inevitably turn to ideology, artistry and narrative—like a fairy-tale lens without which we cannot see—serves well as the final metaphor.

III >

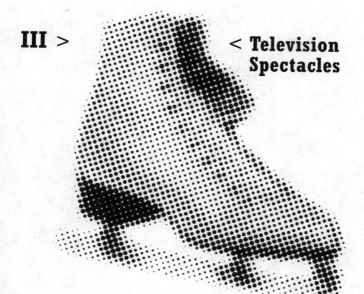

< Television
Spectacles

Tales of the Ice Princess and the Trash Queen

Cultural Fictions and the Production of "Women"

"[T]he woman as icon, displayed for the gaze and enjoyment of men...always threatens to evoke the anxiety it originally signified. The male unconscious has two avenues of escape...investigating the woman, demystifying her mystery counterbalanced by...devaluation, punishment, or saving...or turning the represented figure itself into a fetish...hence over-valuation, the cult of the female star. This second avenue, fetishistic scopophilia, builds up the physical beauty of the object.... The first avenue, voyeurism, on the contrary, has associations with sadism: pleasure lies in ascertaining guilt.... This sadistic side fits well with narrative. Sadism demands a story, depends on making something happen...in a linear time with a beginning and an end. Fetishistic scopophilia, on the other hand, can exist outside linear time as the erotic instinct is focussed on the look alone."[1]

In "Visual Pleasure and Narrative Cinema," her now axiomatic article on sexually-encoded systems of looking in the fiction film, Laura Mulvey strategically dichotomizes the cinema's perpetual play of spectacle and narrative, image and story, in order to demonstrate how cultural constructions of "the feminine" drive even the most apparently gender-neutral forms of visual entertainment. The Olympic sport-turned-tabloid-drama involving champion ice skaters Nancy Kerrigan and Tonya Harding is a particularly powerful demonstration of how, even in the *absence* of a fiction film or cinematic production, this process is still—and perhaps more strongly—at work in the larger cultural context of the general social imaginary. For, athletic ability and talent aside, what emerged from the intensive national preoccupation with the two figure-skaters and their woes was nothing other than a series of competing versions of the feminine, the metaphoric duality of "women" played and replayed according to each medium, in whatever aspect of the story was taken up.

But first, before speaking of images and tropes, let me state right from the start that having an opinion about either skater, taking sides, as it were, in the putative rivalry on the ice and beyond, involves the attribution of agency, something that can only arise from a fiction based on media-constructed images. For me, the bottom line is that Tonya Harding had something to do with the brutal injury of Nancy Kerrigan, a teammate who "still has nightmares" about an arbitrary and unexpected assault on her body. Whatever stories one may compose in order to side with the (partial) perpetrator—from working-class sympathies to perverse notions of female assertiveness—the ugly, unadorned fact remains: a woman was violated in a way that we are now accustomed to seeing on television and another woman was, to some extent, involved in the attack. We are so desensitized, inured to the daily diet of violence against women, that the sheer horror of the attack itself has been virtually absented from all discussion of the skaters. We must not forget that even the feminist discourses of advocacy, the debates over which skater is more deserving of our support, must always bear in mind the violence that initiated this complex of events and images. My argument, then, will not deal with real women at all, but with cultural fantasies of female identity as they are mobilized in a particularly forceful way around the figures of Nancy Kerrigan and Tonya Harding.

From the densely complex discursive network of fictions and real events involving the skaters, the proliferation of texts and metatexts, I've chosen two exemplary moments to illustrate how Mulvey's opposition of female representations shaped the social construction of entertainment regarding these events: The "drama of the shoelace" at the 1994 Olympic competition, and "Artistry on Ice," the ice-skating special broadcast in May, some three months after the Olympic Games themselves. In both of these instances, as in their many avatars, from actual event to structured performance and eventually to the constructed fiction of "Tonya and Nancy: The Inside Story" (the made-for-TV movie broadcast April 30 on NBC), the basic polarity of Kerrigan, the icon of perfection, and Harding, the trailer park tramp—fetishistic object and voyeuristic tale, image and narrative—was reiterated and reinforced in ways that, as in all ideological operation, make the characterizations as natural and enduring as they are (or seem to be) unproblematically obvious.

Almost from its inception, the "saga of Nancy and Tonya," as the mediated complex of events came to be known, was really about Nancy's image and Tonya's story. This, in fact, was borne out by the made-for-TV movie which, while purporting to be the "inside story" of both skaters, was actually an exploration of Tonya's lifelong struggles, liberally punctuated with unforgettable public images of a dazzling Nancy, a bewildered and suffering Nancy, a triumphant Nancy, and so forth. In actual fact, there seemed to be a public craving for images of the beautiful, elegant icon of grace who defined herself on the ice, matched only by an equally rivetting public appetite for the stories of abuse, scandalous behavior, and aggressive nonconformity that characterized Tonya's life *away* from the ice. "Sadism demands a story" to be sure, and Tonya's life provided enough material for a salacious tale of epic proportions. But fetishism "is focussed on the look alone," and a purer definition of the Nancy Kerrigan icon would be hard to find. Schematic as it sounds, the culture's ready polarization of the woman's image found fertile terrain in these real events, and proceeded to generate, with all the commonsense logic of ideological production, the "natural" of femininity in the public arena.

Those already familiar with the culture's overwhelming fascination with exquisite female victims and nasty female villains, its endless capacity for captivation by both images of feminine beauty and lurid stories of female degradation, will readily see here the dual desire to contemplate beauty and expose the "truth." Nancy's commodity endorsements, her Kate Hepburn looks and "Marilyn Monroe" dress, the effervescent smile, the luminous wave, the dazzling spin, the elegant pose captured in a single flash, all coincide with the image-icon aspect of the fetish. A product endorsing products, Nancy's "meaning" is apprehended in a way that is both instantaneous and surface-deep. On the other hand, Tonya's multiple narratives that extend back into the past and forward toward the future, the interviews and self-generating incidents, the narrative reconstructions and dramatizations of tabloid TV, the complex tangle of relationships involved in any single moment of her life, all increase the obsession with her story that sadism demands. There is no single image that corresponds to the "meaning" of Tonya; the vision of Tonya has to be *narrativized* as experience in order to be understood.

Take, for example, the "drama of the shoelace," which was arguably as much Tonya's Olympic performance as her Jurassic Park number itself.

Leaving aside the uncanny and even impossible situation that would station a camera unyieldingly *in the wings*, almost the entire story of the malfunctioning skate was played out behind the scenes. In fact, from the very start of the trouble, each intervening performance on the ice (Canada's Josée Chouinard, Japan's Yuka Sato) was intercut with the inevitable return backstage and an update on the progress of Tonya and her ice skate, making it virtually Tonya's drama, plagued by the interruptions of "extraneous" performances on the ice. Invariably, Tonya is a somewhat disastrous spectacle; even when she presents herself in the performance mode, it turns into something of a narrative, as the mini-drama shows, with all the suspense, temporality, camera angles and crosscuts of a cinematic fiction. No fewer than sixteen returns to the backstage area characterized Tonya's performance in the Northern Lights Hall during the determining Free Skate portion of the Olympic competition, creating an unprecedented dramatic conflict in a sport defined by most as the essence of pure spectacle.

Mulvey associates sadism and voyeurism with narration, and Tonya's crisis of the obstinate ice skate contains rich proportions of all three—convoluted narrative complications, sadistic domination of the heroine, and voyeuristic camera angles that emphasize an illicit keyhole view. Very briefly, the "story" begins just minutes before Tonya is to skate her long program, and as we view the confusion in the narrow hallway backstage from an enclosed point curiously above the action, the commentator remarks: "Right now it's Tonya Harding's turn to skate, but the tortured path she's taken to the Olympics continues here." He continues with a catalogue of Tonya's prior mishaps with costume and skate blade, setting the tone for both the suspenseful drama of the bootlace and Tonya's ensuing performance on the ice, and, as a consequence, framing every codified gesture of Tonya's figure skating display within the context of multilayered narrative concerns.

The rest of the story plays itself out against the intractable pulse of the clock ("a battle of will and strength, victory/defeat, all occurring in a linear time with a beginning and an end"[2]) as the commentators note first the two-minute time limit, then the reprieve, and finally, the preferred placement at the end of the grouping, something which provides a kind of resolution to this suspense-filled drama while lending the performance itself the status of an anti-climax. Tonya's skating on the ice is thus liberally surrounded by melodrama behind the scenes, and whether one views the whole episode with satisfaction at poetic justice or with empathy for the embattled skater, one thing is certain. It is not Tonya Harding's ice-skating ability, athletic or artistic, that is of concern here. Tonya Harding has truly become the heroine of a narrative rather than the centerpiece of a spectacle, and this is a characterization that will remain with her long after the Olympics are over.

As Tonya struggles with a broken lace, then is provided one that is, unbelievably, too short, the commentators try bravely to accompany this frantic backstage scene (involving Tonya, her coach Diane Rawlinson, and others) with unaccustomed patter: "This can really throw a skater off.... This bizarre real-life movie continues." Finally, Tonya runs out clutching her Ventolin asthma inhaler, "It's not gonna hold me.... I'm gonna break my ankle," and gamely tries to begin her four-minute free skate to the single word of the commentator: "Amazing!" (an exclamation that, significantly, has absolutely nothing to do with Tonya's performance and everything to do with the suspense of the preceding moments). Then, in what are now familiar narrative images, Tonya starts to skate, singles a triple lutz on an awkward two-footed landing, starts crying, easily slings her foot high up on the referees' podium and explains her problem. When she's given the time to replace the lace, television viewers are afforded some of the most interesting examples of camera voyeurism in media representation. There are two kinds of voyeurism at work in this saga of the bootlace, both reinforcing my argument about Harding's fulfillment of the sadistic-voyeuristic side of the Mulvey polarity.

The first, alluded to before, has to do with the voyeuristic camera angle in the backstage space (or the space immediately outside the rink). Definitions of voyeurism emphasize the hidden, secret vantage point, distinguishing it from scopophilia (the erotic component of looking, which Mulvey associates specifically with fetishism on the other side of the duality) in its specificity as a perversion. Here the voyeuristic camera position can be found in the unusually prurient camera angles that accompany this backstage drama—peering down into the space of the frantic confusion, or over the shoulder as the other women with their fur-lined boots and their manicures scramble to lace up the boot, or hovering unseen in order to disclose stolen moments of panic and despair. Needless to say, this kind of voyeuristic camera is generally not used for the performance aspect of the skating spectacle; what operates here is a particularly secretive and forbidden quality of the sadistic, probing, investigative gaze.

The second kind of voyeuristic camera angle has to do with a type of fetishism, but not the glamorized overvaluation of the female image that Mulvey contrasts with sadistic voyeurism. Here, instead, it is the boot itself which is fetishized by the camerawork, creating a doubling effect of fetishization since the booted ice-skate already exists in the paradigm of classic fetishes. In addition, while Mulvey associates fetishism with the direct, erotic rapport between viewer and object, voyeuristic fetishism emphasizes the status of the camera as a peephole. Thus fetishistic scopophilia is determined from the standpoint of the object while voyeurism involves the *position of looking* itself in its meaning. Once Tonya comes back from the judges and says "I have to tie it right here," the viewer has access to an inordinately close look at an ice-skating boot, as frenzied fingers struggle to release the delinquent lace in order to replace it with a more appropriate substitute. We see those parts of the ice skate necessarily obscured in the smooth representation of competitive performance—the tongue, the fleece lining, the foam ankle inserts, the grommets—while Scott Hamilton explains how important it is for a skater to have a good fit ("It's important that it's comfortable on your foot. When I get my skate on during competition, I don't retie it if it's a little uncomfortable, I just get used to it. Because any change in the comfort...if they're tied too tight your foot can fall asleep. Everything has to be just perfect, *especially* in Olympic competition"), in what amounts to a dazzling demystification of the traditional figure skating performance. In all of these instances the camera's gaze is voyeuristic: shameless, hidden, and intent on uncovering its story.

There are a few more points about the narrative aspects of the bootlace episode that are relevant to Tonya Harding's connection to the narrative trope of sadistic domination. These have to do with 1) the entanglement of other "characters" in the dramatic conflict, 2) the commentators' continual references to the "story" aspects of the situation, 3) the slo-mo replay not of Harding's performance but of the incident itself—the *breakdown* of performance—as she finally takes the ice for her long program, and 4) her comments after the presentation itself. To those who know the saga by heart, of course, the Canadian champion Josée Chouinard is the primary figure to become unwittingly enmeshed in the incidents. Once Tonya is given the time to replace her lace, a surprised and unprepared Chouinard is forced to skate her long program without any of the psychic space afforded by a prior competitor's free skate. By that very fact, the whole complex of events surrounding Tonya and Nancy suddenly becomes international, as what had previously been seen as somewhat of a domestic melodrama takes on world proportions. Verne Lundquist sums up: "[Here is] Canadian champion Josée Chouinard, who never *dreamed* she would be a part of *this improbable story*. And yet *she* has been affected by it." (Emphasis added)

And of course (and here is where that cinematic first principle of crosscutting comes in), while Chouinard prepares, then skates to "An American in Paris," and finally receives her score, the camera includes several backstage "meanwhile" cutaways, including an extremely intimate overhead closeup of Rawlinson and Tonya, heads together, in confidence. The basic figure of crosscutting, alternating between two series of images conceived as simultaneous (as in a chase sequence, for example), has been the cornerstone of narrative cinema since D.W. Griffith first systematized its use. Thus, building a narrative, from the earliest days of cinema onward, meant alternating between sets of images, creating suspense and expectation through a perpetual return to "meanwhile." Here in the Northern Lights Hall, the commentators ease this process by accompanying backstage shots of Tonya sitting, conversing, practicing, pacing with such phrases as, "Meanwhile, backstage, Tonya Harding does not have her boot on." or "The boot is not yet laced and Tonya is battling asthma, and on the ice, unexpected at this point, the Canadian champion..." Chouinard's long program and score are thus turned into one chain of images in an alternating sequence involving Tonya's progress backstage with her skate, culminating in the commentator's final summation which, needless to say, emphasizes the narrative aspects that cling to Harding like so many sequins on her costume: "This extraordinary chapter in the ongoing saga of Tonya Harding continues." This is said over an image of Tonya in the wings, practicing footwork, in a sort of bizarre prelude to Tracy Wilson's interview with a gracious and poignantly bewildered Josée.

When Tonya Harding finally does arrive at the ice for her long program, the slow-motion replay of her earlier interrupted performance demonstrates just how sadistic the narrative pole of the duality can be ("Pleasure lies in ascertaining guilt...asserting control and subjecting the guilty person through punishment or forgiveness"[3]). As if there were not enough narrative already, viewers are given a story-within-a-story by virtue of this slowed-down reiteration of Tonya's public degradation. And while the instant replay in figure skating is most often used to break down and analyze artistic or athletic aspects of a skater's performance, here it is used basically to recount events that pursue, punish, investigate, and tame the troubled Tonya—all those activities associated with sadism in the classic sense. The commentary over this humiliating preface to what turns out to be an unremarkable performance attempts to justify this unnecessary repetition of Tonya's suffering by explaining the logistics of the interruption and the plea. Instead, it unwittingly contributes to the casting of Tonya in the role of catastrophic loser. "Right off the opening jump of her program she quit. She went directly to the referees; that's what a skater is instructed to do.... And if she has an equipment failure, it's completely within the rules to offer her time to recover *or* change the running order so that she can skate later to give her time to recover. It just seems unfair to the rest of the skaters."

Highly unusual as an introduction to a figure skater's competitive performance, this little narrative drama in some sense explains coach Diane Rawlinson's words to Tonya after her long program: "What a brave kid!" Comments on her abilities would miss the point—it's as a troubled heroine of fiction, one who has surmounted many (sometimes self-generated) odds, that Tonya's social presence is understood. The beginning of her competitive long program is already a repetition (Commentator: "*Once again*, her opening jump is a triple lutz."), already embellished with story elements, already a part of a continuing sequence of events. During her post-performance interview, she continues to construct the character mystique, first by answering in a very practical way a question about her bootlace (thus constituting the third version of the events we are now familiar with), then by creating a further set of possibilities to be investigated when asked why she only singled the triple axel: "I don't know myself. Does anybody know?" as she looks around jokingly. And finally, as her own assessment of her performance, she slyly, even coyly says, "Who knows, if I don't get my gold here, maybe I'll come back in a few years." While she might not know how to play to the crowd when performing on the ice, Tonya Harding seems prodigiously adept at working the crowd outside the rink, in terms of the stories she constructs about herself and the tantalizing bits of narrative she proffers—when she cares to.

On the other hand, a more appropriate icon of fetishistic scopophilia could not be found than the dazzling image of Nancy Kerrigan in full performance mode. And what better way to approach this than through "Artistry on Ice," the non-competitive skating performance intended to showcase Kerrigan, among other figure skaters, well after the 1994 Olympics themselves. Advertized as entertainment without the anxiety of competition, and indeed, as its title suggests, constructed around popular notions of high art (easel and palette, framed oil paintings, draped fabrics, still-life arrangements with roses), this two-hour skating special deftly constructed a "performance space" that isolated the exhibition far from the daily diet of tabloid crises, and cast it into the lofty realm of pure spectacle. And while there were many other figure-skating performers included in the evening (with the obvious and unsurprising exception of

Tonya Harding), this analysis will focus on Kerrigan's skating alone, in order to elaborate on the initiating duality in female representation established by Mulvey between the sadistic voyeurism of narrative and the fetishistic scopophilia of display.

As Mulvey reminds us, this latter "can exist outside linear time, as the erotic instinct is focussed on the look alone."[4] In fact, narrative elements all but disintegrate as the woman's image is placed "in direct erotic rapport with the spectator. The beauty of the woman as object and the screen space coalesce.... [She is] a perfect product, whose body...is...the direct recipient of the spectator's look."[5] As everything else dissolves around the viewer and the object of desire, looking at the performing woman becomes an activity of intense libidinal investment. And it is this body, this image, and this product that the name Nancy Kerrigan has come to signify in the constructed social imaginary surrounding the two skaters.

Of course there is the much belabored accounting of the commodities Kerrigan has been signed to endorse, each trading on a particular quality that her image represents—athletic stamina, perseverance, effervescence, wholesomeness. The body and persona are broken down into their parts, each signifying unit designated to sell a particular item from soup to sneakers. This reached something of a culmination with the "No Nonsense Pantyhose American Woman Award" print advertisement in February 1994—the same month that *People* magazine's cover shouted, "Tonya's World: As Tonya Harding fights for her future—and possibly her freedom—her parents and friends describe the hard life that shaped her," alongside pictures of an agitated Tonya and a dubious looking Gillooly (February 14, 1994). By contrast, the tasteful and minimalist pantyhose ad featured a single, centered portrait of Nancy and her mom, smiling, tilted heads, with red roses clutched between them, framed in a large female symbol, with an accompanying text (matched in its self-congratulatory ideology only by Nancy's "Golden Dream" music for "Artistry on Ice") that read: "This athletically gifted daughter and legally blind mother share brave determination in the face of tragic setbacks, epitomizing the spirit of international athletic competition." But lest one forget the true purpose of this "award," the product's name, "No Nonsense," appears four times on the page, complete with tiny replica of the pantyhose package. It seems there's plenty of nonsense to go around in this vision, this image of mother and daughter who radiate happiness and health, the instantaneous apprehension of which is used to sell fantasies about woman's image and self-image along with efficient and disposable pantyhose. The "anchoring" text, if one were needed, is a further instance of ideological (over)production, manipulating cliches as easily as snapshots in a photo album: "The 'bio' is awarded each month to a person whose confident belief in the talent and power of women has created an enlightened environment benefitting both womankind and mankind."

Nor is the use of Nancy's image in advertising and promotion something new that arose as recently as her Olympic performance of 1992. Kerrigan was already deemed lucratively photogenic when, as a young teenager, she performed the role of demure Russian ice sylph to a rough and tumble American ice-hockey player in an Olympic Coca-Cola commercial in the 1980s. In short, all of the commodification and circulation of the Nancy Kerrigan icon have been based on an immediate popular recognition of something striking, dazzling, and beautiful in her image, something founded on the *gaze* and deriving its force from that connection. Mulvey speaks of the power of the woman's image in narrative film "to freeze the flow of action in moments of erotic contemplation."[6] For her, the awkward but descriptive phrase "to-be-looked-at-ness"[7] suggests that screen women have a strong visual presence that invites the look as much as it impedes narrative development, making the female figure the automatic object of spectacle and site of spectatorial desire. Fetishism, for Mulvey, puts the highly visible woman at the center of classical narrative film, but this centrality comes at a cost to the sequential flow of the narrative, requiring constant mediation between narrative movement and spectacular display. Spectacle functions to suspend the narrative in favor of the sustained and privileged gaze upon the woman's body, a body fragmented into idealized units, distilled as sign in a flattened nonnarrative space, or fixed as a pose/posture devoid of agency and existing ultimately to be looked at alone. Camera gaze and spectator's look condense in the infinitely available spectacle of the woman's performing body. Jokes about endorsements for the anti-auto-theft device "The Club" aside, Tonya Harding's image does not possess the same kind of immediacy, does not elicit the same kind of desiring gaze, for hers is an image forever captioned by some kind of story. By contrast, the emphatic absence of narrative frame is what makes Kerrigan's presence fit so well among the commodities to be wished for and the female image to be desired.

This can be illustrated in one more way before noting the spectacle function of the Kerrigan icon in "Artistry on Ice." "Skating is my life," was the oft-wielded claim of Tonya Harding, used as defensive armor while she negotiated the road to Lillehammer, and there was no shortage of suppliers for this first-person narrative. In every kind of televised image and print journalism from tabloid items to mainstream news and ultimately to the "inside story" of the made-for-TV movie, each discursive form found a way to elaborate what this life was, what this claim meant, and how it was produced. But with Nancy Kerrigan, whose performance and persona were organized, as with all fetish objects, around a body to be looked at, this first-person narration was mobilized in quite a different way. Another print ad (another endorsement), this time for Reebok's Satellite Lightweight Cross Training Shoe in *Glamour* magazine's May 1994 issue, pictures a classic Kerrigan trademark spiral in softly-lit silhouette, Lillehammer long program pose and Vera Wang costume, on a shining mirror of a disk, against the backdrop of an ethereal mountain sunset: "Some days people expect me to walk on water. SO I DO. Except it's not exactly water. And I'm not exactly walking." The same inspirational message that has come to be associated with Kerrigan either through her choice of performance music, her designation by various service groups or advertisers, or her handlers and image-makers themselves, is here associated quite literally with her singular, signifying figure. "Reach for the stars," suggests the excellent extension of her ideogrammatic pose, but there is nothing subtle about the assertion of wholesome success made possible through the purchase of shoes. Although a "self" is presented four times in the accompanying written text, it is not Nancy's subjectivity that makes the impact. The force of the ad is created, instead, by what "she" represents or symbolizes, in exactly that instantaneous and fascinating logic of the fetish, the dynamic of visible flesh. While "Reebok believes in the athlete. *In all of us,*" we believe in the perfection of form. In Nancy.

"Artistry on Ice" never ceases to engage the vocabulary of the visual as it moves its viewer from one display of talent to the next. But it is precisely in the figure of Nancy Kerrigan that the codified aspects of ice-skating performance meet the mechanisms of over-valuation at work in the cult of the female star, providing the fascination with looking that is the cornerstone of fetishistic scopophilia in film. Traditionally, as Kerrigan glides through her spellbinding numbers, she evokes fantasies of imaginary possession and flight, fantasies which evaporate at the edge of the rink, that is, at the moment the performance is over. In a curious coalescence of skating rink and cinema screen, "Nancy Kerrigan" ceases to exist when she leaves that space, relinquishing her hold on the spectator and breaking the triple illusion of self-sufficiency, inaccessibility, and distance so necessary to the creation of that spell. The (television) camera's alignment with the spectator's gaze is both that which offers Kerrigan to be seen and that which makes her visible, thereby positing Nancy herself as an effect of the constructed gaze of visual representation. Typically, a Kerrigan performance will employ this to advantage, utilizing a series of poses as she glides on display. The modernist sculptures of Constantin Brancusi or Henri Gaudier-Brzeska come to mind as gestures are turned into a series of surfaces designed to catch and hold the gaze. Maximum extension of arms and legs suggests flight where there is stasis, luminous transparency where there is substance. The viewer is transfixed by the representation, captivated by this phantom-image-woman who creates a dream-space through the grace of her performance alone.

As a springtime skating extravaganza, "Artistry on Ice" is concerned with promoting the aesthetic underpinnings of its sport, hence the incessant referencing of high art in the discourses and materials surrounding the actual performances. Yet, like the return of the repressed, Tonya Harding's name (matched by the grainy tabloid images of headline quotes) crops up in tantalizing news promos in some commercial breaks. Thus while this televised special is in many ways Nancy's stage—the place where her image can shine in the firmament of art—repeated returns to the cultural realities of Tonya's narrative remind us that the Nancy icon is, at every moment, only one half of the composite social representation of the feminine. But it is essentially this visible, specularized half that is put into play by the Kerrigan performances, easily encapsulated in Paul Wylie's epithetic paean (in another skating special) and requiring nothing more: "She's graceful, she's athletic, she's beautiful!" For while Tonya's efforts at spectacle somehow always seem to spell disaster, Nancy is the perfect image, the ultimate skater-object whose essence is performance alone. In fact, in those moments when Nancy seems to verge on narrative characterization herself (snarling about Oksana's tears, grousing in the Magic Kingdom), she invariably fails, but not because Nancy seems incapable of sustaining fictional concerns. Rather, it is because these moments of narrative elaboration are somehow *incompatible* with the unperturbed image that we both desire and require Nancy to be. Her reification as fetishistic object of spectacle necessitates her removal from the contradictory dynamics of human behavior so that she might more safely be ensconced in the aesthetic realm.

The introduction to "Artistry on Ice" sets up a discursive matrix that combines the ideologies of performance, personal expression, and individual creativity in a notion of artistic excellence, thereby providing a high art framework for each skater's exhibition. An establishing shot of an art gallery interior (the Walters Art Gallery in Baltimore was used) is matched by a masculine voice which intones over fluid piano music: "The most uniquely human experience, self-expression through art, knows many canvases. There are portraits to paint, and shapes to sculpt. But the elusive perfection of movement also invites interpretation. On display tonight, some of the world's greatest artists; their canvas, the ice." And as the music takes over briefly, the camera rests on an easel, whose blank canvas comes to life with the introduction and mini-performances of several of the evening's stars: Oksana Baiul, Brian Boitano, Nancy Kerrigan, Elvis Stojko, and the team of Goryeva and Grinkov. Others are introduced a bit later, but these first skaters are showcased by virtue of this initiating presentation and the gilt frame that surrounds each. Oksana is the "impressionist of fragile elegance," Boitano the "grand master of proud, powerful brushstrokes," but the vocabulary of luminosity is reserved for Nancy herself. As she first sits demurely surrounded by roses (richly connoting "American Beauty"), then skates her signature spiral in Lillehammer lamé, the commentary foregrounds exactly those properties of the fetishistic process that Mulvey finds so significant (fetishism "builds up the physical beauty of the object, transforming it into something satisfying in itself"[8]): "Beauty and grace are Nancy Kerrigan's legacy. Perfect lines, testament to an artistic precision all her own. Radiant and sparkling, like the star on the ice she has become."

Commentators Verne Lundquist and Tracy Wilson prepare us in one more way for the artistic nature of the performances by noting what is "dramatically different" about the evening: Theatrical lighting can be used, as can vocals in the music (Kerrigan exploits both of these in her piece), and there are no rules—anything goes. This enables the performers to skate for themselves and the audience, rather than the judges, "making the ice a stage where their personalities, their signatures, can truly come through." And then, lest we forget the elevated purpose of the evening's spectacle (where phrases like "glimmering across a frozen canvas, the skaters create memorable works of art" with their "palettes" of "emotion, dance, delicacy and strength" abound) each commercial break is prefaced by a return to one mauve or forest green room of the gallery, where paintings, sculptures, flowers and fountains create both an ambience and an ideological equation of luxury, class, and "aesthetic" inspiration.

Kerrigan combines this inspiration with patriotism for her number, "A Golden Dream," and thereby makes herself not only a signifier of spectatorial desire (as all scopophilic objects are), but a symbol of nationalistic pride. She is introduced as "America's own," and as she assumes poses connoting aspiration, strength, triumphant accomplishment and power, her simple red costume maximizes the flow of her movements while red, white and blue lighting forms spectacular star-shaped spotlights across the ice. "America, spread your golden wings, sail on freedom's rim, cross the sky. Brave bird, with your golden dreams, flying high, flying high.... " In the midst of this musical exhortation ("You must keep dreaming now") and exultation ("Brave bird, keep your spirit free"), immediate and familiar quotes from John F. Kennedy, Martin Luther King, and the U.S. moon landing—fetishized bits of our national collective consciousness—remind ice skating fans of the seriousness of spectacle. Skaters not only represent Americans in competition, they can shape and inspire them through such stirring demonstrations of patriotism. Here, in fact, is the purest kind of total spectacle married to a blatant ideological function, with the message of heroic perseverance made available through the dual means of entertainment and high art.

But perhaps the most interesting thing about this performance is the way that it dramatizes the difference in the intensity and quality of the spectatorial look in that half of the Mulvey dichotomy that Nancy Kerrigan represents. While Harding's Olympic mini-melodrama was often punctuated with the commentators' self-aware foregrounding of vision ("Let's look in on Tonya to see how she's doing"), the very effectiveness of the fetishistic spectacle depends on *hiding* such referential reminders of the act of looking itself. In other words, with fetishistic scopophilia, the gaze of erotic contemplation—with its framing, distance, and compositional care—replaces the investigative look of sadistic voyeurism, driven as this latter is by the desire to know rather than to savor. As Kerrigan performs one statuesque turn after another, we never hear the self-reflective discourse on looking, for even when vision is invoked, it merely evaluates her grace and beauty on the ice ("She's been able to skate beautifully...."), without emphasizing that space from which she is seen. To call attention to the subjective *position* of looking itself would somehow break the spell, would drive a wedge in that "direct erotic rapport" between viewer and object that is the mainstay of fetishistic scopophilia. In order for Kerrigan to continue to evoke a "goddess in motion,"[9] an ethereal, impossible distance must be maintained, her glamorized image produced as if by magic, and the viewer's position obscured in that production.

Tonya and Nancy, story and image. This dichotomy of narrative and spectacle played out across the woman's body never fails to be produced in every version of the Olympic event and in every variation of its diffuse media legacies. Both accomplished athletes, coerced in some sense by the social processes that require women to take up the performance mode,

Harding and Kerrigan dramatize the opposing cultural constructions of the feminine prescribed by the logic of patriarchy. In the context of a struggle between identity and cultural meanings, we can never really know, much less understand, who these women actually are. But we can certainly establish the positions of the "feminine" dictated for each by the economy of masculine thought. Even in the world of commodity tie-ins, this signifying polarity prevails. Nancy gets a Barbie doll in her likeness (or so it is rumored), Tonya gets an action figure (the popular comic rejoinder). Nancy gets trading cards—each commodified image of her with its perfect photo on the front and moronically uninteresting text from "Nancy's Diary" on the back—while Tonya gets a "He Said/She Said" comic book— her version of events competing with ex-husband/accomplice Jeff Gillooly's tale on the flip side, pictures driven by text on every page.

But this is not exactly an equal division of options for, attributions of "visual culture" aside, the image part of the polarity has somehow faded next to the plethora of texts on the narrative side. We seldom catch a glimpse of Nancy these days (with the exception of her advertising chores), while Tonya's story continues to spawn new variants. Starting with the news promos that intersected "Artistry on Ice" (promising "a look into the private world of skating's bad girl" and delivering a story about how difficult it is to find Tonya after the scandal), to one network's summertime promo for the TV newsmagazine *Inside Edition* (which hawks interviews with Tonya Harding, Jeffrey Dahmer, and Reginald Denny along with the Menendez brothers and Rodney King to illustrate its ability to scoop the competition with their "inside stories" and "inside investigations"), and on to the seemingly endless features about Tonya's wedding striptease and her emerging mud-wrestling and action-film careers—the name of Tonya Harding continues to evoke volumes of story material. Her celebrity status is thus tied to the dubious aura of sex and violence surrounding her persona, rather than to athletic prowess on the ice. Any vestige of figure-skating performance has become irrelevant to Tonya's name, while Nancy, who has no story to tell (or to sell), remains in the background as an able skater and unlikely heroine.

A case in point is a *Rolling Stone* article, "Tonya Harding: The Fall" by Randall Sullivan,[10] an article which, for want of material, could never have been written about Nancy Kerrigan, much less used to promote magazine sales if it had been. As with most other accounts of Tonya's saga, the moments of her various skating performances are only details; the real interest lies in the roads leading up to and away from those moments. The public fascination with Tonya Harding's travails is here treated as one among several narrative threads, while the article interweaves account and assessment into a perceptive critique of contemporary tabloid culture. Toward this end, Tonya's "fall" is fertile terrain for an analysis of the ways in which that thin line between mainstream news and exploitation media has become blurred. For as much as Harding wants to define herself as "someone who came from the bottom and worked her way up to the top,"[11] the excessive interest in her many narratives is really about that flashpoint of "tabloidization" in television coverage that now systematically turns sordid anomalies into major journalistic events. It is in this context that the narrative bounty of Sullivan's article is best understood.

It makes compelling reading, this mostly straightforward account. Scrupulously researched and loaded with factual detail, its multilayered convolutions complement (rather than detract from) the driving teleology of Tonya's disgrace. There's the story of her fans, whose loyalty was born in the crucible of identification with her underdog status and hardscrabble life. There's the story of the conspirators, most of whom seem obsessed by a steady diet of confused fantasies of survivalism and action-hero exploits. There's the story of Tonya herself, who, despite abusive parents and abusive boyfriend/husband, demonstrates an indomitable will to excel in competitive sports. And of course, there are the stories embedded in the plotting of the attack itself, as Harding, Gillooly, and friends try out different scenarios for injuring Kerrigan, with Tonya herself suggesting embellishments that will serve to damage Kerrigan's reputation.

The convolutions and ramifications continue, with stories of the FBI investigation, the USOC decisions, the windfall for televised sports (with CBS reporting the highest Nielsen rating for any television show during the past eleven years), the media frenzy and so forth. One can even determine a number of genre film motifs in all of the Harding material: The attack itself is imagined as an action-adventure film, the pursuit of clues after the assault suggests a film noir detective thriller with its atmospheric alleyways and secret meetings, Tonya's relation with her mother suggests a maternal melodrama, the legal issues suggest a courtroom drama, not to mention the film sanctioned by Tonya's self-perception, the triumph of a plucky heroine over incredible obstacles. Thus while Nancy Kerrigan's essence can be summed up in a single shot (either performance or attack giving us all we need to know in the flash of an instant), Tonya Harding's persona both requires and promotes an endless stream of narrative texts.

But, finally, when all is said and done, nothing really lasts much beyond the instant it's evoked in a culture of the present moment such as ours. By the summer days of 1994, most of the winter dazzle of the Olympics had thawed. People nodded wearily as, one by one, the sentences for the Harding-Gillooly gang came down. The July *Rolling Stone*'s Tonya Harding article, safely encased in the preterite tense, read like a familiar catalogue of distant events. Nancy Kerrigan showed up in routine ice shows and a "Saturday Night Live" rerun, where her familiar poses and expressions were easily identified by rote. Here were two ice skaters, two women, who had been the focus of massive popular attention as they momentarily crystalized divergent cultural representations of the feminine, and yet, in less than a year, the public had tired equally of Tonya's story and Nancy's smile. Perhaps it was the excess narrative verbiage, the proliferation of stories, that had a sort of numbing effect with Tonya. Perhaps it was the overload of habitual forms that made Nancy's performances grow dreary. At any rate, one thing is certain. The public has gone on to a more accomodating tabloid spectacle, one in which the woman, as both gorgeous victim and stunning image, reaches her apotheosis—in silence.[12]

< NOTES >

1 Laura Mulvey, "Visual Pleasure and Narrative Cinema," *Screen* 16:3, Autumn 1975, pp. 13, n4.

2 "Visual Pleasure," p. 14.

3 "Visual Pleasure," p. 14.

4 "Visual Pleasure," p. 14.

5 "Visual Pleasure," p. 14.

6 "Visual Pleasure," p. 11.

7 "Visual Pleasure," p. 11.

8 "Visual Pleasure," p. 11.

9 *Time*, February 21, 1994.

10 *Rolling Stone* 686/7, July 14–28 1994, pp. 80–88, 113–18.

11 Interview with Rolonda Watts on "Rolonda!" May 1994, ABC.

12 The beautiful, blonde Nicole Brown Simpson was found brutally murdered in front of her home on June 12, 1994; her ex-husband, former football star and popular celebrity, O.J. Simpson, has been charged.

A Skater is Being Beaten

Why Doesn't Anyone Like Tonya? Beats Me!

When Tonya Harding went out to perform her long program in the women's figure skating competition for the 1994 Winter Olympics, on Friday February 25, she was already effectively beaten. In tenth place after the short program two days earlier, it was virtually impossible for her to win any medal, let alone the coveted gold. In this context, her performance extended and exacerbated the melodramatic tensions played out in the Tonya Harding/Nancy Kerrigan "soap opera" that captured media attention in the weeks preceding the Olympics.[1]

The details of her performance are hardly unfamiliar. Due to a broken bootlace, Tonya barely made it onto the ice within the time allotted after she was publicly announced. Less than a minute into her program, she popped out of her opening jump, burst into tears, and skated over to the judges to discuss her lace problem. They offered her a reskate, shuffling the order of the other skaters, and she ended the evening in eighth place. Tonya's opening fall and deliberations with the judges immediately assumed a prominent place in the evening's visual reportage. On the Chicago CBS affiliate, ad breaks promoting the nightly news broadcast following primetime Olympic coverage repeatedly, obsessively replayed the scene, ending with a freeze-frame on Tonya in full "cry-baby" splendor—one leg extended upwards, resting on the table in front of the judges to display the bootlace calamity, while her face collapsed with the teary disappointment of defeat already in place. This skater was indeed beaten.

The news promo promised to tell the full story later. In the meantime, viewers learned that Tonya left the ice barely 45 seconds into her program. Like a serial melodrama cliff-hanger, the scene culminating with the freeze-frame finish endlessly pretold of Tonya's failure even before the broadcast of the women's skating competition concluded. Of course, the discrepancy in time between Lillehammer and Chicago meant that the competition was in fact complete; the news people already knew the final outcome of the competition before it was shown on the official network coverage, even while they were repeating the clip of Tonya's interrupted performance. Indeed, they knew not only that Tonya's evening didn't end with her fall and "cry-baby" face, but also that she returned to the ice and performed sufficiently well to move up to eighth place. But the competitive narrative and its outcome were, for at least a time, less important than the image of Tonya's utter defeat.

Why was this image so compelling? How come it had to be repeated over and over again? What were the symbolic stakes in confronting viewers with this image of "cry-baby Tonya" throughout the course of the evening's Olympic coverage, including the final event of the women's figure skating competition? In many ways this one image captured a complex and contradictory network of narratives and attitudes surrounding Tonya Harding, Nancy Kerrigan, and figure skating more broadly. This image emerges as a paradigmatic moment in a larger drama, signalling that the event (of Tonya falling, and appealing to the judges for a reskate) was less important than the image of Tonya crying, implicitly defeated before either her routine or the competition was complete. From this perspective I want to unpack the image, reading across it in a number of ways. For it is my contention that this particular image not only crystalizes the idea of Tonya in defeat, but also contains the contradictions of the figure of Tonya Harding and what she came to stand for in the public eye. Even more generally, the image condenses a range of ideas and attitudes about women's figure skating that are rarely articulated all at once, but which inform and cut across much of the reporting.

Tonya cries in public, at the Olympics, having fallen before her program has barely even begun. The image can be read as a stark moment of punishment for, and perhaps even as the expression of guilt from, a skater who has been too cocky, too apparently unrepentant for the harm brought to bear on her biggest U.S. rival. It is unclear, even at this moment (that is, as she performed at the Olympics), how deeply she was involved in the attack on Nancy. But the prevalent tenor of reporting suggests she must have known more than she had said. And in any event, she has not been sufficiently public, loud, or insistent about her own regret over the incident, whether or not she was involved. In the aftermath of the attack on Kerrigan, Tonya says too little, and skates too much (at a public arena to boot). With that unstable conglomeration of built up guilt, stress, and regret it is no wonder she quickly slips on the ice; no doubt this behavior can be read as a kind of performed hysteria, symptomatically embodying whatever she has not verbalized. The broken bootlace, initially something of a metaphor for her own interior state, is quickly exteriorized in the fall and the explosion of tears. Freeze frame. This is at least one story to be read in the immobilized teary face.

There are other versions of Tonya as a beaten woman. These are less developed or substantiated, at least publicly, which makes them harder to discern. This is a bivalent representation, involving Tonya's relationship with her mother and her ex-husband. For Tonya, it is widely said, is an "abused" daughter and wife. Her mother's abuse is largely characterized as emotional (though stories of her hitting Tonya with a hairbrush circulate). For example, she is known for harsh carping about the weakness and problems in Tonya's skating routines, while ignoring her daughter's prominent positive achievements. Tonya's marriage is known to be stormy, and included at one point her taking out a restraining order against her husband Jeff Gillooly, and eventually obtaining a divorce. Yet even while the idea of abuse is associated with Tonya through these stories, it is not readily or fully accepted. The nature or degree of the abuse on both counts is challenged.

In this vein, a *Sports Illustrated* story reporting the details of the Kerrigan plot, as told by Shawn Eckert and Jeff Gillooly, disputes Tonya's claims to status as an abused wife, even while it characterizes the confessed conspirators as "goons and buffoons."

> "[Gillooly] reportedly was an abusive husband, but there is little hard evidence of this—no broken bones or black eyes—and Harding herself has been inconsistent on the subject. Though in the past she had been granted restraining orders against him, in her most recent interviews with the FBI, she says she was not abused by Gillooly."[2]

The clear implication is that abused wives are supposed to be pathetic, beaten individuals—with their bruises on display to confirm their pathos. At the same time, they are supposed to somehow know when and how to leave.

The narrative of Tonya's abuse, vague as it is, refuses to conform to the image of appropriate abjection our society commonly associates with abuse. In these terms, she has hardly behaved like an abused wife. In the wake of the attack on Nancy Kerrigan, and her own victory in Detroit, Tonya boldly and brazenly continues to hang out with ex-husband Gillooly, as the two of them proclaim their mutual innocence—at least until Gillooly tells "his side" of the story to the FBI. The question of whom to believe is in turn expressed in sources such as a *Time–CNN* poll: 54% of respondents found Gillooly's version of events, directly implicating Tonya in the attack on Kerrigan, more believable than Harding's. (In the same poll, 52% of respondents said Tonya should be expelled from the Olympic team, while 38% thought she should remain on the team.)[3] And these responses persist in the very midst of reporting that perpetuates the impression of Gillooly and the male co-conspirators as "goons and buffoons"; they nonetheless apparently remain more credible than Tonya.

References to her abuse, such as the one in *Sports Illustrated*, suggest that she had her chances to leave and willfully refused them, "proving" that she could not possibly really be abused in the first place, in which case she cannot be believed at all. This is further complicated by the stories of Tonya's involvement in the attack on Kerrigan. These cast her, implicitly, as an abuser herself, to the degree that she was involved in a woman's beating that did leave clearly visible bruises. At the same time, an array of former friends, including an ex-fiance, appeared on talk shows sharing tales of Tonya's volatile and abusive behavior in interpersonal relations: the time she threatened another driver with a baseball bat; her brash taunting of Gillooly when she arranged for a friend to buy her favorite pickup truck from Gillooly that he had kept from her during the official divorce settlement. In these and other stories, Tonya is not merely *not* an abused wife; she is cast in the role of abuser.

Similarly, although her childhood background is constantly implicitly problematized, especially with the repeated references to her mother's many husbands, the nature and extent of her mother's "abuse" remains equivocal. In these terms her mother is certainly domestically, sexually, and familially unstable, perhaps even something of a floozy. But abusive? The stories of her mother's dismissive and coldly critical responses to her competitive performances are diluted, via displacement, in Lillehammer.

For Tonya's problems on ice there are widely circulated failures which are repeatedly linked to the mindless support of her coach and choreographer. For example, *Sports Illustrated* reported:

> She never ran through even half of her program, either short or long. She was at her worst when her music was playing. In those rare moments when she did successfully complete a triple jump, her coach, Diane Rawlinson, a Stepford-wife grin plastered on her face, and her choreographer, Erika Bakacas, would applaud mindlessly, as if Harding were six years old.[4]

The coexistence of two narratives of response to Tonya's performances by those closest to her—mother's harsh criticism in the past versus Stepford-coach's mechanical applause in the present—opens up a space for comparative reading, with distinct implications for the alleged maternal abuse. Notably, events in Lillehammer recast the ways in which it is possible to understand the function of supportive and critical responses to skating performance. In the version cited above, which is not an isolated account, there is the clear implication that certain kinds of encouragement and support are for young children, not for mature competitive skaters. In light of Tonya's inability to perform successfully, there is even the implication that more honest, if harsher evaluation of her work—along the lines of her mother's so-called abuse—might be better for her than the "mindless" support she was shown by her Olympic contingent. This is subsequently confirmed by her poor showing in the competition. All of this at least allows the possibility that the mother was never really "abusive" at all, but a loving, if unstinting supporter of Tonya's competitive career.

Thus eliding the complex psychology of abuse, all these stories combine to imply that it cannot be true, and at the very least question the extent or degree to which Tonya's status as an abused woman can be taken seriously. This in turn becomes an (additional, supporting) instance of Tonya's lack of credibility. The stories of spouse abuse—nowhere confirmed with images of a beaten body—affirm the truth of Gillooly over Tonya. The stories of maternal abuse are ambivalent from the outset, since her mother is as often discussed as a strong, motivating supporter as she is an emotionally disheartening "abuser." In the end, it is never fully clear whether Tonya is an abused daughter or simply an ungrateful one.

This process of questioning the truth of the abuse stories, in implicit and explicit terms, is integrated into the more general questioning of Tonya's credibility, especially when it comes to her version of her role in the attack on Nancy Kerrigan. It indicates the extent to which mass opinion seems eager to derogate Tonya, as well as the unease and distrust that the very concept of abused women provokes in our culture. Indeed, there may be a structural or theoretical connection between these two positions. When Tonya cries—especially at a moment when she is so apparently, visibly defeated at the skating competition—she assumes the visage of abjection more conventionally associated with popular ideas of abuse victims. Not only a beaten skater, the frozen frame of her crying face holds forth the possibility of being read as the face of a beaten wife/daughter.

Tonya's tearful face seems at once to belie and confirm a set of identities that cut across her: guilty and innocent at the same time that she enacts a more "proper" response to the implications of her "abused" status. For whether she is guilty or innocent, the pressure *must* be too much; to cry in this very public setting expresses this. At the same time, the very meaning of the tears is open to equivocation. That is to say, tears can be seen as a genuinely expressive eruption or as a manufactured product of feminine wiles.[5] Both of these are identified with a female position; after all, big boys don't cry. But in one case the woman is so overcome by emotions that the tears emerge, even unbidden, as a sign of her excessive feelings, thus signifying an interior truth. In the other, the woman "turns on the tears" in a bid to win the emotional upper-hand because they will be (mis)taken for genuine feelings. Unsurprisingly, this puts the woman who cries in a lose-lose situation: she is liable to be seen as overly subject to her emotions (or out of control) on the one hand, and as manipulative and untrustworthy on the other. In either case she cannot be trusted. In this sense tears never lie, as long as they are associated with a female position, since they always bear testimony to a fundamental feminine inadequacy, especially when it comes to the possibilities of female expressivity.

Tonya Harding's situation in the wake of the attack on Nancy Kerrigan enacted this in full relief—nothing she said or did was not open to suspicion. The success of the image of her crying at the Olympics lies in its uncanny ability to contain and intersect all the Tonyas that circulated in the weeks preceding its appearance, at the same time that it unequivocally relegates her to a decidedly feminine position. In the process, the Tonya that doesn't get beaten one way ends up getting beaten in another, in one more version of the lose-lose proposition for women.

Fantasia: Hot Tears on Cold Ice

Tonya's Olympic tears are hardly her first, nor is she the only skater to cry. Indeed, it is quite startling when you start thinking about all the instances of crying skaters before, during, and after this competition. The first public instance in this particular crying game narrative occurs just before the U.S. National figure skating competition in Detroit. When Nancy Kerrigan is hit on the leg above the knee, she cries out. As reported in *Sports Illustrated,* "The videotape of the stricken Kerrigan tearfully screaming, 'Why me? Why now? Help me! Help me!' seconds after being smashed by a crowbar or blackjack—some sort of short, black weapon—will be the single, lasting image retained from these championships."[6] Despite the magazine's predictions fixing the iconography of crying for competitive skating, this image proved to be only the first moment in the ongoing circulation of tears, and beaten women, that permeated coverage of the Tonya/Nancy soap opera, and of the Olympic competition more generally.

Nancy and Tonya both cried publicly in the weeks following the attack on Kerrigan, usually in the course of formal television interviews. Later, at the Olympics, Nancy Kerrigan is quoted about her feelings attending events, watching her friends at a short-track speed skating event, unable to talk to them directly because security insisted she remain in a glass booth above the crowds: "I almost cried there."[7] Of course, the most persistently visible tearful skater on the ice was Oksana Baiul, the eventual gold medalist from the Ukraine, who cried after her long program was successfully completed, and during the awards ceremony, to say nothing of her tears during the often-repeated tape of her previous championship victories. Indeed, Kerrigan's silver-golden image began to visibly tarnish when the media repeated her crack about Baiul redoing her makeup for the Olympic awards ceremony; what was the point, since she was just going to cry again anyway? Unsurprisingly Nancy makes the remark only after she has been beaten, this time on the ice by Baiul (one wonders if she would have been so snide had Oksana been fixing her make-up to receive the silver medal, and Nancy the gold).

Beating. Crying. These become persistent motifs of women's skating in 1994, culminating with the Olympics. The wide circulation of stories around Tonya, condensed in the crybaby face, along with the circulation of crying among many individuals in the skating story, suggest that the meaning of the face and of skaters crying is not stable or fixed, either for participants in the events or for the viewers. The varying and mobile configurations of beaten and crying characters in these scenarios readily recall ideas about fantasy developed by Elizabeth Cowie in "Fantasia," following the work of Freud and Laplanche and Pontalis.[8] Cowie emphasizes the nature of fantasy in terms of staging, as the *mise-en-scène* of desire. "The scenario, the *mise-en-scène* of desire thus emerges for us not just in the story, but rather in its narrating: that series of images bound into the narrative structures, in the devices, delays, coincidences etc. that make up the narration of the story."[9]

The prototypical image of Tonya (as well as related images of Nancy) as a beaten/crying skater is an integral part of the narration of Olympic competitive coverage. It is also curiously integral to the delays of that event, since Tonya had to interrupt her performance; and her appeal to the judges led to shuffling the order of the skaters. It equally contributes to a larger narrative of coincidence, in Tonya's persistent "bad luck" on the ice, since this was not the first time in her career that she had problems with her skates or had to request a reskate.[10] During the Olympic competition commentators noted that there was "just something" about Tonya's whole career, as she seemed to have an inordinate degree of these sorts of incidents associated with her competitive performances. Once again, the implications are at least bivalent. On the one hand, discussion along these lines can be understood as expressions of sympathy for Tonya as she suffers excessive mishaps of this sort, although it is a sympathy that can only emerge once she has properly displayed her beaten status. On the other hand, it also has the capacity to imply that Tonya is somehow complicit in making her own "bad luck."

In this way the image of Tonya in tears almost literally enacts the workings of fantasy, at the same time that it functions as a condensed staging of multiple narratives that had been circulating since the attack on Kerrigan: "The subject is present or presented through the very form of organization, composition, of the scene."[11] Indeed, the freeze-frame of Tonya in tears may serve as something of a meta-fantasy, insofar as it holds these multiple narratives and stagings in balance (as it was repeated during promotions for the local Chicago nightly news, it also functions in these terms, as a narrational device to delay network coverage of the Olympics while holding out the promise of something yet to come, both in Olympic coverage and in the news to follow). Fantasy introduces a number of issues which are of interest in this context. First of all, it engages social, public, or conscious forms with preconscious and unconscious desires. In this sense it is, Cowie says, "a unique concept in psychoanalysis in referring to a psychic process which is both conscious and unconscious, and which juxtaposes the social and the psychic processes."[12]

Fantasy also involves mobility of subject positions, as delineated by Freud in "A Child is Being Beaten," in which he analyzes the common permutations of female fantasies of being beaten. These are routinely expressed in three phases, two of which are available to conscious elaboration, and one of which is a construction of the analytic process.

Kaja Silverman provides a cogent and concise summary, in the course of her analysis of male masochism:

> Here is the complete sequence, after it has been "doctored" by Freud (the phrases within square brackets represent either his interpolations, or additions made by the patient at his prompting):
> Phase 1: "My father is beating the child [whom I hate]."
> Phase 2: "I am being beaten by my father."
> Phase 3: "Some boys are being beaten. [I am probably looking on.]"[13]

In moving through these phases, the mobility of the fantasy refers to subject placement, as the subject is variously positioned as onlooker and participant in the scene; to sexual identity, through variable identification with masculine and feminine positions in the scene; and to libidinal investment, with shifts from sadism to masochism. Freud explains:

> The little girl's beating-phantasy goes through three phases, of which the first and third are consciously remembered, the middle one remaining unconscious. The two conscious phases appear to be sadistic, whereas the middle and unconscious one is undoubtedly of a masochistic nature; its content consists in being beaten by the father, and it carries with it the libidinal cathexis and the sense of guilt. In the first and third phantasies the child who is being beaten is always someone else; in the middle phase it is only the child itself; in the third phase it is almost invariably only boys who are being beaten.... Another fact, though its connection with the rest does not appear to be close, is that between the second and third phases the girls change their sex, for in the phantasies of the latter phase they turn into boys.[14]

By raising questions of fantasy and female masochism, Freud's essay resonates uncannily with the image of Tonya, as it condenses other narratives and their unfolding through *mise-en-scènes* in the form of public skating, crying, and beating performances, raising a range of questions: Who is being beaten, on and off the ice? What is at stake for viewers in these scenarios? Who watches whom? And what subject positions does all of this encourage or facilitate? As different skaters take up the position of skating, crying, and/or being beaten (which, as we have seen, are intimately connected), the mobility of subject positions and identifications for the participants in these scenarios helps configure spectators' relations to the events represented.

In this regard it is interesting to consider the extent to which the skaters were positioned as spectators for one another, whether and how they watched each other during practice sessions and during the formal competition. News stories discussed the fact that Nancy did not plan to watch Tonya's performance, and would probably not even be in the arena when she was skating; and there were shots on television of Tonya's unenthusiastic applause for Nancy's program. In relation to the understanding of fantasy and female masochism developed above, Nancy's inability or refusal to watch another beaten skater is among other things a strategy to avoid inadvertently finding herself in the scene. Of course, it is a position she already occupied, when she was attacked in Detroit. And in the end she also got beaten in Lillehammer, by another skater (a repetition of the previous winter Olympics, when she was beaten by Kristi Yamaguchi), who nonetheless cried more than she did. With her victorious outpouring of tears, Oksana Baiul also assumes the *mise-en-scène* more commonly and familiarly associated with beaten women. In other words, not only is Tonya not the only skater that cries, she is also not the only skater to get beaten.

In all these contexts, crying is the expression and release of the affective and psychic pressures of competitive skating in the form of hot tears on cold ice. As a quintessential expression, the teary face affectively encapsulates the *mise-en-scène* of figure skating, which is otherwise embodied in the performances discussed elsewhere in this volume. It also offers a more visible, emotive figuration of the very structure of the sport, wherein the pressure of the blade which propels the skater provisionally melts the ice, which ideally refreezes fairly quickly, leaving only a trace of the action. In this way, crying, beating, and skating are inextricably connected. The image of Tonya crying at the Olympics condenses the complex images and stories about her that circulate, but also link up with all other women skaters in an elaborate staging of a crying game on ice, with implications for psychic formations of female masochism. These associations may be cause for interrogating the fascination and interest of women's skating when it comes to admiring the sport and/or participating in it. For it seems that whether they win or lose in formal competition, women skaters are all too susceptible to being beaten.

< NOTES >

1 The term "soap opera" here is taken directly from *Sports Illustrated,* which was hardly the only media source to engage in this sort of labeling. Steve Rushin, "As the World Turns: Together Again, Tonya Harding and Nancy

Kerrigan Starred in Their Own Soap Opera," February 28, 1994, p. 32.

2 E. M. Swift, "Anatomy of a Plot," *Sports Illustrated*, February 14, 1994, p. 28.

3 Martha Duffy, "With Blades Drawn," *Time*, February 21, 1994, p. 52.

4 E. M. Swift, "Silver Belle: Nancy Kerrigan Conquered Her Demons but Couldn't Overcome a Pixie from Ukraine," *Sports Illustrated*, March 7, 1994, p. 20.

5 The ambivalence of tears, especially in relation to Tonya Harding, was suggested by Mary Desjardins.

6 E. M. Swift, "Violence: The Place was Detroit. The Victim Was Figure Skater Nancy Kerrigan. The Act was Another Bizarre Assault on an Athlete," *Sports Illustrated*, January 17, 1994, p. 16.

7 E. M. Swift, "Silver Belle", p. 20.

8 Elizabeth Cowie, "Fantasia," *m/f* no. 9 (1984), pp. 71–105; Sigmund Freud, "A Child is Being Beaten," in *Sexuality and the Psychology of Love,* ed. Philip Rieff (New York: Collier Books, 1963), pp. 97–122; J. Laplanche & J.-B. Pontalis, "Phantasy (or Fantasy)," in *The Language of Psychoanalysis,* trans. Donald Nicholson-Smith (New York: W.W. Norton, 1973), pp. 314–319.

9 Cowie, p. 92.

10 In a related vein, one of Cowie's key examples is the film *Now, Voyager.* In her analysis she explains how, through the course of the film, "The gesture of smoking thus accumulates a meaning of transgression and sexuality across the film, which is reorganized at the end to mark an asexual commitment which is nothing of the kind." (p. 92) I cite this in relation to another of Tonya's often noted transgressive behaviors: despite her asthma, and her athletic aspirations, she smokes!

11 Cowie, p. 80.

12 Cowie, p. 87.

13 Kaja Silverman, *Male Subjectivity at the Margins* (New York: Routledge, 1992), p. 201.

14 Freud, p. 114.

< Lynn Spigel

Cool Medium on Ice
Tonya, Nancy, and TV

Most TV stars are men, that is, "cool characters," while most movie stars are women, since they can be presented as "hot" characters.

—Marshall McLuhan[1]

"Heh-Heh—The only way this could be cooler is like if it was on TV—Heh-Heh"

—MTV's Beavis and Butt-head[2]

In 1964, media critic Marshall McLuhan called television a cool medium. According to McLuhan, who thought that all media had certain intrinsic values, television was essentially a medium of "low definition" participatory communication, and those who used it best would understand this from the start. Taking the 1960 presidential debates as a case in point, McLuhan argued that President Kennedy was the epitome of TV cool while Nixon's hot, too sharp image rendered him the quintessential phony politician and cost him the fight (and some even argue, the presidency itself). The way to compete on television, then, was by being as cool as the medium itself.

Obviously, back in 1964 McLuhan wasn't thinking about the 1994 Winter Olympics. For despite the frosty Norwegian winter, this holiday on ice was anything but cool—at least on TV. Instead, television, fanned by the flames of a host of tabloid papers, profited most from the hot tempers and fiery passions that engulfed the names of its two most famous skaters— Tonya Harding and Nancy Kerrigan. The Winter Olympics, as I heard numerous people say, seemed more like TV wrestling, daytime soaps, or a tabloid movie-of-the-week than a respectable Olympics event (and in this light it seems inevitable that Tonya was offered a wrestling gig in Japan several weeks after her infamous downfall). Perhaps it is no small coincidence that these analogies to soaps, wrestling, and scandal-based TV movies conjured up both "femininized" and "working-class" cultural forms rather then the detached, cool presidential debates of which McLuhan spoke. For at least in the way that television portrayed it, female and working-class competitors were anything but cool about the game. In fact, the only people who seemed to be using television as a cool medium were a variety of newscasters and talk show hosts—epitomized by David Letterman—who regularly sported a detached cynicism toward the whole event. In this regard, it seems especially fitting that when formulating his idea of the cool medium, McLuhan compared hot gossip to cool talk shows. Speaking of the original King of Late Night TV, McLuhan wrote, "Jack Paar ran a cool show for the cool TV medium, and became a rival for...the gossip columns. Jack's war with the gossip columnists was a weird example of the clash between a hot and cold medium."[3]

What interests me, however, is not whether McLuhan was right about TV being a cool medium. Obviously, he was wrong to assign essential properties to television. As numerous critics have suggested, television (or any other medium for that matter) is not essentially any one thing by nature. Instead, it is the product of social, economic, political, and cultural struggles; it is the product of the power hierarchies and tactical maneuvers through which people communicate more generally. In the U.S., television (at the most basic level) has been shaped in the image of large corporations, which have used it in a particular way—as a commercial medium—for their own gain. For this reason, rather than relegate the Winter Olympics to the cool atmosphere of television, I am more interested in why television chose to depict Tonya and Nancy in the hot way that it did. No doubt, its choice to represent these women through the melodramatic and/or sensationalist genres of wrestling, soaps, and tabloids had a good deal to do with larger cultural conceptions of female and working-class competition. Indeed, given that the idea of the cool medium was originally linked to John F. Kennedy, the ultimate American aristocrat and father of the nation, it seems obvious that coolness has been in some way associated with both class status and masculine prowess from the start.

But as opposed to our nation's coolest father, in the case of Tonya and Nancy, McLuhan's thermal metaphors of coolness and hotness were, in a quite overdetermined way, presented in relation to the maternal—and especially in relation to the subgenre of maternal melodrama.[4] The skating competition and the surrounding media hype consistently inscribed the athletes in stories about unresolved mother-daughter relationships. By extension, these "mini" maternal melodramas came to suggest that an unresolved mother-daughter relationship resulted in adult female relationships that were essentially pathological—riddled with jealousy, fear, victimization, abuse, and competitiveness—that is, all those qualities that made Tonya and Nancy into the winter's most talked about tale. Meanwhile, and in what I want to argue was a related gesture, Tonya and Nancy were presented as either too hot for the gold (overly competitive) or too cold toward their fans and fellow skaters; but in either case these female athletes were depicted as the antithesis of the "cool" male athlete so typically seen on our nation's TV screens.

As a genre, sports television has, of course, created some of the coolest heroes around. But as in the Kennedy-Nixon debates, the production of a "cool" hero depends upon representing his opposite—the hothead. In respectable sports, bad sportsmanship is penalized not only in the game, but also in spectacles that are staged for the cameras. The competitive game is here attached to the myth of success in American capitalism. Success is measured by the individual's superiority over the "common man," and failure is represented not simply by losing, but more specifically by being a "sore loser." Therefore, respectable sports, if only to represent success, must represent hotheads—people who not only lose, but who haven't properly internalized the rules of the game. These men are often represented as not only losing the game, but also losing their position in the representational economies of manhood. They are either not manly enough or else too manly. In the first case, we get humiliation rituals in which sore losers are publicly infantilized as the camera shows them like school boys, sent to the bench for bad behavior. In the second case, these men often become "excessive" signifiers of masculinity, as in the case of the "macho" Charles Barkley who is often depicted as a participant in a cock fight rather than a respectable hero of the NBA. To be sure, both the humiliation rituals and the cock fights must be considered as part of the pleasure of respectable sports if only because they occur in such conventionalized ways and with such regularity.

But in the "male" domain of respectable sports, these sore losers are the kinks in the system—momentary ruptures in the overall "cool" road to success. Conversely, in the 1994 Winter Olympics, the sore loser was the central heroine through which Americans learned about women's relation to the game: For most journalists (if not the American public) the story of the Winter Olympics was Tonya's story. Tonya was the central narrative vehicle for communicating tales of female competition. In a genre that fluctuates between sport and art, Tonya became the gym class tomboy and

Nancy the prima ballerina. In this scenario, Tonya took the position of the male sore loser in respectable sports; the tabloid press and TV coverage continually depicted her as both a humiliated schoolgirl and an overly agressive thug (although, in this case the media substituted a cat fight for a cock fight). In addition to occupying the sore loser position in the sports narrative, Tonya was also molded into a number of familiar stories about female rivalry and romance. Depending on the myth of choice, Tonya epitomized the Wicked Witch of the West, Cinderella's evil step-sister (or even Cinderella), the ugly duckling, Beauty and the Bitch, and (with her much publicized asthma) the coughing Camille. Through Tonya, the sports narrative was thus condensed with a whole set of storybook figures. This process of condensation made her into an ambivalent signifier of femininity—precisely the kind of cultural construct that is most conducive to the making of a tabloid celebrity. Tonya was representative of so many fractured fairy tales that the media could easily mix and match metaphors in infinite recombinations.

During the CBS coverage of the Winter games, Tonya continually lost her cool, but the press certainly remained cool toward her. The Winter Olympics, and many of the tabloid stories that circulated around them, were narrated from the point of view of hyper-cynical male coolness. The TV movie *Tonya and Nancy, The Inside Story* (NBC, May 1, 1994) is a perfect example of this narrative strategy. Although the publicity for the movie positioned it as a woman's film, the story, in fact, is not Tonya's or Nancy's. Instead, the movie is constructed as a self-reflexive tale narrated from the point of view of a cynical male TV writer. In the opening segment, the writer looks into the camera and tells us that the story of Tonya and Nancy is like a "fairy-tale." His recounting of the tale then intitiates a flashback to the skaters' childhoods. Having established himself as the story's author, the writer later is shown participating in a network story conference during which we learn of NBC's aggressive attempts to exploit the Tonya/Nancy fight as a movie-of-the-week. At the end of the movie, this fictional writer looks philosophically into the camera and concludes, "Tonya and Nancy—we deified one, we demonized the other, and we imprisoned them both in images that we use to sell soup, and newspapers, and Olympic games, and TV movies." In this framing device, the fictional TV writer takes the place of television (and television criticism) itself; he literally becomes a cool medium through which the melodramatic story of a hothead woman is communicated. Moreover, the framing device sets us up as cool spectators by distancing us from any emotional attachment to the story. Throughout the film, spectator identification with the woman's point of view (whether Tonya's or Nancy's) is further distanced as a series of "real-seeming" testimonials by fictional characters (including Tonya's parents, aging ice skaters, sports fans, sixties activists, TV producers, and more) interspersed with the fiction so that it becomes impossible to identify too closely with the story. The movie in this sense is a kind of anti-melodrama melodrama which, in the most cynical terms imaginable, cashes in on the public appetite for scandal while at the same time uses conventions of tabloid journalism to present itself as hipper than the "woman's" genre it seeks to exploit.

However, within the frame of this "cool" masculine detached address, the TV movie is notable for its "inside story" that presents a melodramatic tale of female hotheads. Perhaps not surprisingly, the cynical tone of the male TV writer is here exchanged for mythic tropes of the Cinderella story in which femininity is pathologized through the figure of the evil mother. In the early scenes, the movie presents Tonya as a little girl skating on the ice as her backstage mother berates her for her laziness and clumsiness. It juxtaposes these scenes with images of little swanlike Nancy and her father, who nurtures his fledgling in the most supportive of ways. Later in the film, when Tonya's father announces his plans to leave home, the picture is complete: Tonya is an "ice bitch" because she has been raised by an evil mother and ineffectual father. Compounded with this are the surrogate mother figures that Tonya finds in her female coaches, figures who never seem powerful enough to provide an alternative female support network for the young skater. These women allow Tonya's mother to abuse her, and thus by association they are also evil mothers. Consequently, as the narrative would have it, Tonya grows up into a classic battered woman who chooses a string of male partners who are themselves stand-ins for her abusive mother. Her wife-beating husband Jeff, and the pathologized fat-boy thugs that plot Nancy's attack, become an ambiguous mix of surrogate mother and female replicant: their loss of humanity is associated with their reproduction of Mrs. Harding's pathological mothering. In this case, then, the reproduction of mothering turns into a tale of twisted sisters with twisted laces, but no unexpected plot twists. This is a familiar story of bad women raised by bad mothers, but what stands out is its insipid repetition across a number of television (as well as print media) genres.

Even the news/sports genre of the Winter Olympics was communicated through an excess of parents—especially mothers. Throughout the skating competition, the saga of parenting, and motherhood in particular, became the back story of the athlete's routine. During the Ladies' Technical Program, for example, Germany's Katarina Witt's moment on the ice was framed by a narrative in which parenting and nationhood were intertwined; the sportscasters told viewers that this was the first time that Katarina's East German parents (here presented as victims of East Germany's now fallen communist regime) were allowed to see her compete for the gold. According to sportscasters Verne Lundquist and Scott Hamilton, Katarina wasn't even concerned with winning a medal; instead she used this world stage to put on a show for her parents. France's Surya Bonaly was described as "the adopted daughter of Susana George Bonaly, her ever present mother" whom the camera showed waiting in the wings. And Nancy's legally blind mother cheered from the bleachers, the pathos of her situation underscored by the sportscaster who assured us that "she can sense beauty."

Given this excess of mother figures, it came as no small irony that gold-medalist Oksana Baiul was an orphan. The CBS coverage introduced her technical program with a gripping melodramatic tale of her sad fate. The story begins with scenes from her contemporary teenage life followed by a flashback to her childhood that is introduced by black and white photographs. As sportscaster Verne Lundquist informs us, this is the story of "how much [Oksana] has gained and how much she has lost in this young life." Oksana, we are told, never saw her father and, by the age of 13, her grandmother and mother were dead. She was then embraced by female skating coach Galina Zmievskaya and "became not merely a student but a member of Galina's family." The sportscaster goes on to inform us that Oksana "still has a key to the home where she lived with her mother," but when he asked Oksana to take him there, she "would not show us that place." Just like a heroine of a classic women's weepie, Oksana holds a key to a mysterious dark continent of femininity that is bound up with the trauma of maternal abandonment. To underscore the sense of loss and emptiness that motivates this uncanny tale, the segment ends by telling us, "You have to remember that this 16-year-old, who could be everyone's daughter, in fact is no one's." This statement at once invites us to imagine ourselves as Oksana's surrogate moms, at the same time insisting that, despite Nancy Chodorow's classic formulation, motherhood can never be "reproduced," no matter how hard we try. Mothers and daughters (and for that matter female bonding of any nurturing kind) are forever ripped apart, and in their place lies locked secrets, mourning, melancholia, and the irrevocable loss of a maternal love object—all of which adds up to a pathological explanation for the female skater's desire to compete with other women. For according to the logic of this story, the woman's urge to compete is not the outcome of "normal" female development, but instead tied to an inability to properly separate from one's mother (that is, to overcome separation anxiety).[5] The segment ends with Oksana sitting on the beach, looking out into the emptiness of the expansive ocean. Here, in extreme close-up, she loses complete control of her emotions as she weeps for her dead mother, saying "I feel my mother is with me all the time. That she's still crossing my path. And I feel that if she were alive today she would be as happy for me as I am." After this literal outpouring of female mourning for the maternal, we cut to the arena where Oksana appears poised and ready for the competition. The cut implicitly compares her controlled athletic stance to her uncontrolled emotional breakdown in the framing story. Female competition and mastery over the body is presented not as an end in itself but as a consolation prize for a childhood trauma.[6]

What is particularly interesting in the case of Oksana is that the narrative logic of this story reverses the Tonya Harding saga, but ultimately arrives at the same end-point. In Tonya's case, the evil abusive mother became pop psychology's reigning explanation for her urge to compete (and her alleged assault on Nancy). But in Oksana's Olympics narrative, the terms became somewhat twisted. Now all female competition is traced to the mother-daughter relation (whether that mother be good as in Oksana's case or evil as in Tonya's). In this scenario, a woman's urge to compete is never "normal," but is instead traced back to either too much or too little love for one's mother. Excessive relational bonds with the mother (whether good or bad) cause the woman to compete as a *compensatory act*—not as a "normal" form of female behavior. And, once more, women's sportsmanship is rendered antithetical to cool male reserve and emotional detachment. Instead, it is presented in terms of melodramatic excess: of too much passion, too much emotion, too much desire, especially desire for the mother.

But, in fact, there is one more mother in the mix, a mother who was not packaged through the melodramatic imagination, but rather used in the service of a cool medium. I am referring, of course, to David Letterman's mother, or as she was more typically called, "Dave's mom." TV's ultimate cool hero, Dave understood the significance of mothers from the start, sending his own mother to Lillehammer, Norway for nightly reports on the Winter Olympics.[7] For Dave, motherhood became a foil for his own masculine distance from the passionate "feminized" affect of melodrama and scandal. Making fun of mom—mom as the butt of the cool medium's joke—was the late night twist on the Olympic's melodramatic mother overload.

In the end, the case of the Winter Olympics opens up some more general questions about television's representational regime, especially when it comes to the gendered implications of the cool medium. Is it possible for a woman to be cool on TV? Or is coolness just for the boys? For her part, Nancy Kerrigan tried to keep her cool, denying reporters a full inside story, and resisting her place in the passionate cat fight promoted by the news media. But, Nancy's attempts to be cool were transformed by television into coldness. For despite her working-class origins and average American lifestyle, television turned Nancy into the quintessential ice princess. Nancy even hated Mickey Mouse which, as the TV news continually suggested, was the ultimate proof of her haughty soullessness.

Nancy's cold demeanor was further captured in her markedly stiff performance on *Saturday Night Live* (NBC, March 12, 1994), where she appeared as host to musical guest Aretha Franklin. This unlikely pairing of Queen of Soul and Ice Princess produced a binary opposition that served as the program's racial unconscious. As Richard Dyer has argued, the idea of whiteness (and its connotations of civilization) is dependent upon the desire for its opposite.[8] Whiteness is constituted through its implicit opposition to a more natural state of life (often represented as sensuousness, spirituality, and untamed sexuality), which is in turn typically displaced onto black bodies. In this case, Aretha and Nancy served to mutually reproduce each other as stereotypes of black female sexuality and white female frigidity—a situation that was underscored by the juxtaposition of Aretha's Gospel-blues rendition of "Chain of Fools," which she performed in a low-cut red dress, and Nancy's earlier appearance as Snow White in a parody of her "corny" adventures in Disneyland.

These implicit racial stereotypes become more explicit in a sketch where Kerrigan plays an American exchange student in Mexico. The sketch opens with three men sitting at a table in a Mexican restaurant where exchange student Stacey (played by Kerrigan) has a job as a part-time waitress. The gag in this sketch revolves around one of the men, Don Mateo, whose passionate "macho" ways lead him to the mistaken conclusion that Kerrigan has the hots for him. "There she is," Mateo tells his buddies in a mock Fernando Lamas accent, "the hot-blooded señorita. She has a fiery temper. Her blood runs hot like the lava in a volcano and if you get too close—zzzzzzz—you get burned." The joke, of course, is that Kerrigan/Stacey is the opposite of a red-hot Mexican mama. She is the cold-blooded, midwestern white virgin. In fact, she is the stereotype of the typical Miss America contestant, "a junior at the University of Wisconsin majoring in communication."[9]

To be sure, Nancy and Aretha are not the only victims of the cool medium's temperament toward cool women. There are other instances of hip females who melt in the TV spotlight or freeze on the studio stage. Roseanne, Cher, and Madonna are just a few recent examples. These women may have a certain "cool" cache, but they are engulfed by the hot flames of melodrama and scandal, replete with images of cat fights, evil mothers, and abusive mates.

Still, these scandalous women can sometimes disrupt television's cool breeze. A perfect example is Madonna's infamous appearance on *Late Show with David Letterman* (CBS, March 31, 1994).[10] Just about a month after Dave's Lillehammer jokes had run their course, Madonna graced his stage in her new line of designer fashions, and she proceeded to curse so fluently that the beepers had trouble keeping up. Her performance was for some reason so newsworthy that journalists and Letterman himself compulsively remarked on its catastrophic dimensions. Would Madonna be invited back? Would Dave ever forgive her? These were things inquiring minds wanted to know.

But why was Madonna so scandalous on Letterman? Certainly not because she cursed. After all, just a month before, rock star Bono of U2 said the "F" word on the Grammys which, unlike *Letterman,* was broadcast live and thus not subject to the censor's beeper (at least the East Coast states were receiving live transmission). Instead, I think, Madonna was scandalous because she made Dave lose his cool. Wincing (albeit mockingly wincing) at her excessive cursing and infantile toilet bowl humor, Dave looked "squarely" into her eyes and said, "This is American television. You can't be talking like that.... People don't want that in their homes at 11:30 at night." For her part, Madonna knew exactly how to get Dave steamed. In a teasing voice she told him, "You've changed since the last time I was on the show...you used to be really, kind of like, cool."

But Dave wasn't about to let Madonna get him hot under the collar, nor was he about to let the tabloid press embroil him in the steamy scandal and fiery tempers that Madonna ignited on his show. To recuperate his image, the next night Dave made sure to distance himself from the whole affair with the proper degree of cynicism and cool male wit. Recalling his initial reaction to Madonna's dirty deed the night before, he confessed, "The first thing that came to mind—remember the Olympics, the Winter Olympics? My Mom was on this show every night...she was able to hear every word of every show that she participated in, and [last night when Madonna was on] I got nervous for a second, I thought, Oh my God, what if Mom is listening." Then, he delivered his classic blank punch line,

claiming that his momentary case of juvenile jitters was "a completely unrealistic fear—because you know there's not a chance in hell Mom watches now that she's off the payroll." So in the end Dave restored his place as Late Night King of the cool medium by telling one more joke at mom's expense.

< NOTES >

1 Marshall McLuhan, *Understanding Media: The Extensions of Man.* (1964; New York: Mcgraw Hill, 1965), p. 318.

2 *MTV's Beavis and Butt-head,* Marvel Comics, 1:1 (March 1994), p. 20.

3 McLuhan, p. 29. It should be noted that while I'm obivously playing with the metaphor of the cool medium, McLuhan himelf often played with the term, sometimes using it technically to refer to certain modes of address and other attributes of the media apparatus, while at other times using "cool" in the more colloquial meaning of "hip." In the quote on Paar we already see this slippage.

4 In using the term melodrama, I want to point out that there is a long debate about the existence of this genre on television and its relation to theatrical, literary and film melodrama. Although I am not going to enter this debate here, I use this term mostly to signify television's particular adaptation and ciruculation of the melodramatic form, which is, I will simply state, different from its appearance in other media and at other historical moments. Television melodrama, as I use the term, implies a sense of excessive emotion and also (although differently from cinema) stylistic excess. It also implies an emphasis on the "feminine" (but not necessarily women's) topics of family, domesticity, and personal relationships. Its class and racial dimensions, however, are more difficult to pinpoint as "white" or "bourgeois," even while it often revolves around both of these and addresses the viewer in these terms.

5 With regard to separation anxiety, I am making an argument about the narrative logic of this story more than I am suggesting explanations for all female psychology. Indeed, in terms of female psychology, it might well be argued that an inability to separate from the mother would undermine rather than foster competiveness in women. However, the Olympics narrative simply had it both ways. As I argue in the text, women's competitiveness is traced to excessive relational bonds with the mother (whether good or bad) and is thus depicted as a *compensatory act*—not as "normal" female form of behavior.

6 Later, after her gold medal performance in the final free skate competition, Verne Lundquist once more cast Oksana as the heroine of a maternal melodrama, reminding viewers of her tramautic past. As the camera focused

on the sobbing Oksana in the arms of Galina Zmievskaya, Lundquist remarked, "At this point in the evening Galina Zmievskaya is much more the loving surrogate mom than she is the critical coach."

7　Next to Letterman's two first CBS broadcasts in August 1993, seven of the shows aired during the Olympic Games received the highest ratings. See *Los Angeles Times,* 2 April 1994: F 4.

8　Richard Dyer, "White," *Screen* 29:4 (Autumn 1988): 44–65.

9　It should be noted here that conventions of beauty pageantry were used throughout the Olympics Ladies' skating competition. Their status as national/female spectacles was most apparent in a montage after the Ladies' Technical Program competition in which the clips from the skating routines were edited together to the tune of Frank Sinatra's "Just the Way You Look Tonight."

10　Madonna was exceeded in the *Letterman* ratings only by the first two August 1993 CBS broadcasts and the seven broadcasts aired during the Olympics. In the 30 cities for which ratings were available, the program scored 24%, making it the 10th best rating Letterman has ever received. See *Los Angeles Times,* 4 April 1994: F 4.

13

< Jill Dianne Swenson

Narrative, Gender, and TV News
Comparing Network and Tabloid Stories

In a Times Mirror poll from February 1994, 45% of respondents report paying "very close" attention to the Tonya Harding/ Nancy Kerrigan news reports during the first month of the scandal: the poll reveals that in American minds Skategate eclipsed health care reform, the economy, and President Clinton's first State of the Union address. While this story was reported by a variety of news venues, probably most people followed it on television. As the story spread like wildfire from the tabloids to the nightly network news, grumbling about the "tabloidization" of American journalism could be heard again.

Tabloid television is either dismissed entirely, or denigrated as trashy, sleazy, trivial, gossipy, rumor-filled, and scandal-mongering. These same terms are often used to marginalize and discredit women. The Harding/ Kerrigan story, with its mass penetration of American audiences, thus seems a fruitful one with which to interrogate the distinctions between "hard" and "soft" news, "masculine" and "feminine" news.

Between January and March 1994, NBC and ABC each aired three stories on Harding/Kerrigan during the nightly newscast, while CBS aired four stories. In the same two months of January and February 1994, the tabloid programs of *American Journal* and *A Current Affair* broadcast twenty-one and nineteen stories respectively. These nightly news reports are distinct from the many other network television programs that provided coverage to Harding/Kerrigan across various genres—morning news and magazine shows, specials, sports, interviews, and talk TV. According to the Tyndall Report Tonya/Nancy got 263 minutes of network time clocked over this two month period. This beats out the fall of the Berlin Wall which only received 252 minutes of network time at the peak of coverage on the crumbling of communism.

What kinds of stories were told about Tonya and Nancy in this television coverage? What questions were addressed? What sources were interviewed? Certainly there are generic differences between tabloid shows and nightly network news: tabloids typically have longer reports and more narrative complexity than does an average 90 second story on network news; tabloids also employ more music and re-creations. But I am going to focus here on how tabloids differ from network news in the most fundamental journalistic practices: asking questions, finding sources to answer those questions, and constructing compelling news stories from the material those investigations yield. This essay will examine only the half-hour evening broadcasts of the nightly network news, *American Journal*, selected because it is the longest running tabloid, and *A Current Affair*, because it is the latest to appear on the television landscape.

The engendering of news narratives begins with the distinctions drawn between hard and soft news. The study, practice, and history of journalism in the United States revolves around this dichotomy between hard and soft news in both content and form. Network news is characterized as "hard," important, serious, objective, authoritative, investigative, informative and factual while "soft" news is entertaining powder-puff journalism. Scholars differentiate between "important" and "interesting" news, separate "news" from "human interest" stories, and claim hard news emphasizes information while "soft" news/features are merely stories. The line drawn between the two

blinds us to the way narrative devices are used in all news writing, maintaining the illusion that the structural devices used in hard news are merely neutral techniques that act as a conduit for events to become information, rather than ways in which a particular kind of narrative text is created.[1]

The line between hard and soft news is one which no respectable network journalist should cross. This line, like the one between advertising and editorial content, is one that seems to shift over time and is regularly redrawn. Appearances of network news personalities on *Saturday Night Live*, *Murphy Brown*, *Donahue*, *The Tonight Show*, MTV, commercials for coffee and telecommunications, etc., serve as historical markers of cultural redefinitions of this line.

Telling stories is what journalists routinely do for a living. Yet when journalists tell better stories they suffer professional angst over crossing the line between hard and soft news. The more objectively journalists write, the less likely they will cross that line but the more likely they will lose their audience. Telling stories of individual refugees from Rwanda, Bosnia, or Haiti, or broadcasting news about the personal impact of GATT or NAFTA seem impossible to do without slipping so easily into the subjective.

Network news pledges adherence to the ideals of objective journalism. The myth of objectivity in American journalism has been well-documented. Yet, objectivity remains the central construct used to differentiate hard from soft news. Objectivity serves the illusion that "'hard" news narrative structures are neutral rather than ideologically engendered.

> Objectivity in journalism denotes a set of rhetorical devices and procedures used in composing a news story. Objectivity, in this sense, has no bearing whatsoever on the truthfulness or validity of a story. Nor does it mean that the story is free of interpretation or bias.[2]

The standard technique for objective journalism is to ask rhetorical questions which can be addressed by authoritative sources. The sources to whom a journalist talks on the record determine the substance and sensibility of any news story. Sources provide the narrative conflict and controversy.

So, who are these sources and what is the basis of their authority? Journalists look to sources whose authority is based on 1) knowledge, 2) experience, and/or 3) office. The authority of a source is not determined by gender or genitalia, yet studies consistently demonstrate the overwhelming majority of sources on "hard" news broadcasts are white males. According to the sixth annual "Women, Men and Media" survey, of the people interviewed on network nightly news during February 1994 at the height of the Harding/Kerrigan hype, 76 percent were men. Of the network news stories included in this analysis, 63 percent of the sources used to report the Harding/Kerrigan story were men and 37 percent were women. In contrast, 64 percent of sources appearing in tabloid stories about Tonya and Nancy were female and 36 percent were male.

By comparing the sources used in reports about Tonya Harding/Nancy Kerrigan, the differences between network news and tabloid coverage can be empirically established. Network news relies largely upon sources whose authority primarily resides in their position, role, or office. These sources tend to be "knowns." Herbert Gans documented the reliance of mainstream national news media on "known" over "unknown" sources in news stories.[3] Gans' analysis does not, however, directly address the issue of how an unknown becomes a known. The conferral of this status derives largely from one's office or elected position; however, it may also result from appearing in the news. And who does the media deem worthy of such appearances? Predominantly white men.

Networks suffer from the so-called Golden Rolodex Syndrome: sources frequently used because journalists frequently use them. While these sources may be experts or officials, they no doubt derive some of their authority from their relationships to journalists. Tabloids use sources who derive their authority from their own experience, first-hand knowledge, and relationships to those in the news events instead of connections to those covering the news.

In the stories about Tonya/Nancy, a small circle of sources were common to both network and tabloid stories. This short list of primary characters included Tonya Harding, Jeff Gillooly, LaVona Golden (Tonya's mother), Al Harding, Diane Rawlinson (Tonya's coach), Nancy Kerrigan, her parents, Paul Wylie (Nancy's skating partner and coach), other Olympic skaters, and members of the US Olympic Committee. These sources appeared in network news stories primarily in videoclips shot at press conferences, court appearances and public exhibitions rather than in one-on-one interviews with journalists as they did in tabloid reports.

Only CBS's Connie Chung interviewed Tonya Harding and Nancy Kerrigan eye-to-eye. CBS used footage in the network's newscasts of these interviews largely to promote upcoming *Eye to Eye* segments on the skaters and CBS's exclusive coverage of the Olympics. CBS realized it could cash in on "The Battle of Wounded Knee" and, after some initial sluggishness, finally beefed up its coverage with Connie Chung playing a significant newsmaking role. Assigning this story to the female coanchor is interesting to note. When Connie Chung came on board as co-anchor of the *CBS Nightly News*, Dan Rather gave her a rather public kiss. Later he publicly lamented the demise of broadcast news into mere "powder puff" journalism.

The networks had very few sources the tabloids didn't also use. CBS's and NBC's nightly news reported public opinion poll results on whether

Table 1

Sources Used by Network News and Tabloid Stories

Inner Circle Sources **(sources used by network and tabloid news stories)**

Tonya Harding
Nancy Kerrigan
Jeff Gillooly (Tonya's former husband)
LaVona Golden (Tonya's mother)
Al Harding (Tonya's father)
Diane Rawlinson (Tonya's coach)
Paul Wylie (Nancy's coach and skating partner)
Mr. and Mrs. Kerrigan (Nancy's parents)
Kristi Yamaguchi (former Olympic skater)
Scott Davis (Olympic skater)
U.S. Olympic Committee members

Network News Sources **(sources not included in list of "inner circle sources"**
networks used that tabloids did not)

public opinion polls (commissioned by news organization)
Ed Jones (Tonya's lawyer)
Olympic Athletes' Attorney

Tabloid Sources **(sources used by** *American Journal* **and/or** *A Current*
Affair **that go beyond the list of inner circle sources and not utilized by**
network news)

Stephanie Weber Quintero (Tonya's best friend)
John Quintero (Stephanie's husband and Tonya's friend)
David and Ruth Weber (Tonya's surrogate parents)
Tom and Maggie Dexal (apartment managers of building where
    Quinteros and Tonya Harding resided; Dexals rented apt. next
    door to ABC News)
Bea Owens (neighbor of Quinteros/Tonya)
Wendy Gould (friend of Tonya's)
Allen (Tonya's former next door neighbor)
Debbie Addison (Tonya's cousin)
David Miller (Tonya's new male friend)

(continued)

(Table 1 continued)

Diane Poynter (David Miller's jealous fiancé)
Mike Pliska (Tonya's former fiancé)
Bill Chase (Nancy's former fiancé)
Jerry Solomon (Nancy's manager and contract negotiator)
Vera Wang (Nancy's costume designer)
Cindy Winn (Tonya's costume designer)
Winn's team of seamstresses (all white females)
Erika Bakacs (Tonya's choreographer)
Alan Zell (former fundraiser for Tonya)
Kathy Peterson, owner of Dockside (Portland restaurant where napkin was found in dumpster)
Mark Hyde, Beaverton Police Dept.
Las Vegas oddsmaker (unnamed white male)
Norwegian military/police officer (unnamed white male)
Eyewitness to attack on Nancy Kerrigan (unnamed African American male)
Portland District Attorney (unnamed white male)
Claire Ferguson, Pres., US Figure Skating Association
Video analyst (unnamed white male)
Handwriting expert (unnamed white female)
Panel of 8 expert skating judges (white males and females)
Henry Raider (sports psychologist)
Dr. Jonathan Katz (sports psychologist)
Dr. Eric Morgenau (sports psychologist)
Tiffany Crosswhite (competitive skater)
Domeniza Palandro (competitive skater)
June Scarpa (manager of Stoneham, MA ice rink)
Cindy Petrasso (sports producer)
Richard Sandemeier (New York Times sports writer)
Adam Gutman (New York Post editor)
Philip Bondy (author)
Frank Coffee (author)
News photographer (unnamed white male)
News cameraman (unnamed white male)

Tonya should be allowed to skate for the U.S. at the Olympics. NBC talked to Tonya Harding's lawyer, and ABC interviewed an attorney for Olympic athletes. In contrast, *American Journal* and *A Current Affair* used a wide variety of sources (See Table 1).

Tonya Harding's and Nancy Kerrigan's family and close friends, neighbors, fans, and persons intimately involved with preparing the skaters for competition, were primary sources for tabloid stories. These individuals prior to Skategate were largely unknown to American mass audiences. Sources' authority was based on experience, relationship ties, and/or direct knowledge of the events unfolding around Tonya and Nancy. Tabloids also utilized many unnamed/untitled/unknown sources—predominantly white females.[4] These "unknowns" were interviewed on the sidewalks of streets in New York and Lillehammer, at skating rinks and malls in Massachusetts and Oregon, in queue for tickets at the Olympic village, and watching the skating competition on television in a Portland sports bar. These unknowns were provided opportunities to speak in their own voices by the tabloids—a rare opportunity afforded few unknown sources on network news.

The tabloids included some experts and officials but these sources were utilized for their knowledge and experience rather than the authority of their offices. Tabloids used a number of experts who remained unnamed: a video analyst, a handwriting expert, a Las Vegas oddsmaker, an independent panel of skating judges, and the Portland District Attorney. The tabloids also aired interviews with sports psychologists, President Claire Ferguson of the United States Figure Skating Federation, and United States and International Olympic Committee members. The tabloids' use of some of the same experts and officials can be differentiated from the networks' largely by the kinds of questions asked. The tabloids used some of the same official sources as the networks, but the reporters posed different kinds of questions and, in turn, these sources provided different kinds of information. The tabloids provided less elite-centered coverage that opened up discourse to more participants while addressing a wider array of questions.

By comparing the kinds of questions addressed in network and tabloid stories we can see these differences in journalistic praxis highlighted. The stories told on *American Journal* and *A Current Affair* about Tonya Harding and Nancy Kerrigan answer more HOW and WHY questions than do the networks. The network questions reveal a focus on authority and official procedures. Legal questions rather than moral inquiries predominate the line of network questioning. Lies, conspiracies, coverups—the networks constructed news stories in familiar post-Watergate formulas. Stories tend to be about political processes, grand jury indictments, FBI investigations, official proceedings and hearings. These stock-in-trade narrative forms follow the mainstream practices of professionalized objectivity achieved through the journalistic representation of two opposing sides to a story.

Analyzing the range and nature of questions addressed in tabloid stories suggests a strong contrast to the networks' coverage. WHO questions are asked and answered in terms of personality traits, beliefs, attitudes, behaviors, and life experiences. There is much more character development in tabloid stories. A subset of WHO questions focuses on interpersonal relations and the mitigating circumstances and context they provide. WHERE, WHEN and WHAT questions are answered insofar as they are relevant to HOW and WHY questions.

Why questions are generally answered in tabloid stories by invoking matters of the heart. Character motivations—jealousy, greed, anger, love, retribution, spite, unbridled ambition—are central to finding answers to WHY. The answers to why stem largely from questions about who. The tabloids raised issues about dysfunctional families and domestic violence in their search for answers to WHY questions.

Tabloid stories focused on finding an answer to Nancy Kerrigan's question when she fell screaming to the floor of the ice arena clutching her knee: "Why? Why? Why?" Network news stories were more concerned with "What did Tonya know and when did she know it?" Replace Tonya's name with Nixon's or Reagan's and we can begin to understand the limitations of network narratives. The American public never got to the bottom of Watergate and got sick of hearing about Iran-Contra. In Watergate, the heroes were Woodward and Bernstein embodying the free press as protagonist. The players had little character development and the stories focused on procedural matters and the unspeakable: impeachment. In Iran-Contra, the renegades and circumventors of the constitution (Reagan, Bush, Poindexter, Ollie North) were cast in protagonist roles. And much of the audience cast the news media as an antagonist.

Both network and tabloid news about Tonya and Nancy posed stories in antagonist-protagonist structures. Two stock characters common to both network and tabloid news stories are victim and villain(ess). It is interesting to note the overwhelming majority of stories answered questions about Tonya Harding, not Nancy Kerrigan. In many respects Tonya was both victim and villainess in tabloid stories, but cast only as villainess in network accounts. The tabloids and networks virtually dropped coverage of Nancy Kerrigan once she refused to play the victim role. Stories that ascertain

Table 2
Question Analysis

Questions raised by *network* news stories
What did Tonya know and when did she know it?
Was there a conspiracy to attack Nancy Kerrigan?
How was the attack on Nancy Kerrigan arranged?
Was Tonya Harding involved in the conspiracy?
Was there a coverup of the conspiracy?
Did Tonya Harding break any laws or official rules?
Will this scandal help or hurt Tonya's financial future?
Should Tonya skate? (represent the US in the Olympics?)
Are Tonya's fingerprints to be found in the evidence?
Will Tonya Harding's spin be good enough to get her the gold? (spin
    on the rink/spin on Kerrigan attack)
What did Jeff Gillooly tell the FBI?
Did Jeff Gillooly 's lawyer act unethically by accusing Tonya during
    press conference?
Will Nancy skate?
Is television news protected by the first amendment in regards to the
    subpoenas delivered for videotape of Tonya's denial of prior
    knowledge?
When will the special panel announce its findings?
Why would the U.S. Olympic Committee be hesitant to decide to
    make Harding ineligible?
What forms of redress to the special panel will Tonya have?
If Tonya is found to be innocent but denied the chance to skate, what
    recourse does she have?
If Tonya is found guilty, will she have her titles/medals taken away?
Does Tonya have the protection of her constitutional right to be
    considered innocent until proven guilty?

Questions raised by *tabloid* news stories
Who is Tonya?
Who is Nancy Kerrigan?
Is winning more important to Tonya than anything else?
Is Tonya ill? (How serious is her asthma? ovarian cysts?)
Is Tonya the fiercest competitor in sports we've ever seen?
Is Nancy Kerrigan the comeback kid?

(continued)

(Table 2 continued)

Will/should Nancy win the gold?

Was Tonya born to skate?

Is the ice rink an escape for Tonya or her personal battleground?

What kind of childhood did Tonya have?

How has the shortage of finances affected her skating?

Is Tonya hungry for fame?

Is Tonya greedy?

Does Tonya need a lot of love?

Will Tonya overcome the obstacles facing her now as she has done throughout her life?

Has Tonya fallen or failed?

What makes Tonya tick?

Is Tonya blinded by ambition?

Is Tonya an underdog?

Does Tonya believe God has chosen her to win the gold?

Does Tonya go to church?

Does her church support Tonya?

How confident is Tonya about her Olympic performance?

How does Tonya feel toward Nancy Kerrigan now, after the attack, with the finger pointed to her as the most likely suspect?

Is Tonya sorry for what happened to Nancy?

Why does Tonya leave her truck parked in tow-away zones?

Why does Tonya have two outstanding tickets for moving violations?

Does Jeff Gillooly love Tonya?

Does Tonya love Jeff?

Did Jeff abuse Tonya?

Did Jeff betray Tonya?

Would Tonya do anything for Jeff?

Is LaVona Golden sorry for herself or for her daughter, Tonya?

Why didn't LaVona Golden get to go to the Olympics?

Is LaVona hurt by Tonya shunning her?

Why does Tonya want to be adopted by Stephanie Quinteros' parents, the Webers?

Does Tonya get along with her father, Al Harding?

How did Tonya's half-brother die five years ago? Was it really a hit-or-run or did Tonya have something to do with it? Was Tonya sexually assaulted by her half-brother?

Who are Tonya's friends?

(continued)

(Table 2 continued)

Are Tonya's friends loyal to her?

Who is Stephanie Quintero and why is she Tonya's best friend?

Why did the Quinteros, Tonya and her friends harass the apartment managers?

Did Tonya commit a crime of the heart by stealing away the attentions/affections of David Miller? Did David Miller have an affair with Tonya?

Who will be in Lillehammer to support Tonya?

With whom did Tonya watch the opening ceremonies on TV in Oregon?

When will Tonya Harding arrive in Lillehammer?

How did Al Harding and David Weber (Tonya's surrogate father) get along on their Olympic trip?

Has the media coverage of Nancy/Tonya dominated the Olympics?

Has the media coverage been at the expense of other competitions and the international spirit?

Does the media attention put undue pressure on Tonya or does she work "good" under pressure?

How will the media attention affect Tonya? Nancy? other skaters?

Is the media frenzy out of control?

Why did the apartment managers of the Quinteros' rent out the neighboring apartment to ABC News?

Is Tonya the victim of media harassment?

Does Tonya play on the media and the public with her staged stunts?

How do Tonya's fans feel about her now?

How do Tonya's coach and choreographer feel about her chances to win the gold?

What do other Olympic skaters think of Tonya Harding?

Will Tonya and Nancy see each other off the rink in the Olympic village? If so, how will they interact?

Will Tonya Harding face Nancy Kerrigan on the ice?

Will Tonya win a medal?

What is a triple axel?

When and where did Tonya's skating career start to tumble?

Where and when was the conspiracy to attack Nancy Kerrigan hatched?

How did the attack on Nancy Kerrigan happen?

(continued)

(Table 2 continued)

Who plotted the conspiracy to eliminate Kerrigan from the competition?

What role did Tonya Harding play in planning the attack?

How did the police discover the plot to attack Kerrigan?

What did Jeff Gillooly confess to the FBI?

Who is Shawn Eckhart and who were the two men he hired to carry out the hit on Nancy Kerrigan?

Were the conspirators really so stupid or was this a comedy of errors?

Is there any physical evidence directly connecting Tonya Harding to the attack on Kerrigan?

Was the handwriting on the napkin discovered in a dumpster Tonya's?

Did someone plant the personal documents, including the napkin, to implicate Tonya?

Why would Tonya do such a thing to Nancy Kerrigan?

Why did the attack on Nancy Kerrigan have to happen?

Why would someone attack the "Ice Princess"?

Was Tonya jealous of Nancy?

Will the legal battle end before the skaters are scheduled to compete in Lillehammer?

Why did Tonya file a $25 million lawsuit against the U.S. Olympic Committee?

Just who are the members of the US Olympic Committee and who are they to judge the sportsmanship and ethics of Tonya Harding?

Why did Nike donate $25,000 to Tonya's defense fund?

Will Tonya need money for her legal defense?

Did Tonya want the gold for the glory of skating or were her motives fame and fortune?

Did Tonya lie about her involvement in the attack on Kerrigan?

Who is lying—Jeff Gillooly and/or Tonya Harding?

Is Tonya guilty?

blame/responsibility for events are common to both tabloid and network news. Less common to network news than the tabloids are stories that examine the context of events, explore mitigating circumstances, investigate character, or supply answers to how and why an event occurred.

The differences in narrative forms derive largely from the differences in sources used and questions asked. Network news chronicles world events while tabloid TV tells stories. "News does a great deal of chronicling, recording newsworthy events in a routine fashion...."[5] Telling stories derives from an oral tradition of the people, whereas chronicles stem from the making of official history by those in power. Network news reveals privileged elites reciting noteworthy events to invoke the authority of their offices while tabloid television programs are like other cultural practices of storytelling (particularly soap operas). Traditionally, American journalism has been studied in isolation from other cultural practices of storytelling. Like soap operas, tabloid shows are still constructed mostly by men, but women are allowed to speak; a more feminine discourse is permitted in narrative forms and a larger segment of the audience is female.

It is *how* stories are narrated, not the quality of the events, that distinguishes chronicles from stories. When told as a story, the newsworthy events may be embellished with rhetorical flourishes and personal touches. People really understand news events in human terms when told in story form. Tabloid stories are written with more sensationalistic language than network news. The music and vocabulary keep viewers' emotional involvement higher than in network narratives.

Both chronicles and stories are narrative forms that are "...intimately related to, if not a function of, the impulse to moralize reality."[6] The sort of moralizing for chronicle differs from that for a story. Stories, such as those told in tabloid reports, moralize in a framework of relationships, obligations, and responsibilities, whereas chronicles moralize within a framework of individualism, duties, roles, and rights. In short, tabloids' stories are more akin to feminine moral schemas and chronicles reflect a more masculinist morality.[7] National network news largely focuses on issues of social order—rule- and law-governed behavior with an emphasis on authorities, experts, officials and investigative and legal procedures. Tabloids, like the networks, tell stories that are myths, but tabloid tales are structured more like morality stories with episodic parables. The diegetic structures of tabloid news narratives are more similar to soap operas. The tabloids used videoclips much like soap operas to provide a plot summary with each new episode to clue viewers into the context for the current scene.

Dramatic conflicts in network versus tabloid news stories revolve around personalities, but the construct of personality is different. For networks, personalities are treated as institutionalized roles, i.e., elected office, political appointment, official position, professional, expert, and/or celebrity. For the tabloids, personalities are treated as the intersection of a web of dynamic relationships with others in the world. Whereas network news largely focused on legal issues, the tabloids centered on social issues in terms of responsibilities and the consequences of news events on relationships.

Tabloids, unlike the networks, tell stories with pictures, instead of letting pictures tell the story. The networks rely heavily on press conferences and other staged and scheduled media events to which they either get an invitation, press release, or an assignment from an editor. The overreliance on "known" sources stems from the practice of routine, planned, staged, news. The tabloids, however, focus more on narrative construction and then find images to correspond. The greater range and number of unknown sources allows tabloid journalists access to a variety of narrative possibilities. Both networks and tabloids do a skilled job of matching video and words, but the video texts examined here clearly indicate tabloids match video to words and networks match words to easily available footage.

The lessons to be learned from the tabloids are not about what constitutes news. Network news programs should not become tabloids in their content. Tabloids are not a substitute for national affairs coverage. Sex and violence certainly sell. However, there are other public matters of great consequence about which we as citizens can and should do something. Nor do I suggest networks adopt the practice of paying sources for their stories.[8] Knowing how to invade privacy, sensationalize, self-promote, and market fears, fantasies, and fetishes is not a feature of the tabloid genre worth extolling. Besides, networks already seem to know these lessons. Instead of dismissing tabloids, this comparative analysis reveals why tabloids warrant a closer look and a more critical and feminist reflection on why the genre of tabloid television is so reviled. The "tabloidization" of television news reflects not only masculine bias but a professional process "defined as any particular debased practice that is typical of one's competitors."[9]

The networks might learn important lessons from the tabloids' coverage of Tonya Harding and Nancy Kerrigan about the most fundamental aspects of journalistic praxis. Do your homework. Track down sources not in your Golden Rolodex. Get answers to more how and why questions. Construct narratives that examine social, cultural, and moral issues, not only legal, procedural, and bureaucratic matters. Tell stories with pictures instead of letting the readily available images dictate the direction of the story. Finally, abandon the pretense of objectivity. In professional practice, striving for objectivity means being less subjective. The devaluation of subjectivity is further evidence that feminine narrative and discursive styles of storytelling are pushed to the periphery of professional journalism.

< NOTES >

1. Elizabeth S. Bird and Robert W. Dardenne (1988). "Myth, Chronicle and Story: Exploring the Narrative Qualities of News," in James W. Carey (ed.), *Media, Myths and Narratives: Television and the Press*. Newbury Park, CA: Sage, pp. 67–86.

2. Leon Sigal (1987). "Sources Make the News," in Robert Karl Manoff and Michael Schudson (eds.), *Reading the News*. New York: Pantheon, pp. 9–37.

3. Herbert Gans (1980). *Deciding What's News*. New York: Basic Books.

4. Table 1 does not include 15 white females interviewed on the tabloids without character-generated titles and names at the bottom of the screen.

5. Bird and Dardenne, 1998, op. cit., p. 75.

6. H. White (1981). "The Value of Narrativity in the Representation of Reality," in W.J.T. Mitchell (ed.), *On Narrative*. Chicago: University of Chicago Press, pp. 1–23.

7. Carol Gilligan (1982). *In a Different Voice: Psychological Theory and Women's Development*. Cambridge: Harvard University Press.

8. Because *Inside Edition* paid Tonya Harding for her exclusive story the program's coverage is not included in this analysis. It should be noted that Tonya did not honor this agreement when she agreed to an interview with Connie Chung. The networks' argument against paying sources gets fuzzy when news coverage itself is used as "free" advertising. The financial transactions between tabloids and their sources are more straightforward, but networks regularly pay for "consultant" sources; for example, CBS's employment of skater Scott Davis. Paying for sources is problematic for several reasons. Audiences are not regularly informed of the amount or terms of such financial agreements and such information is used by many to evaluate the veracity of the source. Payment may also change sources' disclosures into performances. Additionally, the stories that get told are those then worth buying.

9. Editorial (1994). "Juicing the News," *Nation*. 259(4), July 25/August 1, p. 112.

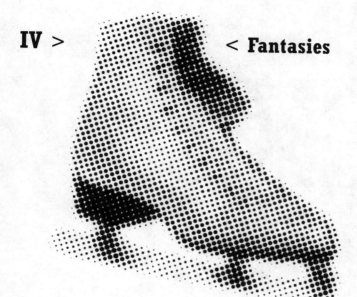

IV > < **Fantasies**

14

An American Tragedy

"I hate the whole *idea* of Nancy Kerrigan," my friend said, putting his finger on what is so terribly off about her: she seems more a package, a prepackage, than a woman. She fits the dress too well. Skating around in circles, waving from the float alongside Mickey, Kerrigan seems to be a living but nonperspiring advertisement for the ease of class mobility in America. Her clean lines are so technocratic, aerodynamic, and gravityless: rising is so simple when you have no body to tie you down. There is something utterly right about the spectacle of Kerrigan's getting her hero's welcome home not in the real city of Boston, but in Disney World, a megalomaniac's idea of a city.

The sport of figure skating itself seems to be an arena for fantasies about class—most of them sad. Let's be frank: spangles are not big in the horsey set. In your average private school, you will find many, many more Picabo Streets than you will Nancy Kerrigans or Oksana Baiuls, no matter how thin they may be. Figure skating, like the Miss America pageant, often resembles some peculiar, outdated girls' school dedicated to preparing its students for a world that doesn't exist. The code, rigidly enforced, appears to be obedience, inoffensive prettiness, wearing your skirts short enough but not too short, and smiling on bound feet. But that is not the ethic of Kelly Klein. That is the ethic of Katherine Gibbs.

And yet, one might argue, the ethic worked: blue-collar Kerrigan won the silver, the endorsements, she's ascended to Disney World while Tonya is sliding down the trash track with her shoelaces untied. (Have you heard this one? Tonya finally got an endorsement after all—for the Club.) Watching Tonya walk barefoot up and down that long, dark corridor Friday night as the other women in their shiny little outfits passed her by, then watching her skate to the music of *Jurassic Park,* a movie about extinct animals, I felt that I was witnessing the final act of an American tragedy.

Theodore Dreiser or Frank Norris could have written it. Tonya, a raging bull on ice, had one magnificent gimmick, her triple axel. But smooth Nancy had the look that gender-paranoid figure-skating judges cream for. Hot with a desperate ambition, Tonya did a terrible thing to her nemesis (and I do think she did, however passively and clumsily), only to be betrayed by her own: her husband, her family, her shoelace. It's so elementary school—it's as if one of the other women broke the shoelace when she wasn't looking and such a perfect image of Tonya's fledgling badness that it's almost a cliché.

Kerrigan skated right over her. "I was flawless," Kerrigan commented from Disney World. Tonya might as well have hit herself on the head with that baton. Kerrigan has never been the most interesting of skaters; she has succeeded by perseverance more than incandescent talent. Although she would've had a good endorsement afterlife anyway, Harding's attack made her a star. It made her glamorous. It added the shadow Kerrigan needed to shine more brightly. Corporate America, as if dancing on Harding's grave, ran Kerrigan commercials over and over and over during the final competition, featuring Kerrigan in that damn Vera Wang dress.

Did you hear this one? Secretly, Tonya and Nancy are lovers and they cooked up this entire scheme together. They're probably spending the money right now. This fantasy embodies a much happier ending than the probable real one, which is likely to be a Minnie Mouse-like petrification on ice for Nancy and a few bad TV movies for Tonya. It also voices the feeling, usually firmly repressed, that Tonya and Nancy are actually deeply connected underneath. Sometimes they seem not two separate women at all, but the before-and-after photo of the same one, Tonya the body Nancy left behind, the negative, the ghost. *Newsday* was criticized for manipulating a photo to make it look like the two women were standing together; the real trick, however, has been to make it appear that they are miles apart, that Kerrigan is not leaving the working class but being restored to Hyannisport while Tonya is inseparable from the grittier precincts of Portland.

But these two women are from the same neighborhood, figuratively speaking. Both are working-class, both driven, both getting the tiniest bit old (mid-twenties) for a sport that fetishizes teenagers like Baiul. Each is in her own way a killer; when Baiul was injured in a collision on ice last week, Nancy didn't stop skating for a minute. They are both striving to get out of their class, one by grinding, the other by shooting.

Figure skating, like Miss Jean Brodie, desperately insists that shooters never prosper, but in the real world this is not true. The corporation may give grinders the job, but the public can't get enough of shooters. They pack the media halls. *Roseanne* is No. 1 in the ratings. Gangsta rap prevails. The display of one's psychic wounds is hardly the route to failure. Tonya might have been able to shoot her way out, but by the time she began to see that her folly, her abusive past, and her attitude put her right on the money culturally, it was already too late. Kerrigan, who was so riveted on skating that she is barely remembered by her high school classmates, is no gilded lily. She may be the tougher of the two.

Kerrigan's survival instincts may have won her a million endorsements, but in terms of media valence she is as cold as the ice she skates on. She couldn't even take a cup of cocoa from David Letterman's mom. Even a quickie trash bio like *The Kerrigan Courage: Nancy's Story* is a deadly dull recitation of where she placed at various events from grade school to the present. The story of Kerrigan's mother, who took up water skiing *after* going blind, has much more drama. However much Campbell's may admire Kerrigan's resemblance to a can of soup, cans of soup aren't very interesting on their own. They need Tonyas beside them to make them look good. And the more we see of this particular can of soup, the more her reserve seems not blandness, but the silent tension of a coiled spring.

My friend told me that in a writing class he attended, the students were most interested in the story from Tonya's mother's point of view, then Tonya's, then Gillooly's. No one at all wanted to imagine Nancy. She is like a whirling blind spot in the cultural vision. Because she did fit the dress so well, we have assumed that she was without those unsightly edges that Tonya could never conceal. How shocking it was when Kerrigan bitched loudly, in camera range, about having to wait around for the medal ceremony while Ukrainian orphan Baiul redid her tear-stained makeup. Did Kerrigan's jaw get bigger overnight, or were we just noticing it for the first time? What big teeth you have, Snow White. No one ever got anywhere without them, my dear.

Postscript, Summer 1994

Four months later, it was all over. In 1994 the US Figure Skating Association stripped Harding of her national championship and banned her from the association for life. The Harding/Kerrigan TV movie is already a summer rerun. Figure skaters, like moths, have very short life spans. What was it about these two that have held my attention so? I find now that it has almost entirely melted away, like ice cream—or, really, like a snowball with a rock inside it. Nancy I can hardly remember, but Tonya, the rock, doesn't slip away so easily. Exiled from ice heaven forever, Tonya gives voice to the middle-class despair Nancy sews up. Look at it all one way, and it's a fairy princess without feet gliding along; look at it another, and it's a woman standing on a knife. And perhaps what still fascinates me most about these two reluctant icons is that both are trailed by enormous clouds of things we can't quite see. All is deduction: Tonya's rage, Nancy's ambition. Both are, in their respective ways, inscrutable. But as Tonya is offered mud-wrestling contracts in Japan, and Nancy, like the Cheshire Cat, dissolves into her smile, I can't help but see the Harding/Kerrigan melodrama as a sort of women's prison movie in tulle. From that vantage, it looks like Nancy is the one who got out without leaving a trace behind.

15

< Sam Stoloff

Tonya, Nancy, and the Bodily Figuration of Social Class

Recollection will sieve the Tonya/Nancy affair until only the large pieces remain—the good girl vs. bad girl confrontation, Kerrigan clutching her knee and howling "Why me?", and Harding frantically fixing her skate lace in the corridor behind the Hamar rink. But how rich in symbolic silt the story was, in pathos and absurdity: Shane Stant crashing through the plexiglass; Eckardt the would-be spook in a trenchcoat, playing his tape recording for a minister classmate in a fit of conscience or bravado; Eckardt's father bragging of his son's exploits to his phone-sex partner; the tale which surfaced of Tonya brandishing a baseball bat at a woman after a traffic mishap; the incriminating napkin discovered in a dumpster outside a Portland restaurant; Tonya's mother singing a maudlin song to "her baby" on *A Current Affair*, and then collapsing on a talk show; the eerie symmetry when Tonya twisted her ankle, as if making a bid for a share of the sympathy Kerrigan had won—and then Oksana Baiul too skating on an injured leg, after she crashed with another skater in practice (Tanja Szewczenko of Germany, another Tanya!); Nancy complaining to Mickey Mouse that Disney World was "corny."

The Tonya Harding/Nancy Kerrigan episode had everything to make it sensational: fascinating characters, personal rivalry, violence, villainy, and buffoonery, intrigue and cover-up, investigative drama, legal strategy, a distinct dramatic climax, sports spectacle, high stakes, and moments of exquisite foolishness. But absorbing as these qualities were, they do not in themselves explain why the episode riveted our attention—why, in fact, the affair assumed the proportions of national myth. Why did it produce such emotional extremes? Why did it inspire expressions of such revulsion and dismay, as well as glee? Why did it become a drama, not merely of personal ambition, but of national corruption and moral ruin?

It will be my argument here that, more than anything else, the episode tapped profound contemporary anxieties about social class in the United States. These anxieties were most discernible in the newspaper and magazine commentary that surrounded the events, spanning the range from sermon to satire. The anxieties focused in particular on Tonya, on her personal history, on her persistence, on her speech, her habits, her hometown, her friends and husband, and, not least, on her body. But these anxieties were rivaled by other emotions, which signalled a different kind of investment in the affair—a pleasure in the up-ending of the outwardly decorous world of figure skating, and in Tonya's brash challenge to the reigning proprieties.

Of course, it's not news that the Tonya/Nancy affair concerned social class; even where class was not an explicit theme of the commentary, it provided a subtext, an allusive ground, or the material for ridicule.[1] Still, as an analytical category, social class suffers from a thorough confusion about its functioning, its significance, and even its existence in the United States, and the Harding/Kerrigan commentary was mired in this confusion. Only occasionally was the centrality of class in the affair directly addressed; for example, writing in *Rolling Stone*, Randall Sullivan argued that class was in fact the basic category for understanding the furor:

> Nearer to the heart of the matter was America's profound denial of (and subterranean fascination with) social class. A cultural apparatus that had substituted race for class was engaged in a willful indifference to the millions of fair-skinned Americans who work for a living that is meager at best. Tonya Harding was the skeleton in the country's closet.[2]

Although I am arguing for the priority of class over gender in the way the media constructed the Harding/Kerrigan episode, the two should not really be seen as exclusive categories; rather, it was their entanglement that was one of the affair's most absorbing qualities. The categories were confused, mapped onto one another, reversed and exchanged. Just to cite the most obvious example, Tonya, when placed in juxtaposition to Nancy, was perceived to be rather stocky, therefore unfeminine, therefore low-class. All of the epithets used to describe Tonya participated in this slippage: she was a smoker, a pool-player, a truck-driver, and so on, and all of these terms were markers of both class and gender. However, it's not as simple as saying that the lower term in one binary can be exchanged for the lower term in another, although this certainly happens; femininity, for example, while a signifier of female weakness when opposed to masculinity in men, may function as the higher term in a class binary. In the Tonya/Nancy episode, femininity appeared as an element of figure skating's "classiness," where femininity is signified by graceful motion and certain forms of balletic gesture. Femininity, in this context, reveals itself as a class style—as a signifier of leisure and cultural capital. To the commentators, Tonya revealed her class origin, in part, through her failed attempts at "high-class" femininity.

The axis on which all these terms hinged, in both their gender and their class connotations, was the body.[3] Tonya's apparent density, in opposition to Nancy's slenderness, evoked carnality, and especially a sense of bodily excess, or lack of bodily discipline. In the terms of cultural hierarchy, the controlled body figures the superior position in binarisms of class, gender and race, while the excessive or uncontrolled body figures the lower position. The deployment of this kind of body imagery in the Tonya/Nancy episode suggested fierce anxieties, particularly on the part of the middle class (represented by most of the mainstream media) which the commentary served to manage.[4] But what we must also not forget is that this same body imagery can convey a very different set of social implications when viewed, not "from above," but "from below." In the remainder of this essay, I will try to sort out some of these competing class readings of the Harding/Kerrigan affair, exploring first the middle-class view, then an alternative view that might be called the carnivalesque, and finally the class configuration of commercial spectator sport, and how Tonya and Nancy adopted roles within that configuration.

White Trash and Blue Collar

The opposition between Tonya and Nancy was frequently construed as a class rivalry.[5] Such commentary focused on the different class cultures from which the two skaters had come: Harding as low-class, defined in terms of cultural attributes, and Kerrigan as her opposite (although what that opposite term consisted of varied). A long litany of vaguely pejorative or mocking expressions were attached to Harding: she was a "tough cookie," a "trailer park honey," a "bad girl," "terminally tacky," etc., while Kerrigan was "elegant" and "classy." In fact, although some writers acknowledged that Harding and Kerrigan were both "daughters of the working class,"[6] much more attention was focused on Harding's class than on Kerrigan's. Harding was from a class culture which required explication, while Kerrigan seemed to come from a culture more familiar to the imagination of the middle class. Both as an object of scorn and of fascination, Harding was the stronger emotional pole in the drama, because, for the middle class, she represented the class Other.

For the middle-class commentators, the land from which Harding came was paradoxically both familiar and strange. It could be dismissed with the flick of a stereotype ("trailer park," "K-Mart"), but it was also *terra incognita*, requiring the services of an interpreter. There was, for example, Susan Orlean's essay in the *New Yorker*, which explored Clackamas County, Oregon, with the following lead: "People who say that Tonya Harding lives in Portland have missed the point. She comes from a place that's tougher and more intractable."[7] The essay's tone was distinctly anthropological, as it described the physical geography of Clackamas in dismal colors. At the margins of the article were advertisements for Italian vacation homes and "country club living in Santa Fe," the more familiar habitats of *New Yorker* readers.

Descriptions of Tonya relied heavily on the bodily register to figure such class categories, dwelling on the ways in which Harding satisfied the stereotypes of the undisciplined lower classes, their lack of bodily containment and control. Consider, for example, the matter of the asthma inhaler. The image of a breathless Tonya sucking on an asthma inhaler was popular in the media, but because it was connected to images of her smoking, the message was not that Tonya had a disability (which might have been seen as an obstacle overcome by heroic tenacity), but that she lacked self-control. Cigarette smoking in itself has rapidly become a signifier of low social class, suggesting a carelessness about the body as well as ignorance about well-documented risks, but in Harding's case that signification of lower-class improvidence was compounded by the way her breathing problems apparently hurt her ability to compete.

Similarly, Tonya's costumes generated a good deal of disapproving commentary, not only because they were judged to be tacky, but because they failed to properly contain her. The story of Tonya "popping a snap" and nearly coming out of her halter at the 1993 national championship[8] suggested poor quality of construction, but more importantly, a sense of bodily surfeit—a grotesque sense that Tonya was swelling beyond the capacity of her clothing to hold her. This sort of thinking led to some rather monstrous images of a gargantuan Tonya bestriding the earth: "*Playboy* offered Tonya $250,000 to pose for the magazine with her tool kit. True story. Ohmigoodness! Can you picture that? I mean, Tonya is wider than I-93."[9]

On the other hand, there was considerable confusion about what class Kerrigan should be assigned to. Was she "middle class," "working class," or (since she wore expensive designer outfits and stood to make a lot of money, and because she was on the threshhold of joining the media aristocracy) "high class"? Or was she moving from one class to another? And if so from which, to which? Confusion about Kerrigan's class provides a good illustration of the ideological filters through which class is perceived in the United States.[10] Without formal markers of class distinction, the white population is seen as a vast undifferentiated social body called "the middle class," with only the obviously indigent and, perhaps, the shadowy "rich" defining the wafer-thin excluded margins at bottom and top. There are gradations within this vast middle, based on income, occupation, place of residence, education, taste, and so on, but since all of these things are theoretically alterable, they are assumed to be voluntary, and thus they do not define essential attributes of persons. The gradations, therefore, may score the national body, but they do not divide it. Anything outside of this body is perceived to be a threat, but almost everything within the nation is part of this undifferentiated body.[11] Even those who are "lower-class" may be contained within it, since the circulation within this body is assumed to be free. Anything that threatens to block the circulation, however, or which asserts that the body is in reality partitioned—like "white trash," which is tantamount, in this figurative case, to saturated fat—will be the object of revulsion and anger. Harding's apparent attack on Kerrigan was just such an assertion of division.

While this vision of a classless United States has deep cultural roots, the particular configuration described here is of fairly recent vintage, a product of post-war prosperity in the 1950s and 1960s. The model is a middle-class view, and one which becomes increasingly parochial, as it less and less accurately describes contemporary social reality. The ideal of classlessness rationalizes the position of the successful stratum which can still be called "middle class" with some justice—what the Ehrenreichs call the "professional-managerial class," more colloquially referred to as "the upper-middle class." This class, which is in fact a relatively small minority, dominates the means of social representation, including (most importantly for present purposes) television and journalism.

Kerrigan, although she comes from a working-class family, was thus presumptively middle class, and therefore included within the national body. The telltale expression in her case is "blue collar," which is not precisely synonymous with "working class," but instead has come (in the Nixon-Reagan era) to represent that *faction* of the skilled working class which is understood to be socially conservative, and comfortably if shabbily well-off; the blue collar belongs, in effect, as the bottom bracket of the middle class, and represents the post-war fantasy of universal prosperity, with home ownership for all, and families supported on a single industrial income.

It's possible that ethnicity also plays into this idea of the blue collar—the Kerrigans were identifiably Irish, while the Hardings were "white trash," i.e. ethnically indeterminate. Tonya's mother's many marriages probably also contributed to the idea of mongrelization and ethnic decay, signified by Tonya's being called a "mutt," fallen away from the white ethnic purity which is a classic ingredient of the integrationist trajectory of upward mobility[12] (this, however, is a contradictory view, since integration itself implies the decay of isolated ethnic identity, and its incorporation into the undifferentiated national body).

What commentators found most distressing was Harding's putative attack on the supposedly superior athlete: the threat she posed, therefore, was to the natural aristocracy of talent, i.e. the assumption of free circulation within the social body. This, too, is paradoxical, since the undifferentiated body should not admit of a concept like "aristocracy." But, on the contrary, it is precisely because of the absence of *a priori* classes that something like a "natural aristocracy" can theoretically emerge. This is why such a fuss was made about Harding's remarks concerning money. Her open declaration of pecuniary interest violated the sham conventions of amateurism which give figure skating its veneer of aristocracy (such declarations have always gotten athletes in trouble; Harding is by no means the first to trangress norms of amateur idealism). Kerrigan, on the other hand, made sure to recite the athlete's media credo: "Take any of [the endorsements] away and I would still do it. I didn't know there was any money to be made in the sport except for teaching until two or three years ago, when I got a couple of endorsement contracts. I had no idea. I do it because I love it."[13]

The more the blue-collar reality erodes in the "post-industrial" United States, the more hysterically attached to the idea of the blue collar the middle class has become. Harding and Kerrigan represented competing middle class fantasies of the poor—Harding the threatening fantasy of a resentful lumpenproletariat, something outside and beneath the national corpus, and Kerrigan the reassuring fantasy of the conservative, assimilationist blue collar. According to Joe Klein, in a *Newsweek* column: "Tonya and Nancy are made-for-TV versions of two dominant, American working-class predispositions. It's not just lady and the tramp; it has more to do with assimilation and rejection, faith and resentment. Assimilation— the possibility of upward mobility—is the bedrock American faith. Nancy's faith."[14] These are not only "working-class predispositions," however, but middle-class fantasmatic projections. This is not to deny the class realities of cultural disparities. On the contrary, class anger and resentment really seem to have motivated the assault on Kerrigan, and to have defined the emotions of some of Harding's supporters. It is merely to observe the emotional and ideological investment that middle-class commentators have in believing the country is full of Kerrigans, while being occasionally attacked by a lone-gun Harding—in believing, in other words, that their own privileged position is a matter of justice, not accident.

So far I have considered only what I'm calling the middle-class view, which by and large sided with Nancy, even if sometimes reluctantly. But there was another view, one that I've hinted at, and one which was poorly represented in the mainstream press. Following Mikhail Bakhtin and those who have developed his ideas, I will call this the carnivalesque view.[15] Some qualification of Bakhtin's vision of the popular, festive, utopian mode of carnival must undoubtedly be made for the contemporary U.S. context, in which the middle class assumes the dominant position, at least in popular ideology, against the extremes of high and low. The carnivalesque will have a different charge when it is addressed to the dominance of the fantasmatic middle-class body which claims an all-encompassing universality rather than claiming a class exclusivity (as a formal aristocracy would). Liberal political ideology in the U.S. does not allow much of a position for alternative cultures of any sort, but particularly not those of class. There has also undoubtedly been considerable attenuation of the carnivalesque mode in modern commercial culture: class cultures are absorbed, mitigated, diluted, and dissected in commercial popular culture. Where, after all, could an autonomous class culture reside within the totality of the media? The fragmentation of broadcasting by cable notwithstanding, television is still the foremost medium of, and figure for, the undifferentiated social body.

But the carnivalesque persists nonetheless, if not as a coherent class culture, then as the vestigial remnants of a festive world view which Bakhtin traced back to the European middle ages. That view emphasizes

the grotesque body, especially the lower bodily strata: the feet, the legs, the organs of sexual reproduction and defecation, the belly and the rump, as opposed to the head and heart; it prefers the animal to the angelic; it elevates the low, and diminishes the high; it revels in reversal, in obscenity, in the open and the excessive. This kind of cultural repertoire was evident throughout the Tonya/Nancy affair, in its satirical subversion of the class hierarchies in skating, sport, and U.S. culture generally. Tonya represented the carnivalesque, although sometimes in a somewhat disappointing fashion. The same recklessness, trash-talking, and bodily excessiveness that the moralists found repugnant are the stuff of which carnival is made.

To get this view, you had to read between the lines of newspaper reports, or watch the tabloid TV programs instead of the network news. Even there you would have to read carefully. As Barbara Ehrenreich notes, "Ideas seldom flow 'upward' to the middle class, because there are simply no structures to channel the upward flow of thought from class to class."[16] The flow is one-way, down: the middle-class media represent their views as universal, while in fact they circulate and recirculate information and opinion among themselves.

But the carnivalesque view comes bubbling up, betraying its presence even in the middle-class media. The "man in the street" gets his say; the tabloid programs include all sorts of odd ephemera; the networks have moments of inadvertent hilarity (of course, there would not have been so much comic potential if the attack on Kerrigan had been more damaging. The carnivalesque took root in the attack's failure, and flowered more fully as the misadventures of the perpetrators became public. After the initial shock of the attack had worn off, and once it was clear that Kerrigan was only superficially harmed, there was greater license to laugh at the clumsiness of the conspirators).

Harding was thus a pole of identification as well as an object of repudiation. Given that the carnivalesque version of the affair was poorly represented in the media, this assertion of Tonya's appeal has to remain somewhat hypothetical. While it is clear that Tonya had her fans, and while it is also clear that the affair expanded the class base of the normally "upscale" audience for Olympic figure skating, it would require empirical research to establish certain class allegiances to Harding.[17]

It should also be pointed out that there were those among the journalistic commentators who sided with Harding, most conspicuously in the progressive press.[18] Although I have been attributing a unified ideological perspective to the middle class, a less reductive account would have to acknowledge what Erik Olin Wright calls the "contradictory locations within class relations" that characterize the middle class.[19] The middle class, situated as it is between the high and the low, between capital and labor, occupies a peculiarly ambivalent position, and does not have a simple, unified class interest. But those in the media who allied themselves with Tonya were a distinct minority, vastly outnumbered by the revilers.

The Legs of the Skater: Sport and the Carnivalesque[20]

In the remainder of this essay, I want to explore the particular ways in which competing class cultures are invested in the field of popular sport, and the ways in which Harding and Kerrigan came to represent those cultures.

It shouldn't be a surprise that such a conflict erupted in sport, and particularly in ice skating. Sport is a fertile field for such conflicts; it inherits rival traditions of the classical and the carnivalesque, and the two traditions, figuring different cultural attitudes, are bound to clash. Among sports, skating is particularly well suited to manifestations of the carnivalesque, because of its open connections to other fields of commercial "show" culture.

Cultural commentary in the United States has both celebrated and dismissed sport, when it has regarded sport at all; to some it is civil religion, to others it is pacification of the masses by a capitalist elite.[21] In fact, of course, neither the celebration nor the condemnation offers a suitably complex account of sport, which is a widely various cultural field, vehicle for different ideological investments—not indoctrination, but conflict. John Hargreaves, a historian of British sport, for instance—arguing against a Marxist, determinist position which holds that contemporary Western sport is necessarily an instrument of capitalist hegemony—describes the ideological heterogeneity of sport in this way:

> There is no sense [in the strict Marxist position] in which people might quite consciously value sports as meaningful and beneficial aspects of their lives, while at the same time being aware that ruling groups attempt to use sport as an instrument of control. In [the determinist] approach sport has to be the exclusive possession of one class rather than another, and so there is no room for conceiving that it might be an arena of uneasy accommodation and conflict between them.[22]

Sport, in other words, is an open field of social representation, and not a set of fixed social meanings.

Having said that, however, it must be admitted that in the U.S., mass spectator sport has frequently served as a vehicle for conservative ideologies.[23] It has served to rationalize hierarchy, through its reinforcement of the ideas of the career open to talent, and of natural aristocracy. It has served as a vehicle for nationalist sentiment, and it functions as a primary discursive field for the establishment of the "imagined community" of the nation.[24] And, perhaps most important, it has functioned to signify "tradition" in a culture in which "everything solid melts into air"—it is very often marketed as an exercise in nostalgia for a pre-industrial, pre-capitalist past (despite its clear historical relation to capitalist development). "Tradition," in turn, signifies a fantasized former national body which was not socially differentiated by racial upheaval, immigration, gender conflict, and so on.

However, this is only half of the picture. As Stallybrass and White caution,

> When we talk of high discourses—literature, philosophy, statecraft, the languages of the Church and the University—and contrast them to the low discourses of a peasantry, the urban poor, subcultures, marginals, the lumpenproletariat, colonized peoples, we already have two "highs" and two "lows." History seen from above and history seen from below are irreducibly different and they consequently impose radically different perspectives on the question of hierarchy.[25]

Commercial popular culture, I would argue, is peculiarly a mixture of the two discourses, the classical and the carnivalesque, the high and the low. Even when sport seems most to reinforce conservative ideologies, it may retain popular, utopian, subversive meanings for those who watch.

Sport is in particular an arena of bodily representation, and so is an especially apt carrier of the kinds of bodily figuration of class and gender I've discussed in relation to Tonya and Nancy. There is a strand of thinking about sport which gives it a firmly aristocratic heritage of ascesis, or training of the body.[26] Spectator sport inherits some of this sense of training, but it contains another, competing strand, which emphasizes performance for others. This tension can be described as one between *play* and *dis-play*, sport performed in itself, and sport performed for others, with "play" furthermore suggesting non-pecuniary amateurism, and "display" suggesting the commercial exhibitionism of professional sport.[27] These terms, of course, are highly gendered. Display of the body for visual consumption has been an almost exclusively feminine function in Western culture, and for this reason, in "masculine" sports, the display element is covert; male athletes are reluctant to acknowledge their audience, preferring the fiction that their performance is something they do for its own sake. Sport is supposed to have the status of "event," not "performance," and the sporting body is not an object but an instrument. Only at moments of extreme spectatorial demand will a baseball player tip his cap, for example, and then only grudgingly, in a shrug of embarassment. By acting as if the crowd did not exist, and therefore as if the sport were worth pursuing merely for its own sake, male athletes subscribe to the aristocratic ideal of ascesis, and the classical masculine ideal of bodily self-containment. The display element in spectator sport is often held to be a contamination, often in gendered terms that are reminiscent of modernist condemnation of popular culture earlier in the century.[28]

But play and display are also terms that are clearly class-coded. To the extent that sport contains these two tendencies, it combines elements of the classical body with those of the grotesque body—the high discourses of the nation and the state, with the low discourses of the carnivalesque.

Ice skating, even more than other spectator sports, is not a "pure" sport, but a hybrid cultural form. Skating thus has a decidedly mixed range of class associations, and contains a greater than usual tension between play and display—a more explicit display component than in other sports. One way in which skating manifests this is in the tension between "athleticism" and "artistry." As has been pointed out elsewhere in this volume, these terms are openly gendered, and thus reveal the gendering already latent in the terms play and display, classical and grotesque body. But there is also a class coding involved. For sportswriters, figure skating is suspect because it isn't "pure" sport—it's contaminated by the elements it borrows from other forms of entertainment, such as musical accompaniment and spangled costuming. In other words, high-class sport is degraded by adopting elements of popular spectacle.

The attack on Kerrigan and its aftermath, then, which were perceived to be outside the arena of skating proper, in fact revealed tendencies and contradictions already contained within the sport, and within sport in general. Harding was accused of turning the "dignified" sport of skating into a "circus," but circus—or the carnivalesque—is the inherent flip-side to spectator sport, especially but not only in those sports that emphasize display. We might call skating's tendency to the classical its "balletic" quality, and its tendency to the carnivalesque its "circus" quality. Skating is frequently associated with both ballet and circus in public commentary; reference to ballet is usually an approving association, which tries to align skating with high culture, while reference to circus is usually disapproving, aligning skating with low culture. But this overlooks the ways in which all three cultural forms are mixed.

Like the ballet, and like the circus, skating has incorporated elements of spectacle: costume, music, and fragments of dramatic narrative. Like dance and circus, it is partly a drama of transcendence, and like those other cultural forms, it codes its spaces and bodies according to social class hierarchies. Within the circumscribed rinks, stages, and arenas, a vertical axis organizes the spectacle, with elevation of the body as the figure for transcendence. The axels and toe loops of figure skating have their counterparts in ballet's dancing on point, and trapeze and high wire acts in the circus—in all these bodily expressions, the emphasis is on the lifting of the body, and therefore on its denial, or the denial of its weightiness.

But in all these cases, there is the weighty counterpart to the ethereal leap. Ballet was transformed in the late nineteenth and early twentieth centuries into "high culture," as cultural hierarchies were established in the U.S., and so tried to suppress the lower bodily elements, but it is useful to remember that at the moment of its transformation into a commercial form of entertainment, ballet was as much about the display of dancers' bodies as about an aesthetic sublime. The cult of the ballerina emerged historically with the perfection of the technique of dancing on point, which served both to figure transcendence and to emphasize the legs of the dancer. The display of the leg specifically served to suggest sexual availability, a suggestion which could increasingly be taken literally as ballet shifted from court patronage to the commercial sphere, and female dancers were no longer protected from the sexual predations of their male audience. At the same time, therefore, as the romantic ballet appealed to a sense of the spiritual, it was practicing a barely tacit form of prostitution.[29]

In the circus, the trapeze and high-wire artists, who adopted the ballerina's costume, had their counterpart in the clown, with costumes that exaggerated the body into grotesque caricature. The clown represented the materiality of the flesh, emphasizing bodily excess and miraculous bodily reproduction. The clown was earthbound, where the high-wire walker defied gravity; the clown was carnal, while the trapeze artist denied incarnation.

And in skating, there was Tonya. Much of the emphasis on Tonya's "athleticism" covertly referred to Tonya's very fleshiness, and the physical effort she displayed which highlighted that embodiedness. When Kerrigan was described as "graceful," that in turn suggested a feminine concealment of bodily labor, indeed of the body itself. While Tonya wore costumes that seemed to gape open, Nancy wore costumes that were notably discreet. While Tonya fussed with her skate laces, thereby calling attention to the apparatus of her work, Nancy was wearing "sheer illusion," a material which in a peculiar way produced a sense of bodilessness (not exactly the illusion intended by the name of the fabric). If Kerrigan was skating's high-wire act (at least until she was trumped by Oksana Baiul), then Tonya was the clown.

Skating's mixed cultural heritage is marked by its emphasis on the legs of the skater, which echoes the carnivalesque emphasis on the lower bodily strata. As one sportswriter noted in the *New York Times*: "Harding-Kerrigan has more legs than a centipede."[30] Tonya in particular called attention to the lower body, to the turned ankle and the clubbed knee, to the broken lace and the loose blade; Tonya's remark about "kicking Nancy's butt" was tacitly juxtaposed to the often-repeated image of Tonya falling on her own butt after attempting a difficult jump. All skaters fall, but Tonya's falls were happily, ruthlessly detailed.

What we saw acted out in the early months of 1994, culminating in the winter Olympic skating competition, was thus a traditional class drama, of a kind that is formally embodied in various types of commercial culture. Partisans of skating's aristocratic pretensions rely on the association with ballet, on ballet's constricted status as signifier of "high culture." For them, Tonya represented an invasion of trash into this sanctified sphere, and the intrusion of class difference into the fantasy of the classless social body. Tonya's admirers, too, appreciated her challenge to the snobbery of skating's high-cultural ambitions. What detractors and admirers alike misunderstood was that Tonya was no invasion; she was always already there. The carnivalesque continues to be embedded in popular culture, despite efforts at purification.

But already there or not, Tonya came to define an emerging class conflict that is increasingly going to be played out in the fields of culture. In that sense, the middle class is right to be worried. "The nineties finally have their defining figure—and he hates your guts" writes Tad Friend in *New York*'s cover article on the "White Trash Nation." But although the pronoun was "he," it was Tonya who was singled out as "the ultimate icon" of white trash.[31]

< NOTES >

My thanks to Peter Stallybrass, for several enlightening conversations on the subject of Harding and Kerrigan; and to Burl Barr, Paul Downes, Rebecca Egger,

Julie Hilden, Naomi Morgenstern, Laura Murray, and Ed White, for their thoughtful comments.

1 Although there was, too, an occasional denial of its significance, such as one writer's claim that "this has nothing to do with class, manners or 'dysfunctional' families," Dan Shaughnessy, "Don't Fall Victim to Twisted Thinking," *Boston Globe*, Feb. 6, 1994, p. 49. However, what Shaughnessy is really complaining of is the use of class as an exculpation.

2 Randall Sullivan, "The Tonya Harding Fall: The Transformation of a Young Figure-Skating Champion into the World's Most Visible Villainess," *Rolling Stone* 686/687, July 14–28, 1994, p. 114.

3 For an interesting account of the social significance of body management, see Susan Bordo, "Reading the Slender Body," in Mary Jacobus, Evelyn Fox Keller, and Sally Shuttleworth, eds., *Body/Politics: Women and the Discourses of Science*, (New York: Routledge, 1990); for work on how the body serves social symbolic functions in general, see Mary Douglas, *Natural Symbols* (New York: Pantheon, 1982), and *Purity and Danger* (London: Routledge, 1966).

4 The term "middle class," however, needs to be specified; I attempt this specification below.

5 More often, commentary on Tonya/Nancy was merely connotative in matters of class. This was in part because class as a causal frame was taken for granted by the moralists: the argument buried in such commentary took the form *post hoc ergo propter hoc*: she did it and she is low-class, therefore she did it because she is low-class. In this sense, social class was merely assumed, at the same time as it was, for other purposes (particularly in perceptions of Kerrigan), denied.

6 e.g. the *Washington Post*, editorial, Feb. 5, 1994, p. A16.

7 Susan Orlean, "Figures in a Mall," *New Yorker*, Feb. 21, 1994, pp. 48–63.

8 See Abby Haight and J.E. Vader, *Fire on Ice: The Exclusive Inside Story of Tonya Harding*, (New York: Times Books, 1994), pp. 66–67.

9 Mike Barnicle, "Media Wobbles on Skater Story," *Boston Globe*, Feb. 15, 1994.

10 The necessarily brief discussion of class which follows is influenced in parts by Barbara Ehrenreich and John Ehrenreich, "The Professional-Managerial Class," *Between Labor and Capital*, ed. Pat Walker, (Boston: South End Press, 1979) pp. 5–45; Barbara Ehrenreich, *Fear of Falling: The Inner Life of the Middle Class*, (New York: Harper Perennial, 1989); and Richard Sennett and Jonathan Cobb, *The Hidden Injuries of Class*, (New York: Vintage, 1972). See also Benjamin Demott, *The Imperial Middle: Why Americans Can't Think Straight About Class*, (New Haven: Yale Univ. Press, 1990).

11 This may help to explain the particular reliance of Americans on foreign

villains, since, to deny internal division, we require external threat to maintain the bodily integrity of the nation.

12 Richard Cohen, *Washington Post*, Feb. 3, 1994, p. A27: "Harding stands in contrast not only to her rival but to her sport itself. She's a mutt among supposed purebreds." The disclaimer implied in the word "supposed" does not, it seems to me, mitigate the straightforward assertion of Tonya's mongrel status.

13 Quoted in Christine Brennan, "Kerrigan Can't Wait to See What Happens; Interested in Harding Saga, But Intent on Ice," *Washington Post*, Feb. 13, 1994, p. D1.

14 *Newsweek*, Feb. 14, 1994, p. 57. Klein's conclusion, however, is that Nancy's faith is justified, while Tonya's class resentment is just the bad faith of a sore loser. Of course winning justifies the faith of the winners. But for losing not to justify the broken faith of the losers, a belief must survive in the rules by which winners and losers are chosen. In skating, the notoriously arbitrary criteria for judging give good grounds for suspicion on this score.

15 Mikhail Bakhtin, *Rabelais and His World*, (Bloomington: Indiana Univ. Press, 1984); see also Peter Stallybrass and Allon White, *The Politics and Poetics of Transgression*, (Ithaca, NY: Cornell Univ. Press, 1986).

16 Ehrenreich, *Fear of Falling*, p. 139.

17 For a useful discussion of the audience for figure skating, and the internal politics of Olympic broadcasting, see John Powers, "The Crying Games," *Boston Globe Magazine*, Jan. 30, 1994.

18 See especially Katha Pollitt, "Subject to Debate," *The Nation*, March 7, 1994, p. 297.

19 Erik Olin Wright, *Classes*, (London: Verso, 1985).

20 My title for this section is drawn from Abigail Solomon-Godeau's discussion of 19th century photographic fetishism, "The Legs of the Countess," *October* 39, Winter 1986.

21 For the celebratory view, see Michael Novak, *The Joy of Sports: End Zones, Bases, Baskets, Balls, and the Consecration of the American Spirit*, (New York: Basic Books, 1976); for the condemnation, Noam Chomsky's statement about sports in the recent film "Manufacturing Consent" is representative if cursory: "Take sports. That's another crucial example of the indoctrination system. It offers people something to pay attention to that's of no importance, that keeps them from worrying about things that matter." Quoted in "Out in Leftist Field," *The Village Voice*, July 13, 1993, p. 137.

22 Hargreaves, John, "Sport, Culture and Ideology," *Sport, Culture and Ideology*, ed. Jennifer Hargreaves. (London: Routledge, 1982) .

23 I would argue, however, that it often does so as a defensive measure—sport

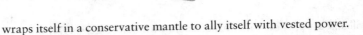
wraps itself in a conservative mantle to ally itself with vested power.

24 Benedict Anderson, *Imagined Communities: Reflections on the Origin and Spread of Nationalism*, (London: Verso, 1983) .

25 Stallybrass and White, *The Politics and Poetics of Transgression*, p. 4.

26 Bourdieu, Pierre, "Sport and Social Class," *Social Science Information* 17:6 (1978), pp. 819–840.

27 Stone, Gregory P., "American Sports: Play and Display," *Sport: Readings from a Sociological Perspective*, ed. Eric Dunning, (Toronto: Univ. of Toronto Press, 1972), pp. 47–65.

28 See, for example, Andreas Huyssen, *After the Great Divide: Modernism, Mass Culture, Postmodernism*, (Bloomington, IN: Indiana Univ. Press, 1986), especially Chapter 3, "Mass Culture as Woman: Modernism's Other," pp. 44–62.

29 Lynn Garafola, "The Travesty Dancer in Nineteenth-Century Ballet," *Dance Research Journal* 17:2 and 18:1, Fall 1985/Spring 1986, pp. 35–40.

30 Jere Longman, "A Pause in Scandal: Now They Will Skate," *New York Times*, Feb. 23, 1994, p. B9.

31 Tad Friend, "White Hot Trash," *New York*, Aug. 22, 1994, pp. 22–31.

16

Tonya, Nancy, and the Dream Scheme
Nationalizing the 1994 Olympics

The night after Nancy Kerrigan won the Silver medal at Lillehammer, she was asked by TV commentator Mark Phillips what she thought about the previous night's "drama" over Tonya Harding's loose skate, a strange episode which nearly led to Tonya's disqualification for lateness but, after a tearful false start, succeeded in getting her a second chance. Nancy replied with restrained irritation, "What drama?.... It happens every time...something...what can I say?" As if disappointed with this inarticulate response, Phillips gave his own *definitive* answer to the question: "What it is is the end of the Olympic chapter in Tonya's sorry saga but not the end of the story!"

What was apparent in both answers was that the competition between Tonya and Nancy was not merely a matter of who was the better skater but whose story was more dramatic—particularly since it was their "sorry saga" that made the 1994 Winter Olympics the most highly watched TV event thus far in the history of television. Tonya's skating may have gotten her no higher than eighth place, but in the competition for the most compelling and cooptive narrative she was clearly the winner. At least, that was the judgment of most of the media—especially of those who made the NBC movie of the week which aired on May 1st, *Tonya and Nancy, The Inside Story.*

Domestic Melodrama

After intercutting even-handedly between the childhoods of Nancy and Tonya, the NBC movie turns from a story of athletic competition to a domestic melodrama about Tonya's stormy marriage to Gillooly, with Nancy relegated to the subordinate role of victim. Thus, the primary struggle for control over the narrative is not between the two skaters but between husband and wife.

This is a familiar story, particularly for avid readers of scandal sheets and loyal fans of musical superstars like Whitney Houston, Tina Turner, and Cher, whose bullying husbands tried to bring them down simply because they resented their fame. And as most TV viewers know, even America's tough, top-rated working-class heroine Roseanne, who (like Tonya) had successfully overcome the early hard knocks of abuse, was still vulnerable to male aggression from a lesser-known husband whom she carried into the spotlight and who lusted after her cultural clout. This is the story that the NBC movie decided to feature, and it obviously had little to do with Nancy Kerrigan.

Tonya's story was clearly more powerful than Nancy's not only because she's had more hardships and became the bigger loser but also because her loss seemed to compensate for male lack—a lack of a father (who abandoned her) and a lack of power in the men who surrounded her—bodyguard Shawn Eckardt (brawn without brains), hitman Shane Stant (strong-arm without aim), and especially husband Jeff Gillooly (drive without talent). As Kaja Silverman has argued in *The Acoustic Mirror*, this "lack" helps position the heroine as a site of displacement for male angst. Thus, Tonya became a battered Queen bee with a swarm of bumbling bullies.

According to *Time* magazine (January 24, 1994), "The picture of Gillooly remains fuzzy; he seems to project virtually no identity beyond that of being Harding's on-again-off-again spouse." Thus when Tonya claimed he once cornered her in a boatyard and threatened, "I think we should break your legs and end your career," it was difficult to tell whether she was merely another female victim like Nancy or a noir femme fatale who, after using Gillooly as one of her henchmen, was now setting him up to take the rap. Because the NBC movie chooses to perpetuate this "mystery" and to hedge on the extent of her guilt (whether she is "little orphan Tonya" or the "wicked bitch of the west"), it focuses instead on clearly defining the formerly fuzzy Gillooly. Dubbed "the average guy" by *Time*, the movie shows him struggling to assert his authority over Tonya and her world-class managers, despite his own feelings of inadequacy. His resentments and frustrations as "Mr. Tonya Harding" are made very understandable—especially to the male writer who frames the movie and who is prominently featured on screen as another cynical young man with big aspirations. Wishing he were a great novelist like Tolstoy instead of a TV hack helping his network win the sweeps, this noirish narrator makes us more sympathetic to Gillooly's doomed drive for power and fame. Though he candidly admits that both skaters are victims of the media, like Gillooly he tries to cash in by giving their story his own personal twist. But because he lacks talent and vision, he restricts both world-class skaters to the familiar moves of domestic melodrama and squeezes their burgeoning saga into the narrow conventions of a made-for-TV movie. Like the "real" writers of this movie, he failed to see the big picture.

Nationalizing the Olympics through Narratives

As Mark Phillips pointed out, part of the power of Tonya and Nancy's saga lay in its seemingly unlimited seriality. It was not merely one of the mini-narratives that enlivened the TV coverage of the 1994 Winter Olympics. Rather, Tonya had succeeded in appropriating that global sporting event as merely one chapter in her own never-ending story. Yet, what the CBS commentators failed to acknowledge is that they (along with other American mass media) used that appropriation to perpetuate their own domestication of an international event. Once again they could demonstrate that it was American media stars and genres that were the biggest draws in the global market.

While the narrative competition between Tonya and Nancy was well known, what was perhaps less apparent is that there was a larger competition going on between nations over whose narrative would succeed in "nationalizing" the Olympics. In most countries this battle was being waged primarily on two fronts—in the sporting events themselves and in documentaries and television coverage of the games. But the scandalous saga of Tonya and Nancy enabled the United States to narrativize the Olympics across the whole gamut of American pop culture, which succeeded (as usual) in capturing world attention. These dynamics did not begin at Lillehammer.

The Olympics have a long history of being the target of competing narratives which have tried to appropriate it for a specific political agenda. Two of the most dramatic examples are the 1936 Olympics in Berlin, where Hitler hoped to demonstrate Aryan superiority—a drama that was subverted by the spectacular performance of African-American athlete Jesse Owens but still documented on film by Leni Riefenstahl—and the

1968 Olympics in Mexico City where the government intended to use the games to demonstrate the nation's progress but ended up massacring student demonstrators who were protesting against their nation's huge expenditures on the event. Only in the United States has this process of narrativization been designed primarily by television networks to boost their ratings for the games and thereby justify their huge investment in buying the broadcast rights—a strategy that reached new heights in NBC's coverage of the 1992 summer Olympics in Barcelona.

By prefacing most of the sporting events with serialized mini-narratives about two or three competitors, the network turned each Olympic event into the climax for what appeared to be a larger story. Even if the featured competitors did *not* win the race (which frequently happened), then it was still interesting for viewers to monitor the reactions of the losers. Not only did this strategy boost ratings, it also helped to justify an almost exclusive focus on U.S. athletes (regardless of their performance), thereby reinforcing American ethnocentrism. Working on the assumption that narrative is the only means of gaining audience identification with the athletes, it also changed the meaning of the event for most American viewers— the Olympics were now about the "drama" and "back story" of the competition (where our nation's media usually excel) rather than the actual performances (where our athletes sometimes fall short).

In 1992 the NBC coverage achieved its greatest success with the story of "the Dream Team," a group of all-star professional basketball players who were playing on the same team together for the first time. Not only did they easily win the gold, but their all-American mini-narrative featured the great Magic Johnson as its star with his heart-wrenching story of having to quit basketball because of being HIV-positive—a story with global appeal that transcended the Olympic games.

In 1992 the United States was certainly not the only country trying to domesticate the Olympics for its own national goals. The host country Spain was using it as the culmination of a year-long celebration of the 500th anniversary of Columbus's discovery of the new world, and Catalonia was using it to globalize its regional television network (TV-3) and to assert its cultural independence from Spain—a goal that was partially achieved when Spain's King Juan Carlos greeted the crowd in Catalan before officially opening the games. The spectacular opening and closing ceremonies were designed to support Barcelona's claim of being "the new cultural capital of Europe" and apparently they partially succeeded, for even several American commentators acknowledged that the city of Barcelona was the most impressive star of the Olympics. This perception was also supported by NBC's coverage, which featured a series of brief vignettes on the city and its massive remodeling for the event. On the other hand, NBC often reduced Barcelona to merely a picturesque backdrop for the Dream Team which attracted huge crowds of fans as they ambled down the Ramblas. The implication was that Spaniards and Catalonians (like most global spectators) would rather get a glimpse of Magic than watch the international competitions and were far more impressed with American superheroes than with local color.

The prospect of matching this American feat for the 1994 Winter Olympics seemed impossible. Since this was the first time it was being separated from the Summer Olympics, it would be taking place only two years after the Winter games of 1992. Moreover, the Winter Olympics were seldom a big draw with American television audiences because the range of sports was narrower and U.S. athletes rarely took home gold. The most popular event, figure skating, was a feminized sport rarely featured in the U.S. press. To turn this around, CBS would need a big story with global appeal. At first, the strongest potential protagonist for an American tearjerker with plenty of twists seemed to be Dan Jansen, the hard-luck skater who fell in the 500 meter race he was favored to win in the 1988 Olympics because of grief over the death of his sister and who had been losing ever since. He would fall again in the 500 at Lillehammer before finally overcoming his "lack" by winning the gold in the 1,000 meter event. But this story of male lack (talent without medals) was dramatically upstaged by the female skaters who figured in "the Dream Scheme"—the kooky plot to cripple Nancy Kerrigan, which soon became the most sensational Olympics melodrama ever told.

It may not have been an "uplifting" story like Magic's courageous confrontation with HIV, yet it transcended the mini-narratives of 1992 by generating a new kind of omnivorous TV series that incorporated and hybridized many of American television's most popular genres. Like *American Gladiators,* it had extravagant spectacle and skimpy costumes. Like soaps, it had intense female rivalries and a never-ending supply of surprising new twists. Like crime shows, it had its line-up of eccentric prime suspects who could be tracked down in real time with the aid of vigilant viewers. Like Court TV, it had clever legal maneuvers and woeful tales of mitigating circumstances. Like magazine shows, it had its real-life Murphy Browns competing over getting an exclusive interview with Tonya. Like talk shows, it had confessions, tears, and profuse professional opinions. And it generated plenty of strange hybrids. For example, on the day of the Oscars, the Geraldo show featured a mock trial with Tonya and Nancy lookalikes and a prosecuting attorney who was an Anglo dressed as a Sikh.

CBS accentuated Tonya's rough edges, showing her take gum out of her mouth, use her inhaler, clench her fists, and bend over awkwardly to tie her defective laces; the best the commentators could say of her run-throughs was that they were "close to clean." Of course, like Roseanne, Tonya created her own character, and she partially controlled the *mise en scène* for her less than sterling performance in the "Ladies Technical Program." Not only did she select the sarcastic "Much Ado About Nothing" for her music, but, like the defiant Scarlett O'Hara, she chose to wear a brazen low-cut bright red costume for that critical moment when she first faced her harshest judges. No one could say she didn't have guts!

In the process of narrativizing and nationalizing the winter Olympics, the Dream Scheme also feminized TV sports—with scandals that could rival the rape by Mike Tyson and with ratings that could elevate the status of the winter games within the wonderful world of entertainment. If the Dream Team could fast-break in the global footsteps of fast-paced action superheroes like Schwarzenegger and Stallone, then Tonya and Nancy could punch the melodramatic female rivalries of world-class soaps like *Dynasty* well over the top. And like *Thelma and Louise,* the Dream Scheme demonstrated that female reinscriptions of popular American action genres definitely had global appeal.

In some ways the Dream Scheme was even better suited than the Dream Team to the project of nationalizing the Olympics. Although the latter drew players from different regions and leagues to form a unified American collective, it was still defeating other nations within the traditional structure of an international event. But the Dream Scheme threatened to transform the games by upstaging the traditional competition between nations with a more sensational personal battle between two long-time rivals from the same nation who represented the two opposing coasts: New England's fancy Nancy as the fairy princess from the east versus Portland's hardboiled Harding as the wicked witch of the west. Meanwhile, other transformative plots were brewing in the east.

The Cold War Legacy

Once Tonya was out of the running, a new narrative emerged—one that put the cold war legacy on ice. In the international competition Nancy Kerrigan lost the gold medal to the Ukrainian skater Oksana Baiul by one tenth of one point. While Nancy was voted number one by judges from three Anglo nations (the USA, Canada, and Great Britain) and their trading ally Japan, Oksana (who was still showing signs of pain from an injury suffered in a freak collision with a German skater) was put in first place by judges from nations with a communist legacy—three former members of the Soviet bloc (Poland, Czechoslovakia, and the Ukraine) and China (whose Bronze medalist Chen Lu learned to skate by watching videotapes because there were no Chinese figure skaters as models). The tie was broken in Oksana's favor by a German judge from the former Democratic Republic, who may have been doubly inclined to help her—out of compensation for the injury caused by the German competitor and out of solidarity with their common historic loyalties. These political dynamics were duly noted by CBS commentators and then promptly dropped.

Although an East European counter-narrative of post-cold war national identity was not emphasized by CBS, it was clearly implicit in the scores. According to this narrative logic, despite the fall of communism, East European nations from the former Soviet bloc were still capable of being world class contenders—even an orphan nation from the former Soviet Union like the Ukraine. Unlike Tonya, their waifish champion Oksana was *truly* an orphan (even her CBS mini-narrative said so)—one who triumphed in the face of both personal *and* political hardship.

The skaters showed their true mettle in the "special performances" following the awards. Gold medalist Oksana demonstrated that (even though she had skated to American Broadway tunes during her winning performance), as a citizen of the former Soviet Union she was the *true* swan, now wearing white and doing a flawless performance to the *real* "Swan Lake." On the other hand, once she had slipped to second place, the supposedly "swanlike" Nancy now loosened up, baring her arms for the first time in a sleeveless low-cut yellow costume as she skated to Barbra Streisand's "With One Look" and promptly fell after one of her jumps.

But the Americans didn't give up; they merely pursued a different narrative strategy that disavowed politics while adopting Hollywood's successful bromo that it was all a matter of entertainment—of simply who put on the best show. Although CBS commentators frequently called the judges from the Eastern bloc "conservative," they accused them not of political favoritism but of being incapable of appreciating skaters at the cutting edge (like Canada's provocative Elvis Stojko, who ended up in second place). While Kerrigan could hardly be called avant-garde, she was pointedly linked to Elvis when one CBS commentator observed, "This will be an Olympics that is memorable for some *silver* medal performances."

Despite the American disavowal of politics, like the Catalonians at Barcelona and the East Europeans at Lillehammer, we certainly had our own national axe to grind. The Dream Scheme occurred shortly after the Europeans succeeded in excluding film and television from the 1993 GATT treaty (General Agreement on Tariffs and Trade)—much to the chagrin of the American entertainment industry and its feisty little lobbyist, Jack Valenti. Thus, there was a new reason to savor the appropriation of the world competition by American mass media and its stories of violent rivalry.

As soon as Oksana got her winning marks, edging past Nancy for the gold, CBS broadcast a strange interlude—part editorial, part commercial—which seemed to challenge the decision of the international judges. As a female voice sang, "A dream is a wish your heart makes ...," we saw a montage of lyrical images from Nancy's stunning performance. Then a male voice-over asked, "Nancy Kerrigan, you've won the hearts of the world, what are you going to do next?" As we heard the voice of the incipient silver medalist coyly reply, "I'm going to Disney World," we saw her (garbed in the same costume that she wore in the final competition) gliding across the ice with none other than Mickey Mouse! This image evoked an earlier bizarre incident that occurred just before her "free skate" performance when she was nearly hit by a teddy bear that someone threw onto the ice. Although Nancy was severely criticized and mocked (especially by David Letterman) for appearing in this Disney commercial, its broader editorializing function was ignored. The ad seemed to proclaim that, despite Oksana's winning of the gold, in the wonderful world of Disney capitalism, Nancy Kerrigan was still number one, for she would make more money in endorsements and her face and voice would be more recognizable worldwide.

This prophecy was fulfilled in the 1994 Academy Award ceremonies (one of the few other television events besides the Olympics that draws such a huge global audience) where Nancy Kerrigan not only presented an Oscar along with Hollywood stars but also appeared as one of the supermodels in a new Revlon commercial. Playing with the superficial similarities between the words *Revlon,* and *Revolutionary,* the ad poses the question: how does a woman become revolutionary? This question is answered by the one model of color, Veronica Wehb, who mischievously quips, "By going without makeup.... Sorry, Revlon!" Providing a new definition of radical chic that redefines politics as a pose, the commercial casts Cindy Crawford as the standard model and surrounds her with others who expand the boundaries of what is acceptable as a supermodel— boundaries of age (Lauren Hutton), color (Veronica Wehb), and context (Nancy Kerrigan). The very inclusion of these others merely calls attention to the boundaries that were supposedly being transgressed. Nancy is an outsider from the world of sports who merely "looks" the part of supermodel and movie star and who is there as a participant only by the grace of a special invitation from the Academy and its sponsors. The same was true of musical superstar Bruce Springsteen, who, when accepting his first Oscar, thanked the Academy for being invited to "your" event, and of Spanish filmmaker Fernando Trueba, who when accepting his award for best foreign film thanked, not God, but Billy Wilder—another outsider who made good in Hollywood. My point is that these inclusions merely demonstrated that this global event was strictly a Hollywood affair—a point that was also underscored by the selection of Whoopi Goldberg as host. As an African-American woman, she helped make the event look culturally diverse (at least in the national context), but her in-jokes were addressed primarily to the American audience and were virtually incomprehensible to most foreign viewers. When compared with Oscar ceremonies of previous years (which sometimes even had cutaways to acceptances in other nations as well as tributes to foreign filmmakers), the telecast of the 1994 Academy Awards seemed as nationalistic as the 1994 broadcast of the Olympics. This shift may be related to the surprising defeats that America suffered at GATT and at Lillehammer, despite the captivating "Dream Scheme" of Tonya and Nancy.

17

< Zillah R. Eisenstein and
Patricia R. Zimmermann

The Olympics and Post-Cold War Femininities

Tonya and Nancy

Femininities and Nationalities

Most of the noise and news of the Nancy Kerrigan/Tonya Harding rivalry, assault, and competition coverage focused on the two women. They constituted the melodrama.

We want to shift the narrative to the larger political, cultural, transnational context of the Tonya/Nancy episode and explore the story as a narrative about post-communist varieties of racialized nation building and transnational constructions of femininity. The narrative simply enlarges the episode by contextualizing the Kerrigan/Harding affair as it simultaneously interfaces with the racialized and sexual politics of nation building. Our point is not that Kerrigan and Harding displace and stand in for another "realpolitik" but rather that politics, as in nation building, has become imaginary in and of itself.

The Eastern European revolutions of 1989 exploded the borders of nation states. The global economy now spans an international network that redraws nationhood. As the new nationalisms carve out and invent new patriotisms, the gendered, racialized, and sexualized constructions of nation states are recontextualized historically. The racialized blood lines of Serb nationalism and the horrific destruction of women in rape/murder prison camps bespeak these outlines.

Femininity, as it is positioned against masculinity, defines the contours of nation building. Feminism is positioned against militarism; Islamism against Christianity; colorations of brown against whiteness. And these writings are inscribed on women's bodies, which represent the territories of nationalist identities.[1]

There is no easy read of women or their bodies today. Amidst the cacophony of popular imagery of western womanhood—Hillary Clinton, Jackie Onassis, Anita Hill, etc.—there are still rules to be followed. Women can be president's wives, but not presidents. In sports, women are to remain feminine though athletic, strong though not aggressive, disciplined though not overzealous.

There is no simple causal relation between the Tonya/Nancy affair and the mixed and fluctuating gender relations of the post-cold war era. But the historical complexity and crisscrossing effect of the new nationalisms in Eastern and Central Europe and the racialized/sexualized politics of "the" West resonate in this narrative which both recalls and effaces the memory of the Olympic competitions held ten years ago in Sarajevo, a beautiful old multicultural city that now lies in ruins.

Tonya and Nancy are supposedly two very different women. Yet both come from working-class families. Both are committed skaters. Both are good athletes. Both are white. Tonya is thicker and somewhat stronger. Nancy is thinner and more feminine looking. Tonya talks tough; Nancy does not. Tonya was married; Nancy is not. Tonya was depicted as bad, Nancy as good. Neither one easily fits the unitary mold of femininity prescribed by national figure skating rules. Or nation-building.

Serbs, Croats, and Muslims used to live together; they were more similar than different. Today they only speak their differences. Nations—like gender and race—are always in part fiction. The fiction, part fantasy and part real, allows us to see whatever we need to see.

On Bodies and Nations

The end of the cold war reflects and instigates new visions of "the feminine." And the feminine is always tied to notions of racialized "motherhood" in terms of family or nation. Mothers or "the mother nation" are the subtext, or the text, for mapping out the choices for girls/women.

The Olympics are premised on cold war perceptions of nationhood defined within a superpower network. There are no more iron curtain or clear cut superpower struggles. Instead there are multiple "new-old" nationalisms and an internationalized transnational global web. The '94

Olympics, amidst all the world flux, contrasts greatly with the Sarajevo games set in the cold war order: the Olympics of Tonya and Nancy were held against the backdrop of mass rapes in Bosnia-Herzegovina.

The '94 Olympics offered an escape from the dismantling of nations and the disintegration of the former statist communist regimes. One could pretend that things were no different. The Olympics—the athletic competition between nations—assumes the "fiction" of "the nation." The fiction is real enough but not true; much like the fiction of motherhood itself. Motherhood is real enough; but there are as many types of mothers as there are types of women, as there are types of family.

Nation and motherhood—and their connected fiction of femininity—are treated as stable, unitary, and unchanging. However, nation building and femininity will be anything but singular in the 21st century. They will be defined in plural terms, most often in racialized meanings which are already engendered.

Serb nationalism defines the nation by blood lines; this racialized definition is translated through a masculinist notion of destruction and statehood. The unity of the nation is defined by singularity and exclusivity. And we see the nation as "the mother country." She is also singular; woman is imaged as the nation. She is seen and silenced simultaneously. Nationalism, as a form of familialism, is naturalized by "the mother"; women are the mothers of the race.

Seeing, and the visual, are key to nation building. It is why bodies and physicality are the site for marking difference as borders. The body is unique in its utter intimacy as a location of politics. Nation borders are made of blood/racial lines. Women are needed to reproduce these lines. War is made with this blood; masculinist racialized nationalisms use these bodies of women. The annihilation and destruction of the body is an attempt to smash difference itself.

The symbolizing of the woman's body traces back to racialized and sexual psychic borders where fictions and fantasies are layered. The signs on/of the body seem naturalized as they resonate internally. However, nations are not natural. They are invented. And they are invented as "fictions" of fraternal belonging. These "imagined communities"[2] are really male fantasies of a world with women silenced. They create the outsider border of the community.

Post-cold war nationalisms are defining new-old patriarchal racial origins as their sense of community. It is against this backdrop that Tonya and Nancy skated at the 1994 Olympics. No wonder everyone watched so carefully. Their skating had been laden with the tumultuous and fluctuating meanings of post-cold war politics, where there are no simple winners or losers.

Tarnished Fictions

In the February 21, 1994 issue of *Time* magazine, two adjacent images picture how the Olympics performs as an idealized fantasy of cold war internationalism. The Walt Disney-like, multicultural unity of the Olympics moved aside the dead bodies that mark the civil war in Bosnia. Here, photographs serve as maps of the nationalist psyche. Pictures of dead Muslim, Serb, and Croat bodies mark the remade, racialized borders of the post-cold war. And pictures of Tonya and Nancy mark fantasy projections of superior white femininity that would seem to cross borders without passports or visas.

In the photo on the top of the page, Tonya Harding occupies the center, head abjectly pointed down. A baggy white t-shirt shrouds her. Five newsmen with video and still cameras tower over her. Right below her, an image of a Sarajevo cemetery, obscured with snow. The new, makeshift gravestones jut out like planks, or bleacher seats turned sideways. A bus cruises outside the cemetery fence. Bombed buildings and rubble crowd the frame. *Time*'s cut line reads: "Tarnished ideals are embodied in the Tonya Harding case and the ruin of Sarajevo, site of 1984's Olympic idyll."[3]

These two photographs speak to mythologies of the nation. These images graph how the reality of racialized wars and dead bodies destroy the unified, psychic construct of the nation. These two images rebuild the disordered and disorderly nation state with women's bodies, with Tonya and Nancy. The photographs speak to how the feminized visual reorders the confusions and horrors which mark the current geopolitical landscape.

The two images together execute a series of moves which rewrite as similar the important differences between the national, the international, the multinational, the transnational, and the multiethnic.[4] These two images together erase the important differences between the melodramatic fiction of Tonya and Nancy and the dramatic reality of war. Both the individual, specified in Tonya, and the nation, generalized in Sarajevo, have fallen from the ideal of harmony and obedience. Both are then transposed into each other, denuded of their geopolitical significance(s) and difference(s) as examples of aberrant behaviors. In these images, Sarajevo looms as the end zone for bad girls, the final solution for transgressions of sexuality, propriety, law, and competition. And Tonya becomes a fallen nation-state.

The photo of Tonya outlines the circumscribed territory for women within the nation. The body of woman and the bodies of women are stationed within a continual house arrest of visualization and domination: men wielding cameras like border guards are stationed at the perimeters of Tonya's image. The female body is always snagged within representation. Photographs create borders for the speaking subject. News photographs can sprout fantasy projections of nationalism precisely because they are stripped of the specificity of speech.[5]

Over 200,000 dead, over 20,000 raped women's bodies and over 2 million displaced Bosnian refugees should trivialize the Tonya/Nancy face-off as solipsism and rabid individualism—not as urgent as genocide.[6] Their quest for the gold is play, not a struggle for community and survival. The Muslims, Croats, and Serbs of Sarajevo imaged in the news photo specify racialized wars over who defines the body. The photographic geography of Tonya and Nancy's battles for success present nothing more than bloodless, raceless, white, war stories.

Tonya and Nancy, together and apart, fictionalize civil strife as an individual battle with rules, judges, scores, and resolutions of Olympic competition. The numerous photographs of them image and imagine civil war as civil, not war. The photographs of their strong, healthy, white bodies on ice motor a series of fantasy projections. Superior whiteness triumphs over multiethnicities. Defined borders with no context are erected rather than destabilized ones. One-on-one battle derived from the smooth narrative contours of mythology and melodrama delete collective identities engaged in war. Ulysses-like individual fortitude and the overcoming of mental anguish wipe out political negotiation and ethical positions across nations, identities, and borders.[7]

As fantasies of national unity, the skating, female bodies of Tonya and Nancy glide smoothly through the confined space of the ice rink with defined, non-negotiable borders. The destruction of the multiethnic state of Bosnia is then transposed into just another face-off on the ice and snow. Bosnia is just another example of what happens when you don't follow the rules and break the laws of cold war detente.

"Tarnished ideals" suggests that ideals of physical purity (skating, fecund, female bodies) and national unity (Sarajevo and the Olympics) should be preserved. The invocation of Nazi iconography suffuses the subtext of these two images. The cut line linking the photographs equates Tonya Harding's involvement with the destruction of Nancy's knee with the Serb's destruction of Sarajevo. Nazi iconography utilized an idealized visual culture which invoked classical Greek iconographies: superior bodies, individuals, racial purity, organized spectacles, ritual, the woman as mother.[8] Much Nazi iconography fetishized the idealized, perfect body of sport, as represented in Leni Reifenstahl's notorious documentary, *Olympia*. In Nazi iconography, the ideal depends on generalization and removal from historical context. The Nazi real is muddied by specifities. In *Time*, Scott Hamilton, a former Gold medalist in figure skating, muses on the Tonya/Nancy case: "Olympic athletes are expected to live up to a higher ideal, to remain pure."[9]

Amidst the rise of nationalism in Eastern Europe, and the intensification of neo-fascist movements in Italy, Hungary, Germany, Poland, and Russia, *Time*'s display of these two photographs together traces the persistence of Nazi iconography within our own nation state.[10] The subtext of these photographs is a visual justification for how idealized women's bodies could resolve the destabilizations of race. While democracy in the United States (unlike the newly emerging democracies of Eastern and Central Europe) may appear to keep neo-Nazis in check, it has conceded to the Nazification of the visual domain, where the hallucinations of a revived Nazism seem less noticeable and less disruptive. Nazification, therefore, can simultaneously traverse the public sphere and be outside, on the fringes; and the neo-Nazi movements of Eastern Europe are transposed for the West.

This is not to argue that the Olympics and the U.S. fanaticism around it revitalize Nazism. Rather, we claim that to understand the visualization of nationalism, internationalism, racialized ethnicity, and gender, we need to transnationalize the connections between images and histories. Imagery should be relocated and reread through the complex matrix of the international, the national, the transnational, and the multi-ethnic. The images of Tonya/Nancy, in this line of argument are truly the same. Images of Tonya and Nancy need to be rethreaded through the racialized meanings of gender.[11]

Photographs as Body Borders

Nationalist fantasies, as fantasies alone, lack materiality and location. The discourse of news photography deposits these fantasies in bodies.

These photographs discussed above circulate as the unified psychic capital of femininities and nationalities in a world destabilized by nationalisms in Eastern Europe and the former Soviet Union. News photographs of Tonya and Nancy, skating and falling, smiling and sulking, generalize the female body as the psychic location for the working through of national anxieties about the formation of nation. They specify the female body as a triumphant white physicality. They announce the potency of the whole bodies of white women against the dismembered, raped, mutilated, shot, amputated bodies jamming every news image from Bosnia.[12]

While photographs from Bosnia depict bodies bombed into fragments, images of Tonya and Nancy exalt the body as whole, unique, cherished. While photographs from Bosnia draft how racialized wars assault and maim the body, images of Tonya and Nancy show bodies isolated in space, intact, cutting through the ice—not other bodies—with blades. While images from Bosnia depict the bodies in racialized, horrific chaos, the images of Tonya and Nancy show the body as orderly, in control. Read against each other, these two sets of images record how photographs install body borders.

The February 21 cover of *Time* demonstrates how the privileging of the perfect, strong, white female bodies of Nancy Kerrigan and Tonya Harding displace the multiple dead bodies of Bosnia.[13] The headline proclaims "The Star-Crossed Olympics." The center of the frame features Nancy Kerrigan, one arm up, the other extended from her shoulder. The small skirt of her white and black skating outfit flies up to reveal her pubis, covered in white, heralding her virginal heterosexuality. She is the perfect breeder for the nation: her body is open, awaiting the embrace of the nation. Her body writes grace, perfection, strength. She is suspended, outside of defined space, floating without context and without geography. She is alone, triumphant in her physical control.

A large blow-up of Tonya's face fills half the page as cloudy background. Tonya's face becomes the territory upon which, quite literally, Nancy skates. Tonya's face stands in for a location that could be within other, more specific war iconographies, defined by place, borders, maps, territories. Over the left hand corner, an insert reads "Life and Death in Sarajevo."

This *Time* magazine cover envisions the linkage of skating women and Sarajevo. The image demonstrates how the female body rewrites America as a triumphant nation which has provided both psychic and geographic space for female physical perfection. If Nancy and Tonya can occupy the domain of the visual, then Sarajevo is displaced into the realm of words of discourse. Sarajevo, that place of dead bodies, is exiled from the visual. Nancy's full body banishes the dead bodies. She is the United States. She is democracy, *par excellence*.

Tonya and Nancy become the vessels into which ideals of national unity are deposited in contradistinction to the disunities of Europe. Nationalist ideology circulates around both Tonya and Nancy: which kind of woman will represent the nation? Discussing Tonya, *US News and World Report* asks "whether she should compete for her country."[14] Discussions about who has won or will win "nationals" allow for the playing out of repressed nationalisms in the U.S. Paul Wylie, another former Olympian, assessed Nancy's mental preparedness for competition: "it helps that she knows the whole country is behind her."[15]

Further, the fantasy constructions of nation which undergrid these images assume the form of paranoid, deluded fantasies that erupt in the narrative subplot. Shawn Eckardt, the bodyguard who masterminded the attack, operated under delusions that he was a C.I.A. agent involved in foreign espionage. His résumé is reputed to have claimed he "successfully tracked and located targeted terrorist cells through the Middle East, Central America, and Europe."[16] *Time* magazine wondered if sporting events featuring women would have to be reconfigured within more international security domains: "The question is whether sports such as skating and tennis will have to start treating every event like a gathering of foreign dignitaries."[17]

One humorous article by Joe Klein in *Newsweek* suggested that the Tonya Harding story and President Clinton's personal story were the same stories of dysfunctional families, perseverance, upward mobility, hard work. The conflation of President Clinton with Tonya Harding here suggests the collapse of the nation into the body of the woman. Klein argues "She (Tonya), like the President, can rise up and become a member of the aristocracy."[18]

Tonya and Nancy, although differently similar in class and athletics, are actually the same in the visual economy of nationhood: they spin and jump and perform for the nation and for the flag. Tonya and Nancy's gendered bodies—engaged in sequin-clad costumes exposing their legs—perform the fantasy of potential white motherhood as they also reproduce racial privilege.

Through their visualization, these stories of Tonya and Nancy merge the body of the woman with the body of the nation. These bodies then narrate the nation similarly: narratives of upward mobility, supreme physicality, familialism, and individualism skate through these iconographies.

Transnationalism and Skating as Melodrama

If capital knows no borders within the transnational economy, then news photography conversely rewrites old borders of nation states on the new bodies of young women. If the new information technologies of satellite, modems, computers, and transnationalized media operations like CBS or CNN promote a fantasy of technology freed from the ambiguities and conflicts of race, gender, and nation, then the news images of Tonya and

Nancy become the repositories for projections about strong, white, female bodies exempt from multinationalism or multiculturalism.[19] Melodrama here is not simply a genre encoding the news, but is rather a psychic fiction retrofitting the massive economic changes wreaked by transnationalization into the more recognizable, stable, and nostalgic borders of the cold war.

This deployment of melodrama to obscure the new/old borders of the post-cold war world was not only a feminist theoretical construct. Even the *New York Times* and the news magazines openly discussed their fascination with the melodramatic components of the Tonya/Nancy narrative.[20] Melodrama was obvious; what was not so obvious was how this melodramatic trope disposed of current histories. In the 1950s, melodrama served as the cultural site where the contradictions of woman and home could be detonated. It proliferated during the cold war era as the feminized underside of conflicts between the west and communism.[21]

The use of melodramatic conventions (good girl/bad girl, troubled sexuality, familial conflicts, tensions between the public sphere of work and the private sphere of the home) to frame the Tonya/Nancy debacle effectively steadies the destabilizing threats of various kinds of women in the 1990s within a more coherent, defined historical fantasy imported from the 1950s. It fabricates a place with only two kinds of women, rather than many. The invocation of melodrama removed Tonya and Nancy as women from the complexities, ambiguities, and multiplicities of 1990s femininities. It catapulted them back to a 1950s United States where women and home needed to be defended against communist incursions. Conflicts were not between countries, but between the inner and outer worlds of women. In the post-cold war period, melodrama has vacated movie and television narratives and has instead narrativized the news.

The problems of the post-cold war period on the global scale were fixed by Dan Jansen, the speed skater who kept falling but who finally won a gold medal. He occupied the place that Tonya and Nancy could not, as women and as representations. He brought back order. He redefined the nation through familialism: he skated around the rink with his Gold medal, his daughter Jane, and an American flag.[22] All was well with patriarchal nationalism and globalized familialism.

This rewriting of contemporary geopolitics within patriarchal cold war fantasies continues to flourish. In a series of full page Macy's ads which ran in the *New York Times* the week before Father's Day, 1994, Dan Jansen and his daughter Jane modeled Guess and Polo clothes in the same poses as the famous *Newsweek* photo of Dan and his daughter during the Olympics.[23] But these were not simply images of a sensitive, caring, family-identified man of the 1990s. They catapult women and mothering out of the picture. They also translate exactly what good fathering is for us: it is linked to the good men who fought the last good war against fascism. The images ran the same week as news coverage of the 50th anniversary of D-Day, and often were printed on pages opposite tributes to veterans. Post-war nationhood and post-cold war fatherhood collapse into each other.

This multinational fantasy of the Olympics summons the visual domains of the cold war and silences the new world disorder. An editorial in *Time* bespeaks this: "For two weeks the whole world is young and strong and fearless, sporting and peaceful and clean. That is the Olympic myth and the well-spring of the Games' enduring appeal. They are like national patriotic day for the whole world, a day when flags wave and people march and the grim realities of the past and, often, the present are forgotten in a global surge of pride and unity."[24]

Dreams, Nightmares, and the Political

Dreams and nightmares imprint the brief political moment Tonya and Nancy crystalized. There are really two narratives about the geopolitical gliding through their story like two skaters doing triple loops: their dreams of success and the nightmare of Sarajevo. Tonya and Nancy blabbed incessantly about their Olympic dreams, a dumb mantra propelling their own avaricious narratives of coveting money and fame. The news photographs create mirages of female physical vigor that show that their perfect bodies, too, are dreams of wholeness, strength, and self-containment.

There are many nightmares that could anchor Tonya and Nancy in the reordered post-cold war world. But the nightmare which has become Sarajevo is historically inscribed. The site of the 1984 Olympics formed the undercurrent of the Lillehammer Olympics. Ten years earlier, Katarina Witt of East Germany won her first Olympic gold medal in Sarajevo. In the 1994 Olympics, Witt, an older skater with less flashy jumps than her younger rivals, skated to the anti-war anthem "Where Have All the Flowers Gone," sung by herself and Pete Seeger. She wore a blood red dress. She dedicated her performance to the people of Sarajevo, not Disney or Campbell's Soup.[25]

Sarajevo and Lillehammer juxtaposed cold war with post-cold war politics: a multinational city versus the isolation and insularity of Lillehammer, Central and Eastern Europe versus Northern Europe, racialized territories versus white ones. In each of these couplings, the Tonya/Nancy fiction dictates we should always chose the newer version.

And the newer version is more nationalistic, more isolated, more removed from the racialized instabilities of the east, and more white. In the *Wall Street Journal*, dignitaries in Lillehammer said, "we're not used to welcoming foreigners, and now the world is coming."[26]

Before the Olympics began, a mortar attack on a market in downtown Sarajevo on February 6, 1994 killed 68 people and wounded 200.[27] The triumphant, named bodies of Tonya and Nancy, sprawled all over the *New York Times*, *Time*, and *Newsweek* cover up the dead of Sarajevo. Tonya and Nancy's bodies are phantoms from the cold war that waft through the psychic territory of the fantasized white nation. Their melodrama is less messy than the bombing of Bosnia. Their bodies have identities and stories. The dead of Sarajevo have no names and no stories. Their fantasies and dreams have been shelled to pieces.

A series of oppositions evolve as we transnationalize Tonya and Nancy.

These are not binary oppositions requiring deconstruction. Instead, they perform as an orchestrated series of differences that help us to see how both the East and West need each other for definition. The east and the west are the inside and outside of each other.

Against the healthy bodies of Tonya/Nancy—the dead bodies of Bosnia. Against the fantasies of strength, perfection, health and perfect food—mutilations and starvation. Against the mythology of internationalism—the defeat of a multiethnic nation in the war in Bosnia. Against whole bodies of Tonya and Nancy—body fragments, pieces of flesh, blood. Against a narrative reviving the cold war—the post-cold war complexities. Against the Walt Disney fantasy of internationalism which defined the Olympics—the disputed borders of Bosnia.

Afterthoughts

Months have passed since the Olympics. Tonya plea bargained and claims she was not a participant in the assault against Nancy. She made some money and seems to have lost everything else. Nancy went to Disneyland and made fun of Mickey Mouse. And then some decided she really was not all that nice afterall. She won the silver but lost the war.

The war in Bosnia has its intermittent cease-fire agreements. But the devastation and desperation continues.

And then there is Rwanda. Another horror filled war with the maiming and hacking to death of bodies. New border wars. And there is no Olympics melodrama to protect the fiction of the new world order.

< NOTES >

We would like to thank William Hooper for his research assistance.

1 See Zillah R. Eisenstein, *Hatreds in the 21st Century: Nationalism, Globalism, and Feminism* (forthcoming, Routledge).

2 Benedict Anderson, *Imagined Communities: Reflections on the Origin and Spread of Nationalism* (New York: Verso, 1983, 1991).

3 William A. Henry III, "The Star Crossed Olympics," *Time*, February 21, 1994, p. 50.

4 For discussions of transnationalism, nationalism, and multiculturalism, see Inderpal Grewal and Caren Kaplan, editors, *Scattered Hegemonies: Postmodernity and Transnational Feminist Practices* (Minneapolis: University of Minnesota Press, 1994); Leslie Sklar, *Sociology of the Global System* (Baltimore: The Johns Hopkins University Press, 1991); Andrew Parker, Mary Russo, Doris Sommer, and Patricia Yeager, editors, *Nationalisms and Sexualities* (New York: Routledge, 1992); and Jonathan Rutherford, editor, *Identity: Community, Culture, Difference* (London: Lawrence and Wishart Limited, 1990).

5 For analysis of the political relationships between representation, speech, and feminism, see Trinh T. Minh-Ha, *When the Moon Waxes Red: Representation, Gender and Cultural Politics* (New York: Routledge, 1991); Bill Nichols, *Representing Reality* (Bloomington: Indiana University Press, 1991); Paul Yirilio, *War and Cinema: The Logistics of Perception* (London: Verso, 1989); B. Ruby Rich, "The Sound of Silence," *Village Voice*, May 3, 1994, p. 16.

6 Slavenka Drakulic, *The Balkan Express: Fragments from the Other Side of the War* (New York: Harper Perennial, 1994); Rabia Ali and Lawrence Lifschultz, *Why Bosnia?: Writings on the Balkan War* (Stony Creek, Connecticut: The Pamphleteer's Press, 1993), pp. 86–132; Alexandra Stigmayer, editor, *Mass Rape: The War Against Women in Bosnia-Herzegovina* (Lincoln: University of Nebraska Press, 1994).

7 See for example Daniel Pedersen, "Where Do We Go From Here?" *Newsweek*, March 7, 1994, p. 60; Tom Callahan, "Careers on Ice and Snow," *U.S. News and World Report*, February 28, 1994, p. 64; Shannon Brown Lee, "Tonya's Nightmare: Should that Raw Bundle of Talent Represent the Red, White and Blue in Lillehammer?" *U.S. News and World Report*, February 14, 1994, p. 44; Mark Starr, "A Five Ring Circus," *Newsweek*, February 28, 1994, p. 46–50.

8 See George L. Mosse, *Nazi Culture: Intellectual, Cultural, and Social Life in the Third Reich* (New York: Schocken Books, 1966).

9 Scott Hamilton, *Time*, Febrary 14, 1994, p. 61.

10 For a discussion of the relationship between war iconography and

nationalism, see Douglas Kellner, *The Persian Gulf TV War* (Boulder, Colorado: Westview Press, 1982).

11 For analysis of the complexities of mapping how representation condenses and rewrites race and gender, see Lester D. Friedman, *Unspeakable Images: Ethnicity and the American Cinema* (Champaign: University of Illinois Press, 1991); bell hooks, *Yearning: Race, gender and cultural politics* (Boston: South End Press, 1990); and Toni Morrison, editor, *Race-ing Justice, En-gender-ing Power: Essays on Anita Hill, Clarence Thomas, and the Construction of Social Reality* (New York: Pantheon Books, 1992).

12 For example of this contrast between the whole bodies of Tonya and Nancy and the wounded of Sarajevo, see photo "Bosnians Airlifted from Sarajevo to Germany," *New York Times*, February 7, 1994, p. 1; photo, "Survivors removed a body yesterday from Sarajevo's Main Market," *New York Times*, February 6, 1994, p. 1; cover, "The Star Cross Olympics," *Time*, February 21, 1994; cover, "Thin Ice: Skater Tonya Harding," *Newsweek*, January 24, 1994; photo "Sarajevo's Disabled Brave the Snipers," *New York Times*, February 16, 1994, p. 6.

13 Cover, *Time*, February 21, 1994.

14 Shannon Brown Lee, "Tonya's Nightmare: Should that Raw Bundle of Talent Represent the Red, White and Blue in Lillehammer?" *U.S. News and World Report*, February 14, 1994, p. 44.

15 Martha Duffy, "With Blades Drawn," *Time*, February 21, 1994, p. 56.

16 "Another Skate Drops," *Newsweek*, January 31, 1994, p. 53.

17 Martha Duffy, "Why? It Hurts So Bad! Why Me?" *Time*, January 17, 1994, p. 45.

18 Joe Klein, "Hi, I'm Joe and I Love Tonya Too Much," *Newsweek*, February 14, 1994, p. 57.

19 Richard Barnett, *Global Dreams*, (New York: Simon and Schuster, 1994); Herbert Schiller, *Culture Inc.*, (New York: Simon and Schuster, 1994); Mark Poster, *The Mode of Information: Poststructuralism and Social Context* (Chicago: University of Chicago Press, 1990).

20 Katha Pollitt, "Subject to Debate," *The Nation*, March 7, 1994, p. 297; Shannon Brownlee, "Surrealism on Ice," *U.S. News and World Report*, January 24, 1994, pp. 64–66; Mark Starr, "A Five Ring Circus," *Newsweek*, February 28, 1994, pp. 46–48; Richard Sandomir, "Thirty Seconds Over Lillehammer on Air Tonya," *New York Times*, February 22, 1994, sec. B, p. 9; Jere Longman, "This Time It's a Slip as Jansen Fails Again," *New York Times*, February 15, 1994, sec. B, p. 7; Richard Sandomir, "Competition, Storytelling and No Trolls," *New York Times*, February 6, 1994, p. 12; Emily White, "Thin Ice," *Village Voice*, March 1, 1994, p. 13.

21 Laura Mulvey, "Melodrama Inside and Outside the Home," in *Visual and Other Pleasures* (Bloomington: Indiana University Press, 1989), pp. 63–77; Jackie Byars, *All That Hollywood Allows: Re-reading Gender in 1950s Melodrama* (Chapel Hill: University of North Carolina Press, 1991); and Marty Jezer, *The Dark Ages: Life in the United States 1945–1960* (Boston: South End Press, 1982).

22 Photo, "A Man, A Baby, A Medal," *Newsweek*, February 28, 1994, p. 41.

23 Macy's Ad, "Put Your Dad First on June 19," *New York Times*, June 9, 1994, p. 9; Macy's Ad, "Put Your Dad First on June 19," *New York Times*, June 10, 1994, p. 9.

24 "Finally, the Games," *Time*, February 21, 1994, p. 50.

25 Martha Duffy, "End of the Winter's Tale," *Time*, March 7, 1994, pp. 64 and 65.

26 Roger Thurow and Lee Lescaze, "Winter Olympics Hosts are Known for Skiing, Not Sunny Disposition," *The Wall Street Journal*, January 17, 1994, p. 1.

27 John Kifner, "61 Die as Shell Wrecks Sarajevo Market," *New York Times*, February 6, 1994, pp. 1 and 10; Elaine Sciolino, "Clinton Rules Out Quick Response to Bosnia A Hack," *New York Times*, February 7, 1994, pp. 1 and 8; John Kifner, "Sarajevans Mourn and Rage While Life and Death Go On," *New York Times*, February 7, 1994, p. 8; John Kifner, "Mourners Fear Gunners Even at Burials," *New York Times*, February 8, 1994, p. 15; R.W. Apple, Jr., "The West Moves to Silence the Guns and Change a State of Mind," *New York Times*, February 13, 1994, section 4, p. 1.

18

Dreaming of Tonya

The day before the attack on Nancy Kerrigan, there was a big blizzard in upstate New York. A visiting friend of mine, who had planned to leave that day, was snowed in, and I had a cold. We stayed inside and when two guys, approximately in their twenties, came to the door asking for shovelling work, we pooled our money and paid them. After they finished, we thanked them and complimented their work, maybe too warmly, because at the end of their day of shovelling, they came back and asked us out. "I got a fortune cookie last night that said I would meet a woman with long dark hair," one of them said.

The next day, my dark-haired friend sped away across the ploughed roads, and my cold was a little better. I started cleaning up my apartment, with the radio on. I was only half-listening to the sports news as the report came that Nancy Kerrigan, a figure skater, had been attacked at the National Championships in Detroit. As I heard about how she had been clubbed on the knee, I sank into a chair in my kitchen. I frequently listen to National Public Radio when I am cooking or cleaning, and occasionally, a heart-rending story (the woman whose AIDS-sick husband committed suicide with sleeping pills in yogurt—she held him in their bed until his heart stopped; the mother of the soldier who died in the Gulf War, opposing some new US intervention) will make me turn off the water in the sink and put down my sponge. I've gotten teary, once or twice, snug in my kitchen, with steam rising from a pot on the stove, or the refrigerator defrosting. After a description of the attack and the injury, I heard an interview with Nancy's coach (though I didn't at that time feel familiar enough with her to call her "Nancy"), saying that she still ought to be allowed to go to the Olympics, and I heard that the championships had been won by a skater from Portland Oregon, named Tonya Harding. I was particularly moved and disturbed by this story. I thought of my friend, driving across the interstate, where the upstate New York winds would be blowing snow from fields onto the ploughed roads. The bodies of those we cherish can seem so fragile. Somehow the injury to Nancy's knee was particularly disturbing. Maybe it was because some years ago I had trouble with my knees—not enough muscle around the knee caps—and had worked for years to get them stronger. The knees are one of those places on the body that seem a particularly vulnerable target; all those moving pieces—you have a funny bone there, and tales of kneecapping can make you feel a twinge the way the thought of a lemon can make you pucker. I thought of all the reasons that some crazy vicious man would inflict this pain on a woman's body: anxiety, threat, the desire to be intimate with the body in whatever way possible. John Lennon's killer was his fan, and seemed to want intimacy with his body; it was an erotic fantasy, that penetrating the physical body, or making an impression on it, could satisfy the extreme desire to be close to a person. Hearing Nancy Kerrigan's plucky voice at a press conference, I felt passionate admiration for her. How many hours of exercising it had taken me to get my knees in shape— a big investment of time, but nothing compared to Nancy's.

As a child, I took skating lessons for a while, riding lessons, and I went skiing a few times—but I was never very good at any of these sports: I was always afraid of falling—deeply afraid of falling. Swimming was the only sport I was any good at, and it still is the one I love—the sport in which you are always supported and will never fall. Gentle though I knew the water was, I was never able to learn to dive, even though I was given private lessons. "Just fall forward. Just let your body fall," my instructor would say, as I stood on the side of the pool, bent over, my palms pressed together, arms arched downward to the water. But I couldn't let my body fall; I stood immobilized on the wet tiles. Finally the diving coach told my mother to forget it—"if she's ever ready, she'll learn"—but I never got ready and I never learned. I admired the girls who weren't afraid of falling—who didn't fear that loss of control, who didn't fear pain, who didn't think of the fragility of their bones and their flesh. I can think of reasons for this fear: my leg was broken when I was two in a car accident in the days before seat belts were mandatory, car seats for children, and locking seat backs were mandatory. As a child I suffered from various orthopaedic maladies requiring numerous x-rays and several surgeries, so I grew up paying a lot of attention to my bones; I thought of my bones as exceptionally vexed.

Today I admire these skaters who are so unafraid of falling—or maybe they are afraid, but the fear doesn't stop them from racing across a hard, cold surface, from leaving the surface, wearing only the skimpiest of clothing—no gloves! No kneepads! I hadn't seen Nancy skate—I watched the Winter Olympics only sporadically—but that strong leg wounded— the leg that I wanted to have, with the wound that I felt I could have— was vivid in my imagination.

But, a few days later, like everyone else, as the rumors began to circulate, I started to think about Tonya. I began to watch the sports news more avidly than ever before; I bought *People* and *The National Enquirer* and watched *A Current Affair*. I talked about the events with my friends— particularly my feminist friends.

In the midst of all of this, I had a dream about Tonya.

There is a tendency among those of us in cultural studies to begin consuming a text or film as part of the vast audience that is riveted by the event. We quickly move into the analytical position and begin to focus on what the text or event means, not necessarily to us, but to other people—to that vast audience which perhaps lacks our skills, our training, our political sophistication, our time for reflection, our resources. Perhaps in reflecting on what the text means to the audience, we find ourselves as one of them. But we can also forget exactly what it was that compelled *us* to watch the TV show, to buy *People*, to read the Tonya/Nancy story in the *Times* before we read anything else—before we read the stories on the issues that we should really care about. It is difficult to consume the event from both positions—that of the analyst and that of the audience, fan, or consumer; that can be as hard as seeing the duck and the rabbit at the same time.

There is a tendency in psychoanalytic criticism to analyze the text in terms of our understanding of psychic constructs in women (or men) in general: what does this text mean to its audience—based on what we know about general psychic structures? Psychoanalytic criticism is not, after all, a clinical practice, and while it can operate with great specificity with respect to the details of a text, it cannot have that kind of specificity with respect to a reader: it tells us what texts might mean to readers in general, but not what it might mean to a specific person.

This is an effort to say not *what*, exactly, but *how* this text—the text of Tonya and Nancy—held meaning for one specific person—what one person's point of contact with it was.

I had been having problems with my boyfriend, and in my Wednesday therapy session I told my analyst that I didn't feel like seeing him that weekend—things are stalled between us; the relationship doesn't seem that rewarding. So I know I'm not going to call him suggesting that we get together, but I'm doubtful I'll be strong enough to say that I want to stay home and do other things if he calls me. He's been complaining that I don't make enough time for the relationship, and I'm afraid that saying no about this one weekend will lead to us splitting up, and I just can't bear the idea of being responsible for that.

"You can't bear the idea of being the one who killed the relationship."

"No."

Lucy takes a moment to respond. "You still feel so guilty about your brother's death," she says—my brother committed suicide when he was 22—"and your father's death"—he died alcoholic and alone—"as if you were responsible. But you weren't. One person can't keep another alive all by herself." Lucy has, of course, said as much to me many times before, but she can be patient with repetition: "And you have tried to preserve this relationship—but you cannot do it all yourself." And she tells me, very gravely, that she's been thinking again that I might benefit from attending a suicide survivor's group, and that she would look into it for me. She says that I seem very marked by my brother's suicide, and that it might be good for me to be in a group of people who have had a similar experience.

At the next session, Friday, two days later, I tell her that she really struck a chord with me when she said that I couldn't bear the self-reproach of being the one to kill off the relationship, but that the idea of this suicide survivor's group makes me uneasy. I like her; she's helping me; isn't she enough? And I suddenly remember that I had a dream on Wednesday night:

I am driving to my session and in my dream it takes two days to get there, and I stop over in a run-down hotel in a depressed town, where, during the night, my car is stolen. The next day I go to the Honda dealer and look at cars and wonder if I'll be able to buy a new one, or just a used one, with the money I get from my insurance. Later I find out that a woman whom an old boyfriend of mine is seeing—the woman he left me for—knows who stole it; the thieves are shady friends of hers. The scene shifts to a party and she is there. I accuse her of colluding with stealing my car. I hit her. I get her down on the floor and try to strangle her. Later, she writes me a letter saying she wants to be friends.

"I really don't know what this is all about," I say. "All that violence."

"What about the two days?" asks Lucy. "Two days."

And I get her drift—she is looking at the transferential aspects of the dream, at what has to do with her.

"I had this dream the night of my Wednesday session, and it's two days until the next session."

"It takes you two days to see me and you have experienced losses during that time." She pauses. "Last time I suggested the suicide survivors' group, and you say the suggestion makes you uneasy. What does the dream have to do with that?"

I have no idea what the dream has to do with her suggestion of the group—all I can do is elaborate on how I feel about the suggestion of the group. "I guess I just dread telling my story to these people. I've told it so many times. I can tell my sad little story glibly, and when I do, people seem surprised—they say 'you seem so together.' I just don't want to go through that again, seeming together and then this new group of people will get me all worked up about my brother, and I'll go to pieces and feel like a mess. I've worked really hard to get together, and I don't want to seem like a mess."

Lucy looks at me, and in her calm gaze I feel fortified to tell her something that I'd been holding back: the other woman in the dream did not in fact look like her real-life prototype, my old boyfriend's new girlfriend; she looked very much like Tonya Harding.

This is the first time that I have mentioned Tonya or Nancy or anything about the whole affair in a session, and the mention of it is tinged with the strange sense of transgression, of experimentation, of pushing the envelope, that attends mentions of events outside the immediate purview of the analysis: my past and present relationships and work. For, of course, Lucy and I are not friends or colleagues: we don't chat; we don't compare notes on movies and politics; I don't know what her interests, tastes, and habits are beyond this room. Lucy is scrupulous in maintaining her analytic stance: I long ago learned not to ask her questions about herself because she always answered with some version of "What are your fantasies about...my training...my background...my marriage...my daughter?" And so, for her even to acknowledge that yes, she has heard of Tonya Harding, seems a violation of these rules and boundaries. It's as if Lucy is telling me something intimate about herself: that she watched this show.

"The story really has fascinated me," I tell her, shyly, shamefacedly, and she nods and murmurs with the same demeanor that might greet a very dark confession.

"What fascinates you about it?" she asks me.

And I tell her about my identification with Nancy's wounded knee, and how that had since been eclipsed by my identification with Tonya's story: my family wasn't as crazy or as poor as hers, but they were pretty crazy.

"Maybe the dream does have to do with being in this group, and telling your story. These are not people you can tell it to glibly, and who will say 'You seem so together.' These are people who will understand that the effects of suicide can be deep and lasting: they will know what your story means. And Tonya Harding is someone whose life has become evident. She is not just this beautiful creature skating through life. She had a past; these were her friends, this was her family, and it has caught up with her. And you are afraid that you cannot deny your past."

This makes sense to me, and I say so.

"And what about the violence?" Lucy asks.

"I'm attacking the Tonya figure. She's not the attacker here."

"And if Tonya is this shameful part of yourself that you want to split off—this part that threatens to immobilize you; to keep you out of analysis; she and her shady friends will steal your car..."

"Then I want to suppress that part of me."

"But you don't entirely succeed, do you? At least not in this dream. She writes you a letter saying that she wants to be friends. And the question before us is, can you reconcile with that split-off woman, that Tonya?"

When we learn as much as we do about someone like Tonya Harding—hearing her mother sing to her, seeing her wedding night videos, seeing her picture in the bathtub at age ten, seeing her in a backstage monitor, as well as seeing her bodily self-expression on ice—we are given so many possible points of identification with this figure, and so many nodes around which to organize our fantasies, that the coordination of analysis of the national fantasy and analysis of the individual fantasy can be daunting.

A few weeks later, I had another dream about Tonya—a very short one. And it was a busy time of year; I was swamped with papers and midterms, and I didn't write it down. Months later, I asked Lucy if she would look in her notes and tell me what the dream was—I begged her to—but she refused. Or rather, she analyzed this request and my anger that she would not grant it—as part of a pattern in which I give more than I want to give, and grow resentful and want back what I have given. All I can remember about the dream is the deep mortification that I had felt dreaming about Tonya a second time. Yes, I had already admitted my fascination with the story, but it was embarrassing to keep dreaming about this figure from the *National Enquirer*: why couldn't I dream about characters from Shakespeare, or real cultural heroes, or even Bette Davis?

"Why should you be embarrassed?" asked Lucy, smiling. "Your unconscious is creatively making use out of what is available to it."

But doesn't my conscious self act as the research assistant, providing material to the unconscious, saying "Hey, get a load of this?" Didn't I choose this story?

Tonya says, "It's my dream."

ELLYN KESTNBAUM

A Glossary of Skating Terms
Quotations are from the 1992–93 USFSA rulebook.

Artistic Impression: The second mark for the free program, also referred to as Composition and Style, taking into consideration "(a) Harmonious composition of the program as a whole and its conformity with the music chosen; (b) Utilization of the area; (c) Easy movement and sureness in time to the music; (d) Carriage; (e) Originality; (f) Expression of the character of the music" (86). As of the 1994–95 seasons the second mark for the free program is called the Presentation mark.

Axel: Also occasionally called an Axel Paulsen or Paulsen jump after its Norwegian inventor, the axel is the only jump with a forward takeoff, from the forward outer edge of one foot to the back outer edge of the opposite foot. The single axel thus consists of one and a half revolutions, placing it at an intermediate level of difficulty between single and double jumps. The double axel involves two and half revolutions, the triple axel three and a half. Most male singles skaters competing at the international level include triple axels in their programs; Midori Ito and Tonya Harding are the only two women to have completed the triple axel successfully in competition. Variations, which are rarely performed and almost never as more than singles, are the inside axel (forward inside to backward outside edge of the same foot) and the one-foot axel (forward outside to backward inside, usually followed with a double or (rarely) triple salchow in combination.

Back Spin: Any spin, or generically one in the upright position, performed on the right foot if rotated counterclockwise (or the left foot if clockwise) so that the heel of the blade leads the rotation.

Biellmann Spin: A variation of the layback spin, invented by 1981 world champion Denise Biellmann of Switzerland, in which the skater grasps the blade of the free leg with one or both hands and pulls it straight up toward the ceiling above her head while holding the torso arched up rather than backward. Only the most flexible female skaters are able to perform this move.

Broken-Leg Spin: A variation of the sit spin in which the free leg is held to the side of the body rather than in front with the knee bent rather than straight.

Camel Spin: A spin in which the upper body and free leg are stretched in opposite directions away from the skating leg, parallel to the ice at hip level, so called because beginners learning the move often drop both head and free leg too low, leaving the hips sticking up like a camel's hump. Variations include the change-foot camel spin, in which the skater moves from a forward to a back camel spin by replacing the spinning foot with the free foot, and the flying camel, a back camel spin entered from the air. The "Hamill camel," named after 1976 Olympic gold medalist Dorothy Hamill, is a flying camel combined with a back sit spin, with the blade of the free foot tapped on the ice as the change of body position is made.

Change of Edge: As the name implies, changing from the inner to outer or outer to inner edge of the blade on one foot by shifting weight (and lean) from one side of the body to the other. This has the effect of reversing the direction of the curve being skated, e.g., right front outer (clockwise) to right front inner (counterclockwise).

Checking: The muscular effort to stop (or check) the rotation of a jump or spin for a still body position on the exit, or to maintain control of the curve of an edge without overrotation. Although the whole body is involved in this effort—and in landing a jump, a controlled swing of the free leg from in front of the body to behind is necessary—strength in the back and shoulders are particularly important.

Combination Spin: A spin involving at least one change of foot and/or of body position.

Death Drop: A flying spin in which the limbs and torso are extended at the highest point in the air, then closed in while descending to a low back sit spin, so that the body has further to fall than in an ordinary flying sit spin. Formerly known as an "open axel flying sitspin."

Edge Jump: A jump in which the takeoff is initiated from the inner or outer edge of one blade only: salchow, loop, and axel (and half loop and walley). Opposed to toe jumps.

Edges: The ice skate blade is sharpened with two edges separated by a concave hollow on the bottom of the blade. Skating upright in a perfectly straight line, both edges are on the ice at once (known as skating on the flat of the blade). Most skating moves, however, are skated on curves, with the body and skating blade tilted toward the center of a circle either toward or away from the center of the body and the free foot, on the inside or outside edge of the blade respectively. Two edges per blade times two directions each can travel (forward and backward) times two feet, yields a total of eight edges: right forward outer, left forward outer, right forward inner, left forward inner, right back outer, left back outer, right back inner, left back inner, abbreviated RFO, LFO, etc. In general, outer edges provide more stability than inner edges. The most stable edge, used for exiting most jumps and spins, is the back outer edge in the direction of the skater's natural rotation (right back outer for the majority of skaters who rotate counterclockwise).

Flip Jump: A jump from the back inner edge of one foot to the back outer edge of the other, assisted by the toe pick of the free foot at takeoff. Although the flip is essentially a "toe salchow," it is more difficult as it is performed from a straighter, shallower edge and requires exact timing to coordinate digging the toe pick into the ice and pushing off into the air, initiating the rotation with the arms and shoulders, and transferring weight from the takeoff skating side of the body to the landing side. (Not to be confused with a backflip, which is illegal in amateur competition.)

Flying Spin: Any spin initiated with a jump. A clear chosen position must be obtained in the air and the same or a different position maintained upon landing.

Footwork: Art intricate sequence of steps (turns and edges) performed on the ice. See Step Sequence.

Free Leg: The leg which is not currently engaged on the ice and so is free to be carried in any position in relation to the rest of the body that facilitates the move being performed and/or adds visual or artistic interest. The entire side of the body opposite the skating foot is known as the free side, so one might refer to the free foot, the free arm, etc. See Skating Foot.

Free Program: A singles skating program, four minutes for women and four and a half for men, worth two-thirds of a skater's total score for the competition. A free program should include jumps, spins, steps, and other skating movements of the skater's choice. No specific moves are required, but the program should be well balanced and there are limitations on the number of triple jumps that may be performed or repeated in the program. Only those moves that are successfully completed count toward the technical merit score.

Half Loop: Actually a full (single) revolution jump, from the backward outer edge of one foot to the back inner edge of the other foot. It is generally used as a transitional move in the middle of a jump sequence or, followed by a double or (rarely) triple salchow, in a jump combination.

Ina Bauer: A two-footed gliding move, named for its inventor, in which the front knee is bent with the skate traveling forward at a right angle to the body, and the back leg is straight with the skate turned at right angles from the facing of the body, 180 degrees opposite from the front skate and traveling backward. In other words, the legs are in a ballet fourth position lunge and the body is traveling sideways relative to the direction of facing.

International Skating Union (ISU): The international governing body of amateur competitive figure skating.

Jump: Any move in which the skater propels herself into the air by pushing off the ice with one skate blade or one blade and the toe pick of the other blade. Small jumps with no, half, or one revolution may be used as transitional moves in step sequences and aren't always named. For the larger, more important of these seen in competition, see Split Jump and Walley. The jumps that can be performed with multiple revolutions have become increasingly important as a test of competitors' athleticism (and the technique to perform them has become increasingly refined), so that whereas in the 1930s Sonja Henie could win Olympic gold medals without any of the double jumps pioneered by her male contemporaries, by the 1980s women as well as men were expected to perform more and more triples. For full credit, these jumps must be landed on a controlled backward edge on one foot. See Axel, Flip, Loop, Lutz, Salchow, and Toe Loop.

Jump Combination: Two or more jumps performed in immediate sequence, with no intermediate steps, so that the landing edge of the first jump becomes the takeoff of the next—most often a double toe loop.

Because it takes off from the standard landing position (back outer edge with the free leg swung behind to tap into the ice) the toe loop is the most common second jump in a combination. The loop jump also takes off from the back outer edge and so can be added after a landing, but it is much more difficult in combination because it must be initiated immediately while the free leg is still in front and doesn't benefit from the extra impetus of the toe loop's two-foot takeoff or the longer preparation of the uncombined loop jump. The salchow can be executed in combination following a one-foot axel or half-loop jump, which are landed on the weaker, less stable back inner edge.

Since the amount of momentum on the landing of a jump is always diminished somewhat from the amount at takeoff, the second or third jump of a combination is harder to perform than the first. Thus, a double-triple combination is harder than triple-double, and triple-triple is harder still.

Any turns on the ice or changes of foot between the two jumps preclude a true combination and occasion deductions in the required jump combination in the technical program. See Jump Sequence.

Jump Sequence: A series of jumps in close succession, but with some intervening turns or steps. The second or third jump in a sequence is easier than the second or third in a jump combination, but more difficult than if performed in isolation.

Layback Spin: A spin in which the upper body is bent backward from the hips and upper back so that the face looks up to the ceiling. The free leg is either extended straight back and down, or more commonly bent up into a ballet back attitude position. Of all the basic spin positions, the layback is most dependent on the spin being well centered. It is rarely performed as a back spin, and because of the upper back flexibility required, rarely performed by males.

Loop Jump: A jump from the back outer edge to the same back outer edge, with one or more revolutions in the air; so called because if it were performed without leaving the ice the blade would leave a loop-shaped tracing on the ice. More difficult than the salchow or toe loop because the free leg is already in crossed position at takeoff so the rotation is initiated from the upper body and the edge of the skating foot only, but less difficult than the flip or lutz because the coordination of timing need not be quite so exact.

Lutz: A jump from the back outer edge of one foot (on the curve counter to the natural rotation) to the back outer edge of the opposite foot, assisted by the toe pick of the free foot at the time of takeoff. It is usually approached on a long, fairly straight back edge, with the skater looking back over her free shoulder before jumping to gauge the distance to the barrier (or to other skaters during practice). The reversal of the direction of rotation at takeoff is what makes this jump more difficult than the flip, to which it is otherwise similar and with which it shares the necessity of exact timing. Triple lutz is the most difficult jump performed by most top female competitors.

Mohawk: A change of foot accompanied with a change of direction from forward to backward; e.g. right front inner to left back inner (inside mohawk) or left front outer to right back outer (outside mohawk).

Natural Rotation: Just as most people are right handed, on the ice most people have a natural preference to curve in a counterclockwise direction (although some prefer clockwise). This natural preference is magnified in the very fast rotations required for advanced spins and jumps, so that skaters very rarely spin and almost never jump in the direction opposite to the natural rotation.

Ordinals: Judge by judge, each skater's marks for required elements and presentation are added and the skaters ranked ordinally (first, second, etc.) with the highest total first. If a judge's totals for two (or three) skaters are the same, the required elements mark breaks the tie in the technical program, the artistic impression (presentation) mark in the free program. If both marks are the same, the skaters are assigned the same ordinal placement and the next (or next two) ordinal places not assigned. The skater placed first by the majority of judges is first in the event, the competitor placed second or better by a majority is second, and so on. See Appendix II.

Pivot: A move in which the edge of one skate (forward or backward, inner or outer) describes a circle around a center anchored by the toe pick of the other skate, like drawing a circle with a compass.

Presentation: The second mark for the technical program, taking into consideration "(a) Harmonious composition of the program as a whole and its conformity with the music chosen; (b) Difficulty of the connecting steps; (c) Speed; (d) Utilization of the ice surface; (e) Easy movement and sureness in time to the music; (f) Carriage and style; (g) Originality; (h)

Expression of the character of the music" (90). As of the 1994–95 season, the second mark in the program is also called Presentation; see Artistic Impression.

Qualifying Competition: One of a series of competitions a skater must do well at to be eligible to compete at the next level. The United States is divided into three sections (Eastern, Midwestern, and Pacific), each of which is in turn divided into three regions. The top four finishers in each category at the regional competitions move on to compete at the sectionals, and the top four at each sectional competition move on to the nationals. The top finishers in the nationals in the senior events in turn are chosen to represent the United States at the Olympics (in Olympic years) and at the world championships. The number of skaters a country may send to these championships is determined by its highest place finish in the previous year's world championships: countries with a skater in the top three (singles and dance) or top five (pairs) have three international spots in that event, a finish in the top ten allows two spots, and all other countries are allowed only one entry. The United States has usually had at least one medalist in Ladies Singles in the past 40 years; Nancy Kerrigan's fifth-place finish at the worlds in 1993 allowed only two spots in 1994.

Required Elements: The first mark for the technical program, taking into consideration "(a) Jumps and jump combinations: the height, length, technique and the clean starting and landing of the required jumps; (b) Spins: strong and well-controlled rotation, number of revolutions in the required position, speed of rotation (in fast spins), centering of the spin. In flying spins, the height of the jump; (c) Step and spiral sequences: the difficulty of the steps used, the swing, carriage and smooth flow of the movement in conformity with the character and the rhythm of the music" (90). There are mandatory deductions for failing to complete and for omitting any of the required jumps, spins, and step sequences. Extra moves are also penalized. See Technical Program.

Salchow: A jump from the back inner edge of one foot to the back outer edge of the opposite foot, named for the turn-of-the-century Swedish world champion Ulrich Salchow. The jump is usually prepared with a forward outside three turn. Swinging the free leg forward at the takeoff deepens the takeoff edge, slightly reducing the amount of rotation required in the air, and also helps provide impetus for the rotation. The salchow is usually the first jump a skater learns to double and the first or second to triple.

School Figures: Skating exercises performed on two or three circles, elaborated by turns, loops, and changes of edge, in which the emphasis is on precision in tracing exact circles on the ice. Until 1991 skaters had to pass the final (in the U.S., the eighth) figure test, along with a freeskating component, to qualify for singles competition at the senior level and the advanced figures served as the first event of the competitions. As of 1991, the United States has had separate testing and competition tracks for figures and freestyle at the novice, junior, and senior levels; school figures are no longer included in international competition.

Scoring: Each judge assigns each skater two marks for each event: for Required Elements and Presentation in the technical program and for Technical Merit and Artistic Impression (now Presentation) in the free program. Marks are based on a standard where 6.0 is considered perfect. See final section of this book.

Scratch Spin: An upright spin in which the arms and free leg begin extended to the side and are gradually pulled in close to the body to obtain maximum rotational speed. So named because the weight is balanced between the center of the blade and the first tooth of the toe pick, which scratches circles into the ice.

Shoot-the-Duck: A forward or backward gliding move on one foot with the skating leg completely bent so the hips are lower than the knee and the free leg extended straight forward, as in the sit spin.

Sit Spin: A spin performed with the skating leg bent and the free leg extended straight front from the hip. In a good sit spin the hips are lower than the bent knee and the torso straight and tilted forward from the hip joints, not bent forward in the waist or upper back. Arm position is variable, although bracing one or both hands on the skating knee lessens the difficulty. Also known as the Jackson Haines spin after its inventor, the 19th-century American popularizer of artistic skating, Jackson Haines.

Skating Foot: The foot currently in contact with the ice during one-foot (i.e., most) skating moves. The side of the body corresponding to the foot that is on the ice is referred to as the skating side, so one might refer to the skating leg or the skating shoulder.

Spin: A move in which the skating leg forms an axis around which the rest of the body rotates in place. Forward spins, on the foot leading into the direction of rotation, are generally easier than back spins. The basic spin positions are upright, sit, camel, and (for females) layback. A good spin doesn't travel across the ice, but is centered on a single spot. Speed of rotation is important; for reasons of physics it is harder to maintain speed in positions such as the camel where the body is extended than when it is held in a single column as in the upright spin. Changing from one foot to another or changing the basic body position while spinning increases the difficulty; see Combination spin.

Spiral: A forward or backward gliding move performed on one foot with the free leg higher than hip level, classically extended backward in a medium-to-high ballet arabesque position. Although beginners may perform this move on the flat of the blade, a true spiral is done on the curve of an inner or outer edge (which, if held indefinitely, would progressively decrease in diameter due to loss of momentum; hence the name spiral).

Split Jump: A half-revolution jump from a flip jump takeoff (i.e., the backward inner edge of one foot and the toe pick of the other), with the legs opened into a split position at the height of the jump, landed on the toe pick of the leading foot immediately followed by a forward edge of the other. A more difficult variation, known as the split flip, involves a full revolution in the air (half on the way up into the split position and half on the way down), to land on the backward outer edge.

Spread Eagle: A two-footed gliding move in which the feet are turned 180 degrees away from each other, as in ballet second position, so that one is traveling on a forward inner or outer edge and the other on the corresponding backward edge (inner or outer), with the body facing sideways to the direction of travel.

Step Sequence: An extended series of quick changes of foot, turns such as three turns and mohawks, and small jumps of less than one revolution. The sequence may be performed in a straight line from one end of the rink to another, around the circumference of a circle or oval the width of the rink, or in a serpentine pattern consisting of tangent arcs of two or more such circles.

Technical Merit: The first mark for the free program, taking into consideration "(a) Difficulty of the performance (with no credit being given for portions thereof which are missed), (b) Variety, (c) Cleanness and sureness" (86).

Technical Program: A program consisting of eight required elements and lasting no more than two minutes and forty seconds, which counts for one-third of the total score in a singles freeskating competition. The required moves for senior ladies are: "(a) Double Axel; (b) One double jump immediately preceded by connecting steps and/or other comparable free skating movements; (c) One jump combination consisting of two double jumps or a double jump and a triple jump; (d) Flying spin; (e) Layback or sideways leaning spin; (f) Spin combination with only one change of foot and at least two changes of position; (g) Spiral step sequence (serpentine, circular or oval or a combination of the two); (h) Step sequence (straight line, circular or serpentine)" (88). As of 1994–95, senior ladies are permitted to include a triple jump in (b), the jump preceded by steps.

Three Turn: A turn on one foot from forward to backward or backward to forward, with the leading end of the blade and the body turning into the center of the curve, so called because the mark the blade leaves on the ice resembles the numeral 3. The forward three turns are very useful in free skating: in their counterclockwise variations, left front outer to left back inner, and right front inner to right back outer.

Toe Jump: A jump in which the takeoff is initiated from the edge of one skate and the toe pick of the other simultaneously: toe loop, toe walley, flip, split, and lutz.

Toe Loop: A jump from the back outer edge of one foot to the same back outer edge (as in a loop jump), but assisted by the toe pick of the free foot. The turn of the body toward the assisting foot at takeoff slightly reduces the rotation required in the air, and the toe-assisted takeoff adds power, making the toe loop the easiest jump to add a third or even fourth revolution to. (Very few skaters have attempted quadruple-revolution jumps in competition, fewer of them successfully. Surya Bonaly of France is the only woman so far to make the attempt.) Because the takeoff position for the toe loop is the same as the landing position for the standard double and triple jumps, it is the jump most often included as the final element in a jump combination.

Toe Pick: The series of serrated teeth at the front of the figure skating blade, used to add stability in spins and to grip the ice for toe jumps, pivots, and some quick running or turning movements.

Toe Walley: A jump from the back inner edge to the back outer edge of the same foot, assisted by the toe pick of the free foot at takeoff. The toe assist effectively compensates for the reversal of rotation, making the toe walley so similar to the toe loop that the two are counted as the same jump for purposes of limiting the number of repeated triples in a free program.

United States Figure Skating Association (USFSA): The national governing body for amateur figure skating in the United States, based in Colorado Springs, Colorado. The USFSA administers tests and competitions, including the national championships, the top finishers of which are selected to represent the United States in international competition. USFSA rules for qualifying competitions conform with those established by the International Skating Union.

Walley: A single-revolution jump from the back inner edge to the back outer edge of the same foot. This jump has the disadvantages of both the salchow (weak inner-edge takeoff) and the lutz (the rotation in the air and on the exit edge is in the opposite direction to the entering edge), and therefore is almost impossible to double. Often performed in sequence with a double or triple toe walley.

APPENDIX II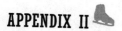

ELLYN KESTNBAUM

Scoring of Singles Figure Skating Competitions
(or how Nancy Kerrigan missed winning a gold medal at Lillehammer)

(Summarized from the United States Figure Skating Association 1992–1993 Rule Book. Passages in quotations are direct quotes from this rule book. USFSA rules conform with those established by the International Skating Association.)

The scores displayed on the television screen after each skater's program are only the first step in determining the skater's overall placement in each phase of the competition, and in the competition as a whole. Once the raw scores are converted to ordinal placements, it's the ordinals that matter. Except in certain sorts of ties, what matters is who gets ordinals of 1 (first) from the majority of judges, not who has the lowest total overall. So it is possible to win with a lower total of raw scores, and even with a higher total of ordinals. And a skater's final placement in the free program counts twice as much as in the technical program. At Lillehammer, Nancy Kerrigan was the clear winner in the technical program. She also had the highest total of raw scores in the free program. However, because Oksana Baiul received more first-place ordinals (one the result of a broken tie) in the free program, it was Oksana who got the gold medal.

Technical Program

Required Elements and Presentation marks:

Each judge awards each skater marks for Required Elements and for Presentation. Marks are based on a scale from 0 to 6:

0 = "not skated"	4 = "good"
1 = "very poor"	5 = "very good"
2 = "poor"	6 = "perfect and faultless"
3 = "mediocre"	

Decimals to one place are permitted to provide intermediate distinctions (e.g., 3.8, 4.4, 5.5).

There are required deductions, taken from the Required Elements mark, if an element is missed:

Element	Failure	Omission
Jumps and jump combination	0.2 to 0.5	0.6
All other elements	0.1 to 0.3	0.4
Extra or repeated elements	0.1 to 0.2	—

There may also be deductions in the Presentation mark if the "harmonious and artistic aspects of the program are involved."

Nancy's scores:	5.6	5.8	5.6	5.8	5.8	5.9	5.8	5.8	5.9
	5.6	5.9	5.7	5.7	5.9	5.9	5.9	5.8	5.8

Oksana's scores:	5.7	5.8	5.4	5.7	5.7	5.6	5.7	5.6	5.5
	5.9	5.8	5.7	5.9	5.9	5.8	5.9	5.9	5.9

Ordinals

Each skater's Required Elements and Presentation marks from each judge are added, and the totals are ranked in order so that each skater receives an ordinal placement (first, second, etc.) from each judge. If the totals are the same but the individual marks are different, the skater with the highest mark for Required Elements receives the lower ordinal (i.e., first rather than second). If both marks are identical, the skaters receive the same ordinal placement and the next ordinal is not assigned.

From this point on, only ordinals matter; the raw scores are no longer taken into consideration.

Nancy	2	1	1	2	1	1	1	1	1
Oksana	1	2	3	1	2	2	2	2	2

Majority

The skater with first place ordinals from the majority of judges is first, regardless of what her ordinals were from the judges not making up the majority. Of the remaining skaters, the one with the majority of second or better ordinals is second, and so on. If the majority of judges (5 on a panel of 9) award the same ordinal numbers to two (or more) skaters, there are procedures for breaking ties based on the distribution of ordinals: however, if the total ordinals from all the judges is the same, the skaters remain tied.

Since Nancy had first place ordinals from seven of the nine judges in the technical program, she was clearly in first place after this phase of the competition, which counts for one-third of the competition as a whole.

Free Program

The scoring for the free program is the same as for the technical program except as noted below.

Technical Merit and Composition & Style/Artistic Impression

There are no required deductions. Skaters are awarded points on the basis of the moves that they actually complete. Repeated moves do not receive full credit. Triple jumps are supposed to be worth 0.1 to 0.3 more than the comparable doubles (and, for instance, triple lutz is worth more than triple toe loop).

Nancy's scores:	5.8	5.8	5.8	5.7	5.7	5.8	5.8	5.7	5.8
	5.9	5.8	5.9	5.9	5.9	5.9	5.9	5.8	5.8

Oksana's scores:	5.6	5.8	5.9	5.8	5.8	5.8	5.8	5.5	5.7
	5.8	5.9	5.9	5.9	5.9	5.8	5.8	5.9	5.9

Ordinals

If two skaters receive the same total score from any judge, the tie breaker is the Artistic Impression mark. If both marks are the same, the skaters receive the same ordinal placement from that judge.

In Lillehammer, Nancy's and Oksana's totals were the same from the ninth judge; since Oksana had the higher artistic mark, she received the first place ordinal from this judge.

Nancy	1	2	2	2	2	1	1	1	2
Oksana	3	1	1	1	1	2	2	3	1

Majority

Same as technical program in the rules.

Oksana had the majority (five) of first place ordinals, so she finished first in the free program. Of the remaining skaters. Nancy had the majority (in fact, all) of the second or better ordinals, so she placed second in this phase.

Competition as a Whole

The technical program counts for one-third of the total competition; the free program counts for two-thirds. Final positions are computed by multiplying each skater's placements in each phase by multiplying factors of 0.5 and 1.0 respectively, and adding the results. The skater with the lowest total wins the competition. However, "when two or more competitors receive the same factored total for technical program plus free skating, the place in question shall be awarded to the competitor with the best place in free skating. If the competitors are also tied in the free skating, they remain tied." Therefore any skater who finishes first, second, or third in the technical program and first in the free program finishes first overall.

Nancy	1 x 0.5 = 0.5	2 x 1 = 2	0.5 + 2 = 2.5
Oksana	2 x 0.5 = 1	1 x 1 = 1	1 + 1 = 2

CONTRIBUTORS

Cynthia Baughman is Assistant Professor in the Department of Cinema and Photography at Ithaca College. She has published articles on screenplays and film adaptation, and is working on a novel.

Stacey D'Erasmo is a Senior Editor at the *Voice Literary Supplement*. Her work has appeared in the *VLS*, *Rolling Stone*, and *The Nation*. She is the recipient of a New York Foundation for the Arts fellowship in nonfiction literature.

Zillah R. Eisenstein is Professor of Politics at Ithaca College. Her most recent book is *The Color of Gender* (University of California Press, 1994).

Abigail M. Feder recently completed her doctoral dissertation, "The Girl That I Marry Will Have To Be: Performing the Feminine in Musical Theater and Film, 1939–50," for Northwestern University's Program in Theater and Drama. She has published articles on gender and sports in *TDR*, the *Village Voice*, and *Pretty Decorating*. She currently works in the Department of Labor Operations at the Metropolitan Opera.

Jane Feuer teaches film studies and cultural studies in the English Department at the University of Pittsburgh. She is the author of *The Hollywood Musical* (second revised edition, Macmillan Press, 1993), and *Seeing Through the Eighties* (Duke University Press, 1995).

Marjorie Garber is Professor of English and Director of the Center for Literary and Cultural Studies at Harvard University. She is author of three books on Shakespeare, and *Vested Interests: Cross-Dressing and Cultural Anxiety* (Routledge, 1992), and *Vice Versa: Bisexuality and the Eroticism of Everyday Life* (Simon and Schuster, 1995). She is co-editor, with Jan Matlock, and Rebecca Walkowitz, of *Media Spectacles* (Routledge, 1993) and with Rebecca Walkowitz of *Secret Agents: The Rosenberg Case, McCarthyism, and Fifties America* (Routledge, 1995).

Sandy Flitterman-Lewis is the author of *To Desire Differently: Feminism and the French Cinema* (University of Illinois, 1990) and co-author of *New Vocabularies in Film Semiotics* (Routledge, 1992). Her work about television can be found in *Channels of Discourse, Reassembled, ReGarding Television*, and *Private Screenings*, as well as *Screen* and *Camera Obscura*. She is Associate Professor of English and Cinema Studies at Rutgers University.

Laura Jacobs writes about fashion for *The New Republic* and *The Modern Review*, reviews dance for *The New Criterion*, and is author of *Barbie What a Doll!* (Abbeville Press, 1994) and *The Art of Haute Couture* (Abbeville Press, 1995).

Ellyn Kestnbaum is a doctoral student in the Department of Theater and Drama at the University of Wisconsin-Madison, writing a dissertation on the cultural meaning of figure skating.

Marsha Kinder is Professor of Critical Studies in the School of Cinema-Television at the University of Southern California. Her latest books are *Blood Cinema: The Reconstruction of National Identity in Spain* (University of California Press, 1993), with a companion CD-ROM containing excerpts from 15 films, and *Playing with Power in Movies, Television and Video Games: From Muppet Babies to Teenage Mutant Ninja Turtles* (University of California Press, 1991).

Judith Mayne is Professor of French and Women's Studies at Ohio State University. She has written several books on feminism and film studies, including *Cinema and Spectatorship* (Routledge, 1993), and *Directed by Dorothy Arzner* (Indiana University, 1994).

Diane Raymond is Professor and Chair of the Department of Philosophy, Simmons College and the author of *Existentialism and the Philosophical Tradition*, and (with Warren Blumenfeld) of *Looking at Gay and Lesbian Life*, as well as numerous articles on law and sexuality, feminist theory, popular culture theory, and ethics. She is presently working on an book on feminist / postmodernist understandings of ethical theory.

Lynn Spigel is Associate Professor at the University of Southern California's School of Cinema-Television. She is author of *Make Room for TV: Television and the Family Ideal in Postwar America*.

Sam Stoloff is a graduate student in American Studies and English at Cornell University. He is completing a dissertation entitled "Stars and

Scandals: The Consolidation of Commercial Culture in Spectator Sports, Silent Film, and Popular Journalism, 1914–1922."

Jill Dianne Swenson is Assistant Professor in the Department of Television-Radio, Media Studies, and Journalism Programs at Ithaca College. She is currently working on a book entitled *Governing Images*, which examines the function of media spectacles in public debates and the democratic process in contemporary America.

Melanie Thernstrom is the author of the non-fiction memoir, *The Dead Girl* (Simon and Schuster, 1990), and is currently completing a novel, *Patterns in Desire* and an article for *The New Yorker*. She has taught creative writing at Cornell, Harvard, and Boston Universities.

Robyn Wiegman is Assistant Professor of English and Women's Studies at Indiana University, and is author of *American Anatomies: Theorizing Race and Gender* (Duke, 1995). She is also co-editor of two anthologies: *Feminism Beside Itself* (Routledge, 1995) and *Who Can Speak? Authority in Critical Identity* (University of Illinois Press, 1995).

Mimi White is author of *Tele-Advising: Therapeutic Discourse in American Television* (University of North Carolina Press, 1992) and co-author, with James Schwoch and Susan Reilly, of *Media Knowledge; Readings in Popular Culture, Pedagogy, and Critical Citizenship* (SUNY Press, 1992). She teaches in the Radio/TV/Film Department at Northwestern University.

Patricia R. Zimmermann is Professor of Cinema and Photography at Ithaca College. She is the author of *Reel Families: A Social History of Amateur Film* (University of Indiana Press, 1995).

Lynda Zwinger is Associate Professor at the University of Arizona, where she teaches American Literature, the novel, and popular culture. She is the author of *Daughters, Fathers, and the Novel: The Sentimental Romance of Heterosexuality*, and has published articles on the *Alien* movies, *Total Recall* and *Blue Velvet*, the *Terminator* films, and Henry James.